Memoir of the Life and Writings of Mrs. Hemans

Merwin

MEMOIR

OF

THE LIFE AND WRITINGS

OF

MRS. HEMANS.

BY HER SISTER.

Owen, née Harriet Mary (Browne),

Not for the brightness of a mortal wreath,
　Not for a place 'mid kingly minstrels dead,
But that, perchance, a faint gale of thy breath,
　A still small whisper in my song hath led
One struggling spirit upwards to thy throne,
Or but one hope, one prayer:— for this alone
　　　　　I bless thee, O my God!
　From "A Poet's Dying Hymn," by Mrs HEMANS.

PHILADELPHIA:
LEA AND BLANCHARD,
SUCCESSORS TO CAREY & Co.
1839.

TO

COLONEL SIR HENRY BROWNE, K. C. H.

THESE PAGES,

WRITTEN UNDER HIS ROOF,

WHICH HAS ALWAYS BEEN A REFUGE FOR THE SORROWFUL,

ARE DEDICATED,

BY HIS SURVIVING SISTER,

IN REMEMBRANCE OF HER,

WHO, DURING MANY YEARS OF TRIAL,

FOUND HER BEST EARTHLY SOLACE

IN HIS CARE AND AFFECTION.

(27)

MEMOIR

OF

MRS. HEMANS.

PERHAPS there never was an individual who would have shrunk more sensitively from the idea of being made the subject of a biographical memoir, than she of whom, by a strange fatality, so many imperfect notices have been given to the world. The external events of her life were few and unimportant; and that inward grief which pervaded and darkened her whole existence, was one with which "a stranger intermeddleth not." The gradual developement of her mind may be traced in the writings by which she alone wished to be generally known. In every thing approaching to intrusion on the privacies of domestic life, her favourite motto was, "*Implora pace;*" and those to whom her wishes were most sacred—in whose ears still echo the plaintive tones of her death-bed injunction, "Oh! never let them publish any of my letters!"—would fain, as far as regards all personal details, have "kept silence, even from good words;" and · in this spirit of reverential forbearance, would have believed they were best fulfilling her own affecting exhortation,—

"Leave ye the Sleeper with her God to rest." [1]

---

[1] See "The Farewell to the Dead."

But it is now too late to deprecate or to deplore.
A part of Mrs. Hemans's correspondence has already
been laid before the public; and the result has been
one which was, doubtless, little contemplated by the
kindly-intentioned editor,—that of creating a very
inadequate estimate of her character, by "presenting, in undue prominence" (to use the words of a
judicious critic,)[1] "a certain portion of the writer's
mind, by no means the portion with which her admirers will best sympathize, and omitting that other
and more exalted division of her nature, in which she
was solely or pre-eminently herself."

The spell having thus been broken, and the veil of
the sanctuary lifted, it seems now to have become the
duty of those with whose feelings the strict fulfilment
of her own wishes would have been so far more accordant, to raise that veil a little further, though with
a reluctant and trembling hand. It has not been
without a painful struggle, that any invasion has been
made on the sanctity of private correspondence, gen-
erously as their treasure-stores have been laid open
by the friends who had hitherto guarded them so
religiously. Such letters only have been selected as
served to illustrate some individuality of character or
temperament, or to exhibit the vivid powers of description possessed by the writer; and it is most earnestly hoped that these unpretending memorials, feeble
and deficient as they are felt to be, may, at least, be
found free from anything which can give pain to
others, or lead to any wrong impressions of the guile-

---

[1] In the leading article of the " Dublin University Magazine"
for August, 1837.

less and confiding spirit, whose bright, and kindly, and endearing graces they so faintly attempt to pourtray. It is acknowledged, indeed, that as to the points of highest moral interest and importance, little more than negative merit is thus attained, and very imperfect redress afforded to a memory on which such partial light had been thrown by previous delineations. But the deficiency is knowingly incurred, as preferable to the use of the only means by which the picture could have been made more complete. For it was in a great measure impossible to render available those positive testimonies to the generous feelings of her heart, and the high principles of her nature, which her correspondence with intimate friends amply supplies, without a breach of those confidences of home and friendship, which no precedent can justify, and which can be reconciled to the feelings of an English family by no increase of public admiration to an individual member, by no craving, however urgent or imperious, of the public taste. With a request, then, that the deficiency thus accounted for may be indulgently borne in mind, a close is now gladly put to these prefatory remarks, and the reader's kind forbearance bespoken for the other imperfections of a biographical sketch, which, it is needless to indicate, has not been drawn by the hand of an artist.

FELICIA DOROTHEA BROWNE was born in Liverpool, on the 25th September, 1793. Her father, a native of Ireland, was a merchant of considerable eminence. Her mother, whose family name was Wagner, and who was of mingled Italian and German descent, was the daughter of the Imperial and Tuscan Consul at Liverpool. The subject of this memoir (the fifth of

seven children, one of whom died an infant,) was distinguished, almost from her cradle, by extreme beauty
and precocious talents. Before she had attained the
age of seven, her father, having suffered commercial
reverses, in common with many others engaged in
similar speculations at that revolutionary era, broke
up his establishment in Liverpool, and removed with
his family into Wales, where, for the next nine years,
they resided at Gwrych,[1] near Abergele, in Denbigh-
shire, a large old mansion, close to the sea, and shut
in by a picturesque range of mountains. In the calm
seclusion of this romantic region, with ample range
through the treasures of an extensive library, the
young poetess passed a happy childhood, to which she
would often fondly revert amidst the vicissitudes of
her after life. Here she imbibed that intense love of
Nature which ever afterwards " haunted her like a
passion," and that warm attachment for the " green
land of Wales;" its affectionate, true-hearted people
—their traditions, their music, and all their interesting
characteristics, which she cherished to the last hours
of her existence. After the loss of her eldest sister,
who died young, her education became the first care
of a mother, whose capability for the task could only
be equalled by her devotedness: whose acquirements
were of the highest order, and whose whole character,
presenting a rare union of strong sense with primitive
single-mindedness, was an exemplification of St. Paul's
description of that charity which " suffereth long and

---

[1] The greater part of this old house has since been taken down,
and Gwrych Castle, the baronial-looking seat of Lloyd Bamford
Hesketh, Esq., erected on the opposite height.

is kind," "seeketh not her own," "thinketh no evil."
Her piety was sober, steadfast, and cheerful; never
displaying itself in high-wrought excitements or osten-
tatious professions, but silently influencing every action of her life, and shedding a perpetual sunshine
over all which came within its sphere. How truly
the love of this exemplary mother was returned and
appreciated, may be traced in many affecting instances through the following pages, from the artless birthday effusion of the child of eight years old, to the
death-bed hymn of agonized affection,[1] in the matured
years of the daughter, herself a matron and a mother.
And when that love had been sealed and sanctified
by death, still more fervent are the yearnings breathed forth in the passionate adjuration to " the charmed
picture" of the

"Sweet face that o'er her childhood shone ;"

and last and deepest, and best of all, in the sonnet
"To a Family Bible," in which the mourner, chastened yet consoled, looks back upon the days when her
mother's lips were wont to breathe forth the sacred
lore of those hallowed pages, and meekly and thankfully acknowledges it to have been—

"A seed not lost—for which, in darker years,
O Book of Heaven! I pour, with grateful tears,
Heart blessings on the holy dead and thee."

It may well be imagined how the heart of such a
mother would be garnered up in a child so gifted as
the bright and blooming Felicia, whose extraordinary
quickness in acquiring information of every kind, was

---

[1] "Hymn by a bed of sickness," written in January, 1827.

not less remarkable than the grasp of memory with which she retained it. She could repeat pages of poetry from her favourite authors, after having read them but once over ; and a scarcely less wonderful faculty was the rapidity of her reading, which even in childhood, and still more in after life, was such, that a bystander would imagine she was only carelessly turning over the leaves of a book, when, in truth, she was taking in the whole sense as completely as others would do whilst poring over it with the closest attention. One of her earliest tastes was a passion for Shakspeare, which she read, as her choicest recreation, at six years old; and in later days she would often refer to the hours of romance she had passed in a secret haunt of her own—a seat amongst the branches of an old apple-tree—where, revelling in the treasures of the cherished volume, she would become completely absorbed in the imaginative world it revealed to her.[1] The following lines, written at eleven years old, may be adduced as a proof of her juvenile enthusiasm.

---

[1] An allusion to this favourite haunt will be found in the sonnet called " Orchard Blossoms," written in 1834.

     ——" Doth some old nook,
Haunted by visions of thy first-loved book,
Rise on thy soul, with faint-streaked blossoms white
Showered o'er the turf, and the lone primrose-knot,
And robin's nest, still faithful to the spot,
And the bee's dreamy chime? O gentle friend!
The world's cold breath, not *Time's*, this life bereaves
Of vernal gifts—Time hallows what he leaves,
And will for us endear spring-memories to the end."

SHAKSPEARE.

I love to rove o'er history's page,
Recall the hero and the sage;
Revive the actions of the dead,
And memory of ages fled:
Yet it yields me greater pleasure,
To read the poet's pleasing measure.
Led by Shakspeare, bard inspired,
The bosom's energies are fired;
We learn to shed the generous tear,
O'er poor Ophelia's sacred bier;
To love the merry moonlit scene,
With fairy elves in valleys green;
Or, borne on fancy's heavenly wings,
To listen while sweet Ariel sings.
How sweet the "native woodnotes wild"
Of him, the Muse's favourite child!
Of him whose magic lays impart
Each various feeling to the heart!

At about the age of eleven, she passed a winter in London with her father and mother; and a similar sojourn was repeated in the following year, after which she never visited the metropolis. The contrast between the confinement of a town life, and the happy freedom of her own mountain home, was even then so grateful to her, that the indulgences of plays and sights soon ceased to be cared for, and she longed to rejoin her younger brother[1] and sister in their favourite

---

[1] Claude Scott Browne, the brother here alluded to, who was one year younger than Mrs. Hemans, died at Kingston, in Upper Canada (where he was employed as a Deputy-Assistant Commissary General,) in 1821.

"They grew in beauty, side by side,
    They fill'd one home with glee;
Their graves are sever'd far and wide,
    By mount, and stream, and sea."
                    The Graves of a Household.

rural haunts and amusements—the nuttery wood, the beloved apple-tree, the old arbour, with its swing, the post-office tree, in whose trunk a daily interchange of family letters was established, the pool where fairy ships were launched (generally painted and decorated by herself,) and, dearer still, the fresh, free ramble on the sea-shore, or the mountain expedition to the Signal Station, or the Roman Encampment. In one of her letters, the pleasure with which she looked forward to her return home, was thus expressed in rhyme.

WRITTEN FROM LONDON TO MY BROTHER AND SISTER IN THE COUNTRY.

Happy soon we'll meet again,
Free from sorrow, care, and pain;
Soon again we'll rise with dawn,
To roam the verdant dewy lawn;
Soon the budding leaves we'll hail,
Or wander through the well-known vale;
Or weave the smiling wreath of flowers;
And sport away the light-wing'd hours.
Soon we'll run the agile race;
Soon, dear playmates, we'll embrace;—
Through the wheat field or the grove,
We'll, hand in hand, delighted rove;
Or, beneath some spreading oak,
Ponder the instructive book;
Or view the ships that swiftly glide,
Floating on the peaceful tide;
Or raise again the carolled lay;
Or join again in mirthful play;
Or listen to the humming bees,
As their murmurs swell the breeze;
Or seek the primrose where it springs;
Or chase the fly with painted wings;

Or talk beneath the arbour's shade;
Or mark the tender shooting blade;
Or stray beside the babbling stream,
When Luna sheds her placid beam;
Or gaze upon the glassy sea—
Happy, happy shall we be!

Some things, however, during these visits to London, made an impression never to be effaced, and she retained the most vivid recollection of several of the great works of art which she was then taken to see. On entering a gallery of sculpture, she involuntarily exclaimed — "Oh! hush!—don't speak;" and her mother used to take pleasure in describing the interest she had excited in a party who happened to be visiting the Marquess of Stafford's collection at the same time, by her unsophisticated expressions of delight, and her familiarity with the mythological and classical subjects of many of the pictures.

In 1808, a collection of her poems, which had long been regarded amongst her friends with a degree of admiration, perhaps more partial than judicious, was submitted to the world, in the form (certainly an ill-advised one) of a quarto volume. Its appearance drew down the animadversions of some self-constituted arbiter of public taste, and the young poetess was thus early initiated into the pains and perils attendant upon the career of an author; though it may here be observed, that, as far as criticism was concerned, this was at once the first and last time she was destined to meet with anything like harshness or mortification. Though this unexpected severity was felt bitterly for a few days, her buoyant spirit

soon rose above it, and her effusions continued to be
poured forth as spontaneously as the song of the sky-
lark.   New sources of inspiration were now opening
to her view.   Birthday addresses, songs by the sea-
shore, and invocations to fairies, were henceforth to
be diversified with warlike themes; and trumpets and
banners now floated through the dreams in which
birds and flowers had once reigned paramount.   Her
two elder brothers had entered the army at an early
age, and were both serving in the 23d Royal Welsh
Fusiliers.   One of them was now engaged in the
Spanish campaign under Sir John Moore; and a vivid
imagination and enthusiastic affections being alike
enlisted in the cause, her young mind was filled with
glorious visions of British valour and Spanish patriotism.   In her ardent view, the days of chivalry seemed to be restored, and the very names which were of
daily occurrence in the despatches, were involuntarily
associated with the deeds of Roland and his Paladins,
or of her own especial hero, " The Cid Ruy Diaz,"
the campeador.   Under the inspiration of these feelings, she composed a poem, entitled " England and
Spain," which was published and afterwards translated into Spanish.   This cannot but be considered as
a very remarkable production for a girl of fourteen;
lofty sentiments, correctness of language, and historical knowledge, being all strikingly displayed in it.

The very time when her mind was wrought up to
this pitch of romantic enthusiasm, was that which
first brought to her acquaintance the person who was
destined to exercise so important an influence over
her future life.   Captain Hemans, then in the 4th, or

King's Own Regiment, whilst on a visit in the neighbourhood, was introduced to the family at Gwrych.
The young poetess was then only fifteen; in the full
glow of that radiant beauty which was destined to
fade so early. The mantling bloom of her cheeks
was shaded by a profusion of natural ringlets, of a
rich golden brown; and the ever-varying expression
of her brilliant eyes gave a changeful play to her
countenance, which would have made it impossible
for any painter to do justice to it. The recollection
of what she was at that time, irresistibly suggests a
quotation from Wordsworth's graceful poetic picture :—

> "She was a phantom of delight,
> When first she gleamed upon my sight;
> A lovely apparition, sent
> To be a moment's ornament.
> *   *   *   *   *
> A dancing shape, an image gay,
> To haunt, to startle, and waylay."

That so fair a being should excite the warmest
admiration, was not surprising. Perhaps it was not
more so, that the impassioned expression of that admiration should awaken reciprocal feelings in the
bosom of a young, artless, and enthusiastic girl, readily
investing him who professed such devotion, (and who,
indeed, was by no means destitute of advantages
either of person or education,) with all the attributes
of the heroes of her dreams. Their intercourse at
this time was not of long continuance; for Captain
Hemans was called upon to embark with his regiment
for Spain; and this circumstance was in itself suf-

ficient to complete the illusion which had now gained
possession of her heart. It was hoped by the friends
of both parties, that the impressions thus formed might
prove but a passing fancy, which time and distance
would efface; but the event proved otherwise, though
nearly three years elapsed before they met again.

In 1809, the family removed from Gwrych to Bronwylfa, near St. Asaph,[1] in Flintshire. Here, though
in somewhat less of seclusion than during the previous
years of her life, her mind continued to develope itself,
and her tastes and pursuits to embrace a progressively
wider range. The study of the Spanish and Portu-
guese languages was added to the already acquired
French and Italian. She also read German, though
it was not until many years later that she entered
with full appreciation into the soul and spirit of that
magnificent language, and wrote of it as " having
opened to her a new world of thought and feeling, so
that even the music of the *Eichenland*,[2] as Korner
calls it, seemed to acquire a deeper tone, when she
had gained a familiarity with its noble poetry."

The powers of her memory were so extraordinary,
as to be sometimes made the subject of a wager, by
those who were sceptical as to the possibility of her
achieving, what she would, in the most undoubting
simplicity, undertake to perform. On one of these
occasions, to satisfy the incredulity of one of her
brothers, she learned by heart, having never read it

---

[1] This place was purchased, some years afterwards, by Mrs.
Heman's eldest brother, Colonel Sir Henry Browne.

[2] Land of Oaks.

before, the whole of Heber's poem of "Europe" in one hour and twenty minutes, and repeated it without a single mistake or a moment's hesitation. The length of this poem is four hundred and twenty-four lines.

She had a taste for drawing, which, with time and opportunity for its cultivation, would, doubtless, have led to excellence; but having so many other pursuits requiring her attention, she seldom attempted anything beyond slight sketches in pencil or Indian ink. Her correctness of eye, and the length and clearness of her vision, were almost as proverbial amongst her friends as her extraordinary powers of memory. She played both the harp and piano with much feeling and expression, and at this time had a good voice, but in a very few years it became weakened by the frequent recurrence of affections of the chest, and singing was consequently discontinued. Even in her most joyous days, the strains she preferred were always those of a pensive character. The most skilful combinations of abstract musical science did not interest or please her: what she loved best were national airs, whether martial or melancholy, (amongst these the Welsh and Spanish were her favourites), and whatever might be called suggestive music, as awakening associations either traditional, local, or imaginary. There are ears in which certain melodies are completely identified with the recollection of her peculiarly soft and *sostenuto* touch, which gave to the piano an effect almost approaching to the swell of an organ. Amongst these may be mentioned Jomelli's *Chaconne*, Oginsky's well-known *Polonaise*, some of

4 *

the slow movements from the Ballet of *Nina,* and a little touching air called the *Moravian Nun,* brought from Germany by her eldest brother, who had learned it by ear.

In after life, when, like "a reed shaken by the wind," her frame had been shattered by sorrow and suffering, the intensity of her perceptions was such, that music became a painful excitement, and there were times when her nerves were too much over-wrought to bear it. Allusions to this state of feeling are found in many of her poems; and in one of her letters, referring to a work of Richter's, she thus expresses herself:—" What a deep echo gives answer within the mind to the exclamation of the 'immortal old man' at the sound of music.[1] 'Away! away!

---

[1] " Once in dreams, I saw a human being of heavenly intellectual faculties, and his aspirations were heavenly; but he was chained, methought, eternally to the earth. The immortal old man had five great wounds in his happiness—five worms that gnawed for ever at his heart. He was unhappy in spring-time, because that is a season of hope, and rich with phantoms of far happier days than any which this Aceldama of earth can realize. He was unhappy at the sound of music, which dilates the heart of man with its whole capacity for the infinite; and he cried aloud,—'Away! away!' Thou speakest of things which, throughout my endless life, I have found not, and shall not find!' He was unhappy at the remembrance of earthly affections and dissevered hearts; for Love is a plant which may bud in this life, but must flourish in another. He was unhappy under the glorious spectacle of the heavenly host, and ejaculated for ever in his heart—' So, then, I am parted from you to all eternity by an impassable abyss! the great universe of suns is above, below, and round about me, but I am chained to a little ball of dust and ashes!' He was unhappy before the great ideas

thou speakest of things which, throughout my endless life, I have found not, and shall not find!' All who have felt music, must, at times, I think, have felt this, making its sweetness too piercing to be sustained.

Some of the happiest days the young poetess ever passed were during occasional visits to some friends at Conway, where the charms of the scenery, combining all that is most beautiful in wood, water, and ruin, are sufficient to inspire the most prosaic temperament with a certain degree of enthusiasm; and it may therefore well be supposed, how fervently a soul, constituted like hers, would worship Nature at so fitting a shrine. With that happy versatility, which was at all times a leading characteristic of her mind, she would now enter with child-like playfulness into the enjoyments of a mountain scramble, or a pic-nic water party, the gayest of the merry band, of whom some are now, like herself, laid low, some far away in foreign lands, some changed by sorrow, and all by time; and then, in graver mood, dream away hours of pensive contemplation amidst the grey ruins of that noblest of Welsh castles, standing, as it then did, in solitary grandeur, unapproached by bridge or causeway, flinging its broad shadow across the tributary waves which washed its regal walls. These lovely scenes never ceased to retain their hold over the imagination of her whose youthful muse had so often

of virtue, of truth, and of God; because he knew how feeble are the approximations to them which a son of earth can make. But this was a dream. God be thanked that there is no such asking eye directed upwards towards heaven, to which Death will not one day bring an answer!" —— *From the German of Richter.*

celebrated their praises. Her peculiar admiration of Mrs. Joanna Baillie's play of *Ethwald* was always .pleasingly associated with the recollection of her having first read it amidst the ruins of Conway Castle. At Conway, too, she first made acquaintance with the lively and graphic Chronicles of the chivalrous Frois- sart, whose inspiring pages never lost their place in her favour. Her own little poem, " The Ruin and its Flowers," which will be found amongst the earlier pieces in the present collection, was written on an excursion to the old fortress of Dyganwy, the remains of which are situated on a bold promontory near the entrance of the river Conway ; and whose ivied walls, now fast mouldering into oblivion, once bore their part bravely in the defence of Wales; and are further endeared to the lovers of song and tradition, as having echoed the complaints of the captive Elphin, and resounded to the harp of Taliesin. A scarcely degene- rate representative of that gifted bard[1] had, at the time now alluded to, his appropriate dwelling-place at Conway ; but his strains have long been silenced, and

---

[1] Mr. Edwards, the Harper of Conway, as he was generally called, had been blind from his birth, and was endowed with that extraordinary musical genius, by which persons suffering under such a visitation, are not unfrequently indemnified. From the respectability of his circumstances, he was not called upon to exercise his talents with any view to remuneration. He played to delight himself and others ; and the innocent complacency with which he enjoyed the ecstasies called forth by his skill, and the degree of appreciation with which he regarded himself, as in a manner consecrated, by being made the depositary of a direct gift from Heaven, were, as far as possible, removed from any of the common modifications of vanity or self-conceit.

there now remain few, indeed, on whom the Druidical mantle has fallen so worthily. In the days when his playing was heard by one so fitted to enjoy its originality and beauty,

"The minstrel was infirm and old;".

but his inspiration had not yet forsaken him; and the following lines (written in 1811) will give an idea of the magic power he still knew how to exercise over the feelings of his auditors.

TO MR. EDWARDS, THE HARPER OF CONWAY.

Minstrel! whose gifted hand can bring,
Life, rapture, soul, from every string;
And wake, like bards of former time,
The spirit of the harp sublime; —
Oh! still prolong the varying strain!
Oh! touch th' enchanted chords again!

Thine is the charm, suspending care,
The heavenly swell, the dying close,
The cadence melting into air,
That lulls each passion to repose.
While transport, lost in silence near,
Breathes all her language in a tear.

Exult, O Cambria! — now no more,
With sighs thy slaughter'd bards deplore:
What though Plinlimmon's misty brow,
And Mona's woods be silent now,
Yet can thy Conway boast a strain,
Unrivall'd in thy proudest reign.

For Genius, with divine control,
Wakes the bold chord neglected long,
And pours Expression's glowing soul
O'er the wild Harp, renown'd in song:

And Inspiration, hovering round,
Swells the full energies of sound.

Now Grandeur, pealing in the tone,
Could rouse the warrior's kindling fire,
And now, 'tis like the breeze's moan,
That murmurs o'er th' Eolian lyre:
As if some sylph, with viewless wing,
Were sighing o'er the magic string.

Long, long, fair Conway! boast the skill,
That soothes, inspires, commands, at will!
And oh! while Rapture hails the lay,
Far distant be the closing day,
When Genius, Taste, again shall weep,
And Cambria's Harp lie hush'd in sleep!

Whilst on the subject of Conway, it may not be amiss to introduce two little pieces of a very different character from the foregoing, which were written at the same place, three or four years afterwards, and will serve as a proof of that versatility of talent before alluded to. As may easily be supposed, they were never intended for publication, but were merely a *jeu d'esprit* of the moment, in good-humoured raillery of the indefatigable zeal and perseverance of one of the party in his geological researches :—

EPITAPH ON MR. W——, A CELEBRATED MINERALOGIST.

Stop, passenger! a wondrous tale to list —
Here lies a famous Mineralogist.
Famous indeed! such traces of his power,
He's left from Penmaenbach to Penmaenmawr,
Such caves, and chasms, and fissures in the rocks,
His works resemble those of earthquake shocks;

And future ages very much may wonder
What mighty giant rent the hills asunder,
Or whether Lucifer himself had ne'er
Gone with his crew to play at foot-ball there.

His fossils, flints, and spars, of every hue,
With him, good reader, here lie buried too—
Sweet specimens! which, toiling to obtain,
He split huge cliffs, like so much wood, in twain.
We knew, so great the fuss he made about them,
Alive or dead, he ne'er would rest without them,
So, to secure soft slumber to his bones,
We paved his grave with all his favourite stones.
His much-loved hammer's resting by his side;
Each hand contains a shell-fish petrified:
His mouth a piece of pudding-stone incloses,
And at his feet a lump of coal reposes:
Sure he was born beneath some lucky planet—
His very coffin-plate is made of granite.

Weep not, good reader! he is truly blest
Amidst chalcedony and quartz to rest:
Weep not for him! but envied be his doom,
Whose tomb, though small, for all he loved had room:
And, O ye rocks!—schist, gneiss, whate'er ye be,
Ye varied strata!—names too hard for me—
Sing, "Oh, be joyful!" for your direst foe,
By death's fell hammer, is at length laid low.
Ne'er on your spoils again shall W—— riot,
Clear up your cloudy brows, and rest in quiet—
He sleeps—no longer planning hostile actions,
As cold as any of his petrifactions;
Enshrined in specimens of every hue,
Too tranquil e'en to dream, ye rocks, of you.

EPITAPH ON THE HAMMER OF THE AFORESAID MINERALOGIST.

Here in the dust, its strange adventures o'er,
A hammer rests, that ne'er knew rest before.
Released from toil, it slumbers by the side
Of one who oft its temper sorely tried;
No day e'er pass'd, but in some desperate strife
He risk'd the faithful hammer's limbs and life;
Now laying siege to some old limestone wall,
Some rock now battering, proof to cannon-ball;
Now scaling heights like Alps or Pyrenees,
Perhaps a flint, perhaps a slate to seize;
But, if a piece of copper met his eyes,
He'd mount a precipice that touch'd the skies,
And bring down lumps so precious, and so many,
I'm sure they almost would have made—a penny!
Think, when such deeds as these were daily done,
What fearful risks this hammer must have run.
And, to say truth, its praise deserves to shine
In lays more lofty and more famed than mine:
Oh! that in strains which ne'er should be forgot,
Its deeds were blazon'd forth by Walter Scott!
Then should its name with his be closely link'd,
And live till every mineral were extinct.
Rise, epic bards! be yours the ample field—
Bid W——'s hammer match Achilles' shield:
As for *my* muse, the chaos of her brain,
I search for specimens of wit in vain,
Then let me cease ignoble rhymes to stammer,
And seek some theme less arduous than the hammer;
Rememb'ring well, " what perils do environ"
Woman or " man that meddles with cold iron."

About this time, also, she wrote, for her second
brother, the following Prologue to the *Poor Gentleman,* as intended to be performed by the officers of
the 34th regiment at Clonmel :—

Enter Captain GEORGE BROWNE, *in the character of*
CORPORAL FOSS.

To-night, kind friends, at your tribunal here,
Stands "The Poor Gentleman," with many a fear;
Since well he knows, who e'er may judge his cause,
That Poverty's no title to applause.
Genius or Wit, pray, who'll admire or quote,
If all their drapery be a threadbare coat?
Who, in a world where all is bought and sold,
Minds a man's worth—except his worth in gold?
Who'll greet poor Merit if she lacks a dinner?
Hence, starving saint, but welcome, wealthy sinner!
Away with Poverty! let none receive her,
She bears contagion as a plague or fever;
"Bony, and gaunt, and grim"—like jaundiced eyes,
Discolouring all within her sphere that lies.
"Poor Gentleman!" and by poor soldiers, too!
O matchless impudence! without a sous!
In scenes, in actors poor, and what far worse is,
With heads, perhaps, as empty as their purses,
How shall they dare at such a bar appear?
What are their tactics and manœuvres here?

While thoughts like these come rushing o'er our mind,
Oh! may we still indulgence hope to find?
Brave sons of Erin! whose distinguish'd name
Shines with such brilliance in the page of Fame,
And you, fair daughters of the Emerald Isle!
View our weak efforts with approving smile!
School'd in rough camps, and still disdaining art,
Ill can the soldier act a borrowed part;
The march, the skirmish, in this warlike age,
Are his rehearsals, and the field his stage;
His theatre is found in every land,
Where wave the ensigns of a hostile band:
Place him in danger's front—he recks not where—
Be your own Wellington his prompter there,

VOL. I.——5

And on that stage, he trusts, with fearful mien,
He'll act his part in glory's tragic scene.
Yet here, though friends are gaily marshall'd round,
And from bright eyes alone he dreads a wound,
Here, though in ambush no sharpshooter's wile
Aims at his breast, save hid in beauty's smile;
Though all unused to pause, to doubt, to fear,
Yet his heart sinks, his courage fails him here.
No scenic pomp to him its aid supplies,
No stage effect of glittering pageantries :
No, to your kindness he must look alone,
To realize the hope he dares not own ;
And trusts, since here he meets no cynic eye,
His wish to please may claim indemnity.

And why despair, indulgence when we crave
From Erin's sons, the generous and the brave ?
Theirs the high spirit, and the liberal thought,
Kind, warm, sincere, with native candour fraught;
Still has the stranger, in their social isle,
Met the frank welcome and the cordial smile,
And well their hearts can share, though unexpress'd,
Each thought, each feeling, of the soldier's breast.

In 1812, another and much smaller volume, entitled
The Domestic Affections and other Poems, was given
to the world — the last that was to appear with the
name of Felicia Browne ; for, in the summer of the
same year, its author exchanged that appellation for
the one under which she has become so much more
generally known. Captain Hemans had returned to
Wales in the preceding year, when the acquaintance
was renewed which had begun so long before at
Gwrych ; and as the sentiments then mutually awakened continued unaltered, no further opposition was
made to a union, on which (however little in accord-

ance with the dictates of worldly prudence,) the happiness of both parties seemed so entirely to depend. They soon afterwards took up their residence at Daventry, Captain Hemans having been appointed Adjutant to the Northamptonshire Local Militia. Here they remained for about a twelvemonth, during which time their eldest son, Arthur,[1] was born. The transition from her "own mountain land," as she would fondly call it, to a country so tame and uninteresting as the neighbourhood of Daventry, was felt by Mrs. Hemans to a degree almost amounting to the *heimweh* (home sickness) of the Swiss. The only scenery within reach of her new abode, which excited any pleasing associations, was that of Fawsley Park, of which the woods and lawns, the old Hall, with its quaint gables and twisted chimneys, and the venerable, ivy-mantled church—always retained a place in her "chambers of imagery," as presenting a happy combination of the characteristic features of an old English ancestral demesne. Her sonnet "On an old Church in an English Park," published in the *Scenes and Hymns of Life,* though written so many years after, was suggested by the recollection of this scenery, of which she had made several sketches.

The unexpected reduction of the corps dissolving their connexion with a place to which they had no other ties, Captain Hemans and his family returned to Wales in the following year, and became domiciliated at Bronwylfa; from which time, till the death

---

[1] This child of many hopes, the first to awaken a mother's love, has been the first to rejoin her in the world beyond the grave. He died at Rome, in February, 1837.

of her mother, Mrs. Hemans was never again withdrawn from the shelter of the maternal wing.[1] Early
and deeply was she taught to appreciate the blessing
of that shelter—the value of that truest and tenderest
friend, "the mother," to use her own words, "by
whose unwearied spirit of love and hope she was
encouraged to bear on through all the obstacles which
beset her path."

For several succeeding years, the life of Mrs. Hemans continued to be a scene of almost uninterrupted
domestic privacy, her time being divided between the
cultivation of her wonted studies, and the claims of an
increasing family.   Her five children were all sons—
a circumstance which many persons profess to have
discovered from her writings, in which allusions to a
mother's love are so frequent, and where the "blessed
child," so often apostrophised or described, is always,
it may be observed, a "gentle" or a "gallant" or a
"bright-haired" *boy*, whose living image might be
found in the blooming group around her.   Her eager-
ness for knowledge of every kind was intense; and
her industry may be attested by volumes, still existing,
of extracts and transcriptions, almost sufficient to form
a library in themselves.   The mode of her studies
was, to outward appearance, singularly desultory, as
she would be surrounded by books of all sizes, in
divers languages, and on every variety of topic, and
would seem to be turning from one to another, like
a bee flying from flower to flower: yet, whatever

---

[1] Her father had, some time before, again engaged in mercan
tile pursuits, and gone out to Quebec, where he died.

confusion might reign without, all was clear and well-defined within. In her mind and memory, the varied stores were distinctly arranged, ready to be called forth for the happy illustration, the poetic imagery, or the witty comparison. She continued the study of languages with undiminished ardour, and made some progress in the acquisition of Latin. A volume of translations published in 1818, might have been called by anticipation, " Lays of many Lands." At the time now alluded to, her inspirations were chiefly derived from classical subjects. The "graceful superstitions" of Greece, and the sublime patriotism of Rome, held an influence over her thoughts which is evinced by many of the works of this period—such as, *The Restoration of the Works of Art to Italy,*[1] *Modern Greece,* and several of the poems which formed the volume entitled *Tales and Historic Scenes.*

At this stage of transition, " her poetry," to use the words of a judicious critique,[2] " was correct, classical, and highly polished; but it wanted warmth: it partook more of the nature of statuary than of painting. She fettered her mind with facts and authorities, and drew upon her memory when she might have

---

[1] This poem is thus alluded to by Lord Byron, in one of his published letters to Mr. Murray, dated from Diodati, Sept. 30th, 1816.

" Italy or Dalmatia and another summer may, or may not, set me off again.   . . . . .

" I shall take Felicia Hemans's *Restoration,* &c., with me—it is a good poem—very."

[2] Written by the late Miss Jewsbury (afterwards Mrs. Fletcher), and published in the *Athenæum* of Feb. 12th, 1831.

5 *

relied upon her imagination. She was diffident of
herself, and, to quote her own admission, " loved to
repose under the shadow of mighty names." This
taste by degrees gave way to one which suggested a
choice of subjects more nearly allied to the thoughts
and feelings of daily life. She turned from the fables
of antiquity,

" Distinct, but distant — clear, but oh ! how cold !"

to the more heart-warming traditions of the middle
ages; imbuing every theme with the peculiar colouring of her own mind—her instinctive sense of the
picturesque, and her intense love of the beautiful.
Her poetry of this class is so eloquently characterised
by the able writer of the article already referred to,
in the *Dublin University Magazine*, that in no other
language can it be more truly and gracefully described.
" Tender and enthusiastic, she fed her heart upon all
things noble, and would tolerate no others as the
aliment of imagination. She created for herself a
world of high-souled men and women, whose love had
no outward glitter, no surface-sparkle, but was a deep,
o'ermastering stream, strong, steady, and unbroken.
The men were made to hold high feast on days of
victory—to lead the resolute chivalry of freedom—to
consecrate banners in ancient churches, solemnized
with rich evening light—to scale the walls of cities or
defend them—to strike with courage—to endure with
fortitude. The women to sing hymns of pensive worship—to sit in antique bowers, with open missals and
attendant maidens—to receive at castle gates the true-
hearted and the brave—to rush amid the spears, and

receive the wound meant for a sterner heart—to clasp
the infant snatched from peril at the peril of life—to
bear uncomplaining agonies—and, above all, to wait
long, long days for the deceiver who will not return ;
to know the deadly sickness of a fading hope, and, at
last, to dedicate a broken heart to him who has
crushed it.   These are the people and the achievements of her pages; here is the fountain and principle
of her inspirations—Honour deepened and sanctified
by religion."

In the year 1818, Captain Hemans, whose health
had been long impaired by the previous vicissitudes
of a military life, determined upon trying the effects of
a southern climate ; and, with this view, repaired to
Rome, which he was afterwards induced to fix upon
as his place of residence.   It has been alleged, and with
perfect truth, that the literary pursuits of Mrs. Hemans
and the education of her children, made it more eligible
for her to remain under the maternal roof, than to accompany her husband to Italy.   It is, however, unfortunately but too well known, that such were not the
only reasons which led to this divided course.   To
dwell on this subject would be unnecessarily painful,
yet it must be stated, that nothing like a permanent
separation was contemplated at the time, nor did it
ever amount to more than a tacit conventional arrangement, which offered no obstacle to the frequent
interchange of correspondence, nor to a constant reference to their father in all things relating to the
disposal of her boys.   But years rolled on — seventeen
years of absence, and consequently alienation—and
from this time to the hour of her death, Mrs. Hemans

and her husband never met again. In a position so
painful, as must ever be that of a woman for whom
the most sacred of ties is thus virtually broken, all
outward consolations can be but of secondary value;
yet much of what these could afford was granted to
Mrs. Hemans in the extending influence of her talents,
the growing popularity of her writings, and the warm
interest and attachment of many private friends.
Amongst the most devoted of these from an early
period of their acquaintance, were the family of the
late Bishop of St. Asaph, the good and lamented Dr.
Luxmore. In this kind-hearted prelate, Mrs. Hemans
possessed a never-failing friend and counsellor, whose
advice, in the absence of nearer ties, she at all times
sought with affectionate reliance, and whose approbation she valued with appreciating respect. His paternal kindness was not confined to herself, but extended
with equal indulgence to her children, who were so
accustomed to the interest he would take in their
studies and sports, that they seemed to consider themselves as having an inherent right to his notice and
favour; and would talk of " their own Bishop" in an
amusing tone of appropriation. Many years afterwards, in a letter from Chiefswood, their mother thus
alludes to the recollection of former days: " I have
been much at Abbotsford, where my boys run in and
out as if they were children of the soil, or as if it
were ' The Palace.' "

The poem of *The Sceptic*, published in 1820, was
one in which her revered friend took a peculiar
interest. It had been her original wish to dedicate
it to him, but he declined the tribute, thinking it

might be more advantageous to her to pay this compliment to Mr. Gifford, with whom she was at that
time in frequent correspondence, and who entered very
warmly into her literary undertakings, discussing them
with the kindness of an old friend, and desiring her to
command frankly whatever assistance his advice or
experience could afford. Mrs. Hemans, in the first
instance, consented to adopt the suggestion regarding
the altered dedication; but was afterwards deterred
from putting it into execution, by a fear that it might
be construed into a manœuvre to propitiate the good
graces of the *Quarterly Review;* and from the slightest approach to any such mode of propitiation, her
sensitive nature recoiled with almost fastidious deli
cacy. Shortly before the publication of *The Sceptic,*
her prize poem, *The Meeting of Wallace and Bruce
on the Banks of the Carron,* had appeared in *Black
wood's Magazine*[1] for September, 1819. A patriotic
individual having signified his intention of giving
£1000 towards the erection of a monument to Sir
William Wallace, and a prize of £50 for the best
poem on the subject above alluded to; Mrs. Hemans
was recommended by a zealous friend in Edinburgh,
to enter the lists as a competitor, which she accordingly did, though without being in the slightest degree
sanguine of success; so that the news of the prize
having been decreed to her was no less unexpected
than gratifying. The number of candidates for this
distinction was so overwhelming, as to cause not a

---

[1] The stanzas on the "Death of the Princess Charlotte," had
been published in the same periodical in April 1818.

little embarrassment to the judges appointed to decide
on their merits. A letter, written at the time, describes them as being reduced to absolute despair by
the contemplation of the task which awaited them;—
having to read over a mass of poetry that would
require at least a month to wade through. Some of
the contributions were from the strangest aspirants
imaginable; and one of them is mentioned as being as
long as *Paradise Lost.* At length, however, the Her-
culean labour was accomplished; and the honour
awarded to Mrs. Hemans on this occasion, seemed an
earnest of the warm kindness and encouragement she
was ever afterwards to receive at the hands of the
Scottish public. One of the earliest notices of *The
Sceptic* appeared in the *Edinburgh Monthly Magazine;* and there is something in its tone so far more
valuable than ordinary praise, and at the same time
so prophetic of the happy influence her writings were
one day to exercise, that the introduction of the concluding paragraph may not be unwelcome to the
readers of this little memorial. After quoting from
the poem, the reviewer thus proceeds:—" These
extracts must, we think, convey to every reader a
favourable impression of the talents of their author,
and of the admirable purposes to which her high gifts
are directed. It is the great defect, as we imagine,
of some of the most popular writers of the day, that
they are not sufficiently attentive to the moral dignity
of their performances; it is the deep, and will be the
lasting reproach of others, that in this point of view
they have wantonly sought and realised the most profound literary abasement. With the promise of talents

not inferior to any, and far superior to most of them, the author before us is not only free from every stain, but breathes all moral beauty and loveliness; and it will be a memorable coincidence if the era of a woman's sway in literature shall become co-eval with the return of its moral purity and elevation."[1] From suffrages such as these, Mrs. Hemans derived not merely present gratification, but encouragement and cheer for her onward course. It was still dearer to her to receive the assurances, with which it often fell to her lot to be blessed, of having, in the exercise of the talents intrusted to her, administered balm to the feelings of the sorrowful, or taught the desponding where to look for comfort. In a letter written at this time to a valued friend, recently visited by one of the heaviest of human calamities—the loss of an exemplary mother—she thus describes her own appreciation of such heart-tributes. "It is inexpressibly gratifying to me to know, that you should find anything I have written at all adapted to your present feelings, and that *The Sceptic* should have been one of the last

---

[1] "It is pleasing to record the following tribute from Mrs. Hannah More, in a letter to a friend who had sent her a copy of *The Sceptic*. 'I cannot refuse myself the gratification of saying, that I entertain a very high opinion of Mrs. Hemans's superior genius and refined taste. I rank her, as a poet, very high, and I have seen no work on the subject of her *Modern Greece*, which evinces more just views, or more delicate perceptions of the fine and the beautiful. I am glad she has employed her powerful pen, in this new instance, on a subject so worthy of it; and anticipating the future by the past, I promise myself no small pleasure in the perusal, and trust it will not only confer pleasure, but benefit.' "

books upon which the eyes, now opened upon brighter
scenes, were cast.   Perhaps, when your mind is sufficiently composed, you will inform me which were the
passages distinguished by the approbation of that pure
and pious mind : they will be far more highly valued
by me than anything I have ever written."

The sentiments expressed in the same letter on the
subject of Affliction, its design and influence, are so
completely a part of herself, that it would seem an
omission to withhold them.   They are embodied in
the following words :—" Your ideas respecting the
nature and degree of sorrow for the departed, permitted us by that religion which seems to speak with
the immediate voice of Heaven to affliction, coincide
perfectly with my own.   I have been hitherto spared
a trial of this nature, but I have often passed hours
in picturing to myself what would be the state of my
mind under such a visitation.   I am convinced, that
though grief becomes criminal when it withdraws us
from the active duties of life, yet that the wounds
made by " the arrows of the Almighty" are not meant
to be forgotten.   If He who chastens those whom He
loves, means, as we cannot doubt, by such inflictions
to recall the Spirit to Himself, and prepare the mortal
for immortality, the endeavour to obliterate such recollections is surely not less in opposition to His intentions, than the indulgence of that rebellious grief,
which repines as if its own sufferings were an exception to the general mercies of Heaven.   Life is but
too dear to us, even with all its precarious joys and
heavy calamities; and constituted even as it is, we
can hardly keep our minds fixed upon a brighter state

with any degree of steadiness. What would it, then, be, if we were not continually reminded that "our all does not lie here;" and if the loss of some beloved friend did not constantly summon our wandering thoughts from the present to the future? I was so struck, a few days ago, with the concluding passage in the *Memoirs* of Mrs. Brunton, that I will not apologize for transcribing part of it, as I am sure you will feel its beautiful and affecting coincidence. It is from a Funeral Sermon on *the Death of the Righteous:*— " Let me exhort you, as you would rise superior to the fear of death, to cherish the memory of those who have already passed from the society of the few who were most dear to them on earth, to the society of the blessed in Heaven. How unnatural seems to be the conduct of many, whose consolation for the loss of a departed friend, appears to depend upon committing his name to oblivion !—who appear to shrink from every object that would for a moment bring to their recollection the delight they once felt in his society! If such conduct be, in any respect, excusable, it can only be in the case of those who have no hope in God. There are few, if any, among us, who have not, ere now, committed to the tomb the remains of some who had been, not only long, but deservedly dear to us; whose virtues are in consequence a satisfying pledge, that they have only gone before us to the mansions of bliss. Some of us have but recently laid in the grave all that was mortal and perishing, of one who may well continue to live in our remembrance—whose memory will be a monitor to us of those virtues, which may qualify us for being re-uni-

ted to her society. Though the body mingle with the
dust, the spirit, in this case, ' yet speaketh ;' it invites,
and, I trust, enables us to anticipate more effectually
on earth our intercourse with the spirits of the just
in heaven.   Great cause we, no doubt, have to mourn
over that dispensation of Providence, which has, in
the mean while, removed from the sphere of our converse on earth, one, from whose converse we had so
invariably derived at once instruction and delight ;—
whose piety was so genuine, that, while never osten-
tatiously displayed, it was, as little, in any case disguised,—whose mental energies communicated such a
character and effect to both her piety and her active
beneficence, that they often served the purpose of an
example to others, when such a purpose was not contemplated by her.   Not to mourn over a dispensation
of Providence, which has deprived us of such a blessing, would be incompatible with the design of Providence in visiting us with such a cause of affliction.
But God forbid that we should sorrow as those who
have no hope of being re-united in heaven to those
who have been dear to them on earth !   God forbid
that we should be unwilling in our hearts to conform
to the design of Providence, when, by removing from
us those who have been the objects of our regard in
this world, it would, in some sense, unite earth to
heaven, by gradually weaning us from the world, and
gradually transferring our hearts to heaven, before we
have altogether completed the appointed years of our
pilgrimage on earth !   Let a view of our condition, as
the heirs of heaven, so elevate our minds, as to make
us now join, with one heart, in the language of our

Christian triumph—'O death! where is thy sting? O grave! where is thy victory?'"

In a subsequent letter to the same friend, and in pursuance of the same subject, there is the following allusion to a poem, which Mrs. Hemans had even then begun to appreciate, though her more perfect and "reverential communion" with the spirit of its author was reserved for later years. "You may remember that I was reading Wordsworth's *Excursion* some time before you left the country. I was much struck with the beauty and sublimity of some of the religious passages it contains; and in looking over the copious extracts I made from it, I observe several, which I think will interest you exceedingly. I mean to copy them out, and send them to you in a few days: the mingled strain of exalted hope and Christian resignation, in which the poet speaks of departed friends, struck me so forcibly, that I thought when I transcribed it, how soothingly it would speak to the heart of any one who had to deplore the loss of some beloved object."

In the spring of 1820, Mrs. Hemans first made the acquaintance of one who became afterwards a zealous and valuable friend, revered in life, and sincerely mourned in death—Bishop Heber, then Rector of Hodnet, and a frequent visiter at Bodryddan, the residence of his father-in-law, the late Dean of St. Asaph, from whom also, during an intercourse of many years, Mrs. Hemans at all times received much kindness and courtesy. Mr. Reginald Heber was the first eminent literary character with whom she had ever familiarly associated; and she therefore entered with a peculiar freshness of feeling into the delight inspired by his conversational powers, enhanced as they were by that gentle benignity of manner, so often the characteristic of minds of the very highest order. In a letter to a friend on this occasion, she thus describes her enjoyment:—" I am more delighted with Mr. Heber than I can possibly tell you; his conversation is quite rich with anecdote, and every subject on which he speaks had been, you would imagine, the sole study of his life. In short, his society has made much the same sort of impression on my mind, that the first perusal of *Ivanhoe* did; and was something so perfectly new to me, that I can hardly talk of anything else. I had a very long conversation with him on the subject of *the* poem, which he read aloud, and commented upon as he proceeded. His manner was so entirely that of a friend, that I felt perfectly at ease, and did not hesitate to express all my own ideas and opinions on the subject, even where they did not exactly coincide with his own."

The poem here alluded to was the one entitled *Superstition and Revelation*, which Mrs. Hemans had commenced some time before, and which was intended to embrace a very extensive range of subject. Her original design will be best given in her own words, from a letter to her friend Miss Park :—" I have been thinking a good deal of the plan we discussed together, of a poem on national superstitions. 'Our thoughts are linked by many a hidden chain;' and in the course of my lucubrations on this subject, an idea occurred to me, which I hope you will not think me too presumptuous in wishing to realize. Might not a poem

of some extent and importance, if the execution were
at all equal to the design, be produced, from contrast-
ing the spirit and tenets of Paganism with those of
Christianity? It would contain, of course, much classical allusion; and all the graceful and sportive fictions
of ancient Greece and Italy, as well as the superstitions of more barbarous climes, might be introduced
to prove how little consolation they could convey in
the hour of affliction, or hope, in that of death. Many
scenes from history might be portrayed in illustration
of this idea; and the certainty of a future state, and
of the immortality of the soul, which we derive from
revelation, are surely subjects for poetry of the highest
class. Descriptions of those regions which are still
strangers to the blessings of our religion, such as the
greatest part of Africa, India, &c., might contain
much that is poetical; but the subject is almost bound-
less, and I think of it till I am startled by its magni-
tude."

Mr. Heber approved highly of the plan of the work,
and gave her every encouragement to proceed in it;
supplying her with many admirable suggestions, both
as to the illustrations which might be introduced with
the happiest effect, and the sources from whence the
requisite information would best be derived. But the
great labour and research necessary to the develop-
ment of a plan which included the superstitions of
every age and country, from the earliest of all idol-
atries—the adoration of the sun, moon, and host of
heaven, alluded to in the book of Job—to the still
existing rites of the Hindoos—would have demanded
a course of study too engrossing to be compatible with

6 *

the many other claims, both domestic and literary, which daily *pressed* more and more upon the author's time. The work was, therefore, laid aside; and the fragment now first published, is all that remains of it, though the project was never distinctly abandoned. About this time, Mrs. Hemans was an occasional contributor to the *Edinburgh Monthly Magazine*, then conducted by the Rev. Robert Morehead, whose liberal courtesy in the exercise of his editorial office, associated many agreeable recollections with the period of this literary intercourse. Several of her poems appeared in the above-mentioned periodical, as also a series of papers on foreign literature, which, with very few exceptions, were the only prose compositions she ever gave to the world; and, indeed, to these papers such a distinctive appellation is perhaps scarcely applicable; as the prose writing may be considered subordinate to the poetical translations, which it is used to introduce. Much has been said of the retirement in which this part of Mrs. Hemans's life was passed; but perhaps the best idea of it may be formed from her own words, in a letter written in October 1820, during a visit she was paying to a happy home circle, at Wavertree Lodge, near Liverpool, the family of the late Henry Park, Esq., whose life of unwearied benevolence and scientific distinction, was then, like the golden sunset of a long bright day, calmly drawing towards its close, in the fullest enjoyment of

"That which should accompany old age,
As Honour, Love, Obedience, troops of friends;"

amongst which friends none were more favoured or

more attached than Mrs. Hemans herself. " I cannot tell you how much I have enjoyed the novelty of all the objects around me. The pastoral seclusion and tranquillity of the life I have led for the last seven or eight years, had left my mind in that state of blissful ignorance particularly calculated to render every new impression an agreeable one; and accordingly, gas-lights, steam-boats, Mr. Kean, casts from the Elgin marbles, and tropical plants in the Botanic Garden, have all, in turn, been the objects of my wondering admiration. I saw Kean in two characters, Richard the Third, and Othello, and can truly say, I felt as if I had never understood Shakspeare till then. I shall never forget the sort of electric light which seemed to flash across my mind from the bursts of power he displayed in several of my favourite passages."

It was either during the present, or a future visit to the same friends, that the *jeu d'esprit* was produced, which Mrs. Hemans used to call her " sheet of forgeries" on the use of the word Barb. A gentleman had requested her to furnish him with some authorities from the old English writers, proving that this term was in use as applied to a steed. She very shortly supplied him with the following imitations, which were written down almost impromptu: the mystification succeeded perfectly, and was not discovered until some time afterwards:—

> The warrior donn'd his well-worn garb,
>   And proudly waved his crest,
> He mounted on his jet-black *barb*,
>   And put his lance in rest.
>
>   PERCY's *Reliques.*

Eftsoons the wight, withouten more delay,
Spurr'd his brown *barb* and rode full swiftly on his way.
SPENSER.

Hark! was it not the trumpet's voice I heard?
The soul of battle is awake within me!
The fate of ages and of empires hangs
On this dread hour. Why am I not in arms!
Bring my good lance, caparison my steed!
Base, idle grooms! are ye in league against me?
Haste with my *barb*, or by the holy saints,
Ye shall not live to saddle him to-morrow!
MASSINGER.[1]

No sooner had the pearl-shedding fingers of the young Aurora
tremulously unlocked the oriental portals of the golden horizon,
than the graceful flower of chivalry, and the bright cynosure of
ladies' eyes—he of the dazzling breast-plate and swanlike plume
—sprang impatiently from the couch of slumber, and eagerly
mounted the noble *barb* presented to him by the Emperor of
Aspramontania.
SIR PHILIP SIDNEY's *Arcadia.*

See'st thou yon chief whose presence seems to rule
The storm of battle? Lo! where'er he moves
Death follows. Carnage sits upon his crest—
Fate on his sword is throned—and his white *barb*,
As a proud courser of Apollo's chariot,
Seems breathing fire.
POTTER's *Æschylus.*

---

[1] An amusing proof of the success of this imitation has recently appeared, in the selection of the first four lines of this
passage for a motto to one of the chapters of Mr. Cooper's
"Homeward Bound," where they are given as a real quotation
from Massinger.

Oh! bonnie look'd my ain true knight,
  His *barb* so proudly reining;
I watch'd him till my tearfu' sight
  Grew amaist dim wi' straining.
                    Border Minstrelsy.

Why, he can heel the lavolt and wind a fiery *barb* as well as
any gallant in Christendom. He's the very pink and mirror of
accomplishment.

                                        SHAKSPEARE.

Fair star of beauty's heaven! to call thee mine,
  All other joys I joyously would yield;
My knightly crest, my bounding *barb* resign,
  For the poor shepherd's crook and daisied field;
For courts, or camps, no wish my soul would prove,
So thou wouldst live with me and be my love!
                        EARL OF SURREY'S *Poems.*

For thy dear love my weary soul hath grown
  Heedless of youthful sports: I seek no more
Or joyous dance, or music's thrilling tone,
  Or joys that once could charm in minstrel lore,
Or knightly tilt where steel-clad champions meet,
Borne on impetuous *barbs* to bleed at beauty's feet.
                        SHAKSPEARE'S *Sonnets.*

          As a warrior clad
In sable arms, like chaos dull and sad,
      But mounted on a *barb* as white
      As the fresh new-born light,—
      So the black night too soon
Came riding on the bright and silver moon,
      Whose radiant heavenly ark,
Made all the clouds beyond her influence seem
      E'en more than doubly dark,
Mourning, all widowed of her glorious beam.
                              COWLEY.

Amongst the very few specimens that have been preserved of Mrs. Hemans's livelier effusions, which she never wrote with any other view than the momentary amusement of her own immediate circle, is a letter addressed about this time to her sister, who was then travelling in Italy. The following extracts from this familiar epistle may serve to show her facility in a style of composition which she latterly entirely discontinued. The first part alludes to a strange fancy produced by an attack of fever, the description of which had given rise to many pleasantries—being an imaginary voyage to China, performed in a cocoa-nut shell, with that eminent old English worthy, John Evelyn:—

Apropos of your illness, pray give, if you please,
Some account of the converse you held on High Seas,
With Evelyn, the excellent author of " Sylva,"
A work that is very much prized at Bronwylfa.
I think that old Neptune was visited ne'er
In so well-rigged a ship, by so well-matched a pair.
There could not have fallen, dear H., to your lot any
Companion more pleasant, since you're fond of Botany,
And *his* horticultural talents are known,
Just as well as Canova's for fashioning stone.

Of the vessel you sailed in, I just will remark,
That I ne'er heard before of so curious a bark.
Of Gondola, Coracle, Pirogue, Canoe,
I have read very often, as doubtless have you:
Of the Argo, conveying that hero, young Jason;
Of the ship moored by Trajan in Nemi's deep basin;
Of the galley, (in Plutarch you'll find the description,)
Which bore along Cydnus the royal Egyptian;

Of that wonderful frigate (see "Curse of Kehama,")
Which wafted fair Kailyal to regions of Brama, }
And the venturous barks of Columbus and Gama.)
But Columbus and Gama to you must resign a
Full half of their fame, since your voyage to China,
(I'm astonished no shocking disaster befel,)
In that swift-sailing first-rate—a cocoa-nut shell!

I hope, my dear H, that you touched at Loo Choo,)
That abode of a people so gentle and true, }
Who with arms and with money have nothing to do.)
How calm must their lives be!—so free from all fears,
Of running *in* debt, or of running *on* spears!
Oh dear! what an Eden!—a land without money!
It excels e'en the region of milk and of honey,
Or the Vale of Cashmere, as described in a book,
Full of musk, gems and roses, and called "Lalla Rookh."

But of all the enjoyments you have, none would e'er be
More valued by me, than a chat with Acerbi,
Of whose travels, related in elegant phrases,
I have seen many extracts, and heard many praises,
And have copied (you know I let nothing escape),
His striking account of the frozen North Cape.
I think 'twas in his works I read long ago,
(I've not the best memory for dates, as you know),
Of a warehouse, where sugar and treacle were stored,
Which took fire (I suppose being made but of board)
In the icy domains of some rough northern hero, ·
Where the cold was some fifty degrees below zero.
Then from every burnt cask as the treacle ran out,
And in streams, just like lava, meandered about,
You may fancy the curious effect of the weather,
The frost, and the fire, and the treacle together.
When my *first* for a moment had hardened my *last*,
My *second* burst out, and all melted as fast;
To win their sweet prize long the rivals fought on,
But I quite forget which of the elements won.

But a truce with all joking — I hope you'll excuse me,
Since I know you still love to instruct and amuse me,
For hastily putting a few questions down,
To which answers from you all my wishes will crown:
For you know I'm so fond of the land of Corinne,
That my thoughts are still dwelling its precincts within,
And I read all that authors, or gravely, or wittily,
Or wisely, or foolishly, write about Italy;
From your shipmate, John Evelyn's, amusing old tour,
To Forsyth's *one* volume, and Eustace's *four*,
In spite of Lord Byron, or Hobhouse, who glances
At the classical Eustace, and says he romances.

Pray describe me from Venice (don't think it a bore)
The literal state of the famed Bucentaur;
And whether the horses, that once were the sun's,
Are of bright yellow brass, or of dark dingy bronze,
For some travellers say one thing, and some say another,
And I can't find out which, they all make such a pother.
Oh! another thing too, which I'd nearly forgot,
Are the songs of the Gondoliers pleasing or not?
These are matters of moment, you'll surely allow,
For Venice must interest all, even now.

These points being settled, I ask for no more hence,
But should wish for a few observations from Florence.
Let me know if the Palaces Strozzi and Pitti
Are finished — if not 'tis a shame for the city,
To let *one* for ages — was e'er such a thing? —
Its entablature want, and the other its wing.
Say, too, if the Dove (should you be there at Easter,
And watch her swift flight, when the priests have released her),
Is a turtle, or ring-dove, or but a *wood*-pigeon,
Which makes people *gulls*, in the name of Religion?
Pray tell, if the forests of famed Vallombrosa
Are cut down or not, for this, too, is a *Cosa*
About which I'm anxious — as also to know
If the Pandects, so famous long ages ago,

Came back, (above all, don't forget this to mention)
To that manuscript library called the Laurentian.

Since I wrote the above, I, by chance, have found out,
That the horses *are* bright yellow brass, beyond doubt;
So I'll ask you but this, the same subject pursuing,
Do you think they are truly Lysippus's doing?

When to Naples you get, let me know if you will,
If the Acqua Toffana's in fashion there still,
For, not to fatigue you with needless verbosity,
'T is a point upon which I feel much curiosity.
I should like to have also, and not written shabbily,
Your opinion about the *Piscina mirabile;*
And whether the tomb, which is near Sannazaro's,
Is decided by you to be really Maro's.

In June 1821, Mrs. Hemans obtained the prize
awarded by the Royal Society of Literature for the
best poem on the subject of *Dartmoor.* On this occasion, as on every other, her chief enjoyment of success
was derived from the happiness it created in those
around her. That "Fame can only afford *reflected*
delight to a woman," was a sentiment she unceasingly
felt and expressed; and she never was more truly herself than in writing to Miss Mitford. "Do you know
that I often think of you, and of the happiness you
must feel in being able to run to your father and
mother with all the praises you receive." In the
" kind, approving eye," the " meek, attentive ear" of
her own fond mother, she possessed a source of pure
happiness, too soon, alas! withdrawn. When absent
from her brothers and sister, almost the first thought
that would occur to her, on occasions like the present,
was a longing impatience for them to hear of her good

Vol. I. —— 7

fortune ; and the tumultuous exultation of her boys, was a far dearer tribute than the praise of the mightiest critic.   On hearing of the success of *Dartmoor*, she thus wrote to the friends who had been the first to communicate it to her.

"What with surprise, bustle, and pleasure, I am really almost bewildered.   I wish you had but seen the children, when the prize was announced to them yesterday.   Arthur, you know, had so set his heart upon it, that he was quite troublesome with his constant inquiries on the subject.   He sprang up from his Latin exercise and shouted aloud, 'Now, I am sure mamma is a better poet than Lord Byron !' [1]

"Their acclamations were actually deafening, and George [2] said that the ' excess of his pleasure had really given him a headache.'   The Bishop's kind communication put us in possession of the gratifying intelligence a day sooner than we should otherwise have known it, as I did not receive the Secretary's letter till this morning.   Besides the official announcement of the prize, his despatch also contained a private letter, with which, although it is one of criticism, I feel greatly pleased, as it shows an interest in my literary success, which from so distinguished a writer as Mr. Croly, (of course you have read his poem of *Paris*,) cannot but be highly gratifying."

---

[1] It is scarcely necessary to remark, that the comparison originated solely with the boy himself.

[2] George Willoughby Hemans, the eldest of her surviving sons, now a promising young civil engineer.

Mrs. Hemans was at this time occupied in the composition of her tragedy, *The Vespers of Palermo*, which she originally wrote, without any idea of offering it for the stage. The sanguine recommendations, however, of Mr. Reginald Heber, and the equally kind encouragement of Mr. Milman (to whose correspondence she was introduced through the medium of a mutual friend, though she had never the advantage of his personal acquaintance), induced her to venture upon a step which her own diffidence would have withheld her from contemplating, but for the support of such high literary authorities. Indeed, notwithstanding the flattering encomiums which were bestowed upon the tragedy by all who read it, and most especially by the critics of the green room, whose *imprimatur* might have been supposed a sufficiently safe guarantee of success, her own anticipations, throughout the long period of suspense which intervened between its acceptance and representation, were far more modified than those of her friends. In this subdued tone of feeling she thus wrote to Mr. Milman:—" As I cannot help looking forward to the day of trial with much more of dread than of sanguine expectation, I most willingly acquiesce in your recommendations of delay, and shall rejoice in having the respite as much prolonged as possible. I begin almost to shudder at my own presumption, and, if it were not for the kind encouragement I have received from you and Mr. Reginald Heber, should be much more anxiously occupied in searching for any outlet of escape, than in attempting to overcome the difficulties

which seem to obstruct my onward path."[1]   These
misgivings were but too well justified by the ultimate
fate of the piece; but, as this remained in abeyance
for two years longer, it will be again alluded to in the
proper order of date.

Mrs. Hemans's familiar letters of this period, exhibit a singular mixture of maternal and literary anxieties.   In one of them, she says—" I have not been
able, I am sorry to say, to pay the least attention to
my Welsh studies, since your departure   I am so
fearful of not having the copying of the tragedy completed by the time my brother and sister return, and I
have such a variety of nursery interruptions, that what
with the murdered Provençals, George's new clothes,
Mr. Morehead's *Edinburgh Magazine*, Arthur's cough,
and his Easter holidays, besides the dozen little riots
which occur in my colony every day, my ideas are

---

[1] " Oh! what troubled billows," wrote she to an intimate
friend, " have I launched my paper boat upon, in writing this
play! If I get through them as well as we did through the awful
hurricane, of which you have given us so many melancholy particulars, it will be marvellous indeed.   We escaped wonderfully,
and, strange to say, every one in the house but myself, slept
quietly the greater part of the night, which, I think, argued great
stupidity.   For me, I have ' given too many pledges to fortune,'
as Lord Bacon says, to feel so tranquil, with ' such a dreadful
pother o'er our heads;' and I must say, I never passed a night
of such awful suspense   The deep, rosy sleep of the children
quite affected me to look at.   Heaven be praised! no accident
of any serious consequence occurred in our neighbourhood, and I
do think there never will be such a storm again, because the
winds must have ' cracked their cheeks,' so as to be quite unable
to blow any more."

sometimes in such a state of rotatory motion, that it is with great difficulty I can reduce them to any sort of order."

In another letter, she writes—"You will smile when I tell you of my having stolen time to-day from much more serious employments, for the very important purpose of making garlands for my little boys to dance with, as it is the birthday of my youngest."

About this time, the return of her sister from Germany, and the ample supplies of new books furnished to her by her eldest brother, then with the embassy at Vienna (the ever ready minister to her tastes, no less than the unfailing support in her trials,) induced her to devote herself with enthusiasm to the study of German, which from thenceforward she may be said to have taken to her heart with a kind of affectionate adoption. She never spoke of it without warmly acknowledging how many sources of intellectual enjoyment and expansion it had opened to her; and could well have understood the feelings of the celebrated Venetian paintress, Rosalba Carriera, who, as we are told by Mrs. Jameson,[1] used, after her return to Italy from Dresden, to say her prayers in German, " because the language was so expressive." In this predilection, as in every other, it was always a true pleasure to Mrs. Hemans to meet with a corresponding taste in any of her friends. In one of her letters, she says—" I am so delighted when I meet with any

---

[1] See " Visits and Sketches at Home and Abroad," vol. ii. p. 115.

7 *

one who knows and loves my favourite *seelenvolle*[1] German, that I believe I could talk of it for ever." And, in another,—" I do assure you, that when any of my friends enjoy what has been a source of enjoyment to myself, I feel all the pleasure of a child who has found a companion to play with his flowers."

She in general preferred the writings of Schiller to those of Goethe, and could for ever find fresh beauties in *Wallenstein*, with which she was equally familiar in its eloquent original, and in Coleridge's magnificent translation, or, as it may truly be called, transfusion. Those most conversant with her literary tastes, will remember her almost actual, relation-like love for the characters of Max and Thekla, whom, like many other " beings of the mind," she had learned to consider as friends; and her constant quotations of certain passages from this noble tragedy, which peculiarly accorded with her own views and feelings. In the *Stimmen der Volker in Lieder* of Herder, she found a rich store of thoughts and suggestions; and it was this work which inspired her with the idea of her own *Lays of many Lands*, most of which appeared originally in the *New Monthly Magazine*, then edited by Mr. Campbell. She also took great delight in the dreamy beauties of Novalis and Tieck, and in what has been gracefully characterised by Mr. Chorley, as the " moonlight tenderness" of Oehlenschlager. Of the works of the latter, her especial favourite was *Coreggio;* and of Tieck, *Sternbald's Wanderungen*, which she often made her out-of-doors companion. It

---

[1] Full of soul.

was always an especial mark of her love for a book, and of her considering it true to nature, and to the best wisdom of the heart,[1] when she promoted it to the list of those with which she would " take sweet counsel" amidst the woods and fields.

But, amongst all these names of power, none awakened a more lively interest in her mind, than that of the noble-hearted Korner, the young soldier-bard, who, in the words of Professor Bouterwek, " would have become a distinguished tragic poet, had he not met with the still more glorious fate of falling on the field of battle, while fighting for the deliverance of Germany." The stirring events of his life, the heroism of his early death, and the beautiful tie which subsisted between him and his only sister, whose fate was so touchingly bound up with his own, formed a romance of real life, which could not fail to excite feelings of the warmest enthusiasm in a bosom so ready as hers, to respond to all things high and holy. The lyric of *The Grave of Körner*, is, perhaps, one of the most impressive Mrs. Hemans ever wrote. Her whole heart was in a subject which so peculiarly combined the two strains dearest to her nature, the chivalrous and the tender.

> "They were but two, and when that spirit pass'd,
> Woe to the one, the last!"

That mournful echo—" They were but two," was,

---

[1] "One of out poets says, with equal truth and beauty, ' The heart is wise.' We should be not only happier but better if we attended more to its dictates."—*Ethel Churchill, by L. E. L.*, vol. i. p. 234

by some indefinable association, connected in her mind with another and far differing brother and sister, called into existence by the magic pen of Scott. The affecting ejaculation, " There are but two of us !" so often repeated by the hapless Clara Mowbray in *St. Ronan's Well*, was frequently quoted by Mrs. Hemans as an instance of the deepest pathos. The lyric in question was, it is believed, one of the first tributes which appeared in England, to the memory of the author of *The Lyre and Sword*, though his name has since become " familiar in our ears as household words." A translation of the *Life of Körner*, with selections from his poems, &c., was published in 1827, by G. F. Richardson, Esq., whose politeness in presenting a copy of the work to Mrs. Hemans, inscribed with a dedicatory sonnet, led to an interchange of letters with that gentleman, and was further the means of procuring for her the high gratification of a direct message, full of the most feeling acknowledgment, from the venerable father of the hero, who afterwards addressed to her a poetical tribute from *Theodore Körner's Father.* Her pleasure in receiving this genuine offering was thus expressed to Mr. Richardson, who had been the medium through which it reached her. " *Theodor Körner's Vater !*—it is, indeed, a title, beautifully expressing all the holy pride which the memory of *die treuen Tödten* [1] must inspire ; and awakening every good and high feeling to its sound. I shall prize the lines as a relic. Will you be kind enough to assure M. Körner, with my

---

[1] The faithful dead.

grateful respects, of the value which will be attached
to them, a value so greatly enhanced by their being
in his own hand.   They are very beautiful, I think,
in their somewhat antique and *treuherzig*[1] simplicity,
and worthy to have proceeded from *Theodor Körner's
Vater.*"

The following almost literal translation of these
lines, is given by W. B. Chorley, Esq., in his interesting little volume, *The Lyre and Sword*, published in
1834 :—

"Gently a voice from afar is borne to the ear of the mourner ;
Mildly it soundeth, yet strong, grief in his bosom to soothe ;
Strong in the soul-cheering faith, that hearts have a share in his
 sorrow,
In whose depths all things holy and noble are shrined.
From that land once dearly belov'd by our brave one, the fallen,
Mourning blent with bright fame—cometh a wreath for his urn. .
Hail to thee, England the free ! thou see'st in the German no
 stranger.
Over the earth and the seas, joined be both lands, heart and
 hand !"

There was nothing which delighted Mrs. Hémans
more in German literature, than the cordial feeling
of brotherhood, so conspicuous amongst its most eminent authors, and their freedom from all the petty
rivalries and manœuvres, on which she herself looked
down with as much of wonder, as of contempt.   In a
letter, in which she speaks of the bitterness, and jea-
lousy, and strife, pervading the tone of many of our
own Reviews, she adds, turning to a brighter picture
with a feeling of relief, like that of one emerging

---

[1] True-hearted.

from the heated atmosphere of a city to breathe the fresh air of the mountains.—" How very different seems the spirit of literary men in Germany ! I am just reading a work of Tieck's, which is dedicated to Schlegel ; and I am delighted with the beautiful sim-plicity of these words in the dedication.

" ' *Es war eine schone Zeit meines Lebens, als ich dich und deinen Bruder Friedrich zuerst kennen lernte ; eine noch schonere als wir und Novalis für Kunst und Wissenschaft vereinigt lebten, und uns in mannigfaltigen Bestrebungen begegneten. Jetzt hat uns das Schicksal schon seit vielen Jahren getrennt. Ich kann nur in Geist und in der Erinnerung mit dir leben.*'* Is not that union of bright minds, *für Kunst und Wissenschaft,* a picture on which it is delightful to repose ?"

Mrs. Hemans's familiar correspondence of the year 1822, contains many humorous complaints of the per-petual disturbance she endured from the inroads of masons and carpenters, who were employed in cer-tain alterations and additions at Bronwylfa. It was in the desperation occasioned by these circumstances that she was at last, as has been elsewhere record-ed, driven to seek refuge in the laundry, from which classical locality, she was wont to say, it could be no wonder if sadly mangled lines were to issue.

---

[1] " That was a bright era in my life when I first learned to know you and your brother Frederick ; a still brighter, when we and Novalis lived united for art and knowledge, and emu-lated one another in various competitions Fate has since, for many years, divided us. I can now live with you only in spirit and in memory."

Some of her lamentations over these grievances were poured forth in such strains as the following: —"I entreat you to pity me—I am actually in the melancholy situation of Lord Byron's 'scorpion girt by fire'—'Her circle narrowing as she goes,' for I have been pursued by the household troops through every room successively, and begin to think of establishing my *métier* in the cellar; though I dare say, if I were to fix myself as comfortably in a hogshead as Diogenes himself, it would immediately be discovered that some of the hoops or staves wanted repair.

"When you talk of tranquillity and a quiet home, I stare about in wonder, having almost lost the recollection of such things, and the hope that they may probably be regained some time or other. I believe I told you that I had been obliged to vacate my own room, and submit to the complete dislodgement of my books, together with the dust, cobwebs, and other appurtenances thereunto belonging. 'If there be any love of mercy' in you, I hope you will feel a proper degree of commiseration towards me in my extremity."

A few weeks later, she writes—" We continue in the same state of tumult and confusion, wherein we have existed, as it appears to my recollection, time immemorial. There is a war of old grates with new grates, and plaster and paint with dust and cobwebs, carrying on in this once tranquil abode, with a vigour and animosity productive of little less din than that occasioned by 'lance to lance, and horse to horse.' I assure you, when I make my escape about 'fall of eve' to some of the green, quiet hay-fields by which we are surrounded, and look back at the house, which, from a little distance, seems almost, like Shakspeare's moonlight, to 'sleep upon the bank,' I can hardly conceive how so gentle-looking a dwelling can contrive to send forth such an incessant clatter of obstreperous sound through its honeysuckle-fringed window. It really reminds me of a pretty shrew, whose amiable smiles would hardly allow a casual observer to suspect the possibility of so fair a surface being occasionally ruffled by storms.'

During these days of confusion, her two eldest boys, Arthur and George, had been sent away for a few weeks to the house of a clergyman, whose pupils they had been, during his previous residence in the neigh bourhood of St. Asaph. It was their first absence from home, and was consequently considered as an era of no small importance. Their mother would often afterwards refer to the day on which she went with her sister to fetch them home, as one of the white days of her life. The little journey (about twenty miles,) was in itself an enjoyable one. The remote village[1] at which they were staying, is quite embosomed amongst the mountains, and only approach-able by narrow shaded lanes, seldom traversed by a carriage. It was one of those glorious summer days when all nature seems to rejoice,

> "As if earth contained no tomb."

The quiet beauty of the "hill-country," with its bright streams and rich verdure smiling in the sun-shine ; the joyous song of the sky-lark (never heard so triumphantly as amongst the mountains,) — the

---

[1] Bettws Gwerfil goch.

peculiar luxuriance of the ferns and fox-glove[1] which
fringed the way-side, and even the grotesque rugged-
ness of the road, which gave to the excursion almost
an air of adventure—were all felt and enjoyed as
such things must ever be by the lover of nature: and
when at last the little parsonage appeared in sight,
and the two happy boys came rushing down a green
slope behind it, flapping their pinafores in ecstasy,
and uttering a thousand joyful exclamations at the
sight of the carriage, it was indeed a bright picture,
and a moment not easily to be forgotten.   Then came
the kind welcome of the host and hostess, the important air of ciceroneism with which the two boys proceeded to do the honours of the village, the church,
the bridge, all the wonders, in short, of the little
world around them—and then the charms of the
evening drive home, the thousand questions to be
asked and answered on each side, and finally, the
gladsome meeting with grandmamma, and the three
merry little brothers in the nursery.

About this time, after reading the then new-novel
of *The Fortunes of Nigel*, Mrs. Hemans had inad-
vertently mentioned it, in a letter to a friend, as giving an admirable picture of the times of James the
Second.   On recollecting her mistake, she lost no time

---

[1] This luxuriance was so remarkable, that, by one of the
party, the fox-glove has never been seen since, without a recollection of that day, and of the information then first obtained,
of its pretty Welsh name, *Menyg Ellyllon*, fairies' gloves, from
which some learned authorities have traced its common appellation as a corruption of *folk's glove;* the fairies being designated
as " the good folk."

in making the following recantation:—"I am somewhat uneasy at having committed myself, as I just
now recollect, by telling you that the scene of *The
Fortunes of Nigel* is laid in the times of James the
Second. If you have read the book, you are not the
person to treat such

> "Misquoting, mis-stating,
> Misplacing, misdating,"

with the smallest degree of compassion. I shall certainly suffer for it, and be the unhappy subject of one
of the three modes of showing disdain, practised in the
days of good Queen Bess, viz., "the broad flout, the
fleering frump, and the privy nip." If you have not
(that is, not read *Nigel*), you may be committing yourself, and that not merely as an individual, but as a
member of the "very noble and approved" Literary
and Critical Society of St. Asaph, by quoting the
anachronism into which I have led you. I therefore
write to-day, for the sole purpose of throwing the bur-
den off my mind, and you may set it down in the list
of my errata, that I told you *Nigel* described the court
and manners of James the Second, instead of the First,
the

> "Bonnie King James who from Scotland came."

I am sure, the very idea of his quilted doublet is
enough to give one a fever such a day as this. I wish
I were with those people in South America, who hold
their assemblies and *conversazioni* every evening in a
river. There they sit, gossiping in their elbow chairs;
and, I dare say, the chief conversation, like that over
our own tea-tables, turns upon the heat or coolness of

the water. But I am quite forgetting that I had not
a word to say to you except about *Nigel,* and moreover, dinner is going in. Dinner! I wonder if "gen-
teel families" are at dinner now in the dog-star.

> "You're hot if you don't eat at all,
>   You're hotter if you do."

Nevertheless, to the latter alternative, I must submit at present; therefore, good bye."

In the autumn of this year (1822), Mrs. Hemans
had the good fortune to make an acquaintance, not
only highly interesting in itself, but most advantageous
in a literary point of view—that of William Jacob, Esq.,
the well-known author of *Travels in Spain and in
Germany,* and of several other valuable statistical
works.

This gentleman, whilst travelling through Wales,
accompanied by one of his daughters, paid a visit to
Bronwylfa, which, leaving nothing to regret but the
shortness of its duration, laid the foundation of a long
series of kind and active services on the one part, and
of grateful appreciation on the other. "Believe me,"
wrote Mrs. Hemans to Miss Jacob, "the few hours
we passed in your society will be long remembered;
and, to use an expression of our old Welsh bards, we
shall look back to them " as to green spots on the
floods;" for our paths, in this retired part of the world,
are seldom crossed by those who leave any deeper impression upon our memory than " the little lines of
yesterday."

The bardic expression above alluded to, with many
others, equally quaint and figurative, was frequently

quoted by Mrs. Hemans, who took infinite delight in
all that related to the ancient days of Wales, and was
at this time engaged in an undertaking, which, from
the course of reading it led to, initiated her into much
that was striking and original in the legendary lore of
her adopted country. The noble motto for all the proceedings of the old Welsh bards,—" In the face of the
sun, and in the eye of light," was one completely after
her own heart, and in perfect accordance with the
transparent guilelessness of a character to which the
conventional insincerities of every-day life were so
unutterably distasteful. It is, indeed, impossible to in-
sist too much upon this peculiar characteristic, which,
rendering her as unsuspicious of evil thoughts in others,
as she was incapable of them herself, laid her open in
a thousand ways to the misconstructions of those
" children of this world" who are, " in their genera-
tion, wiser than the children of light." To return,
however, to her favourite ancient Britons, whom she
thus introduced to the notice of her new friend:—
" The idea entertained of the bardic character, appears to me particularly elevated and beautiful. The
bard was not allowed, in any way, to become a party
in political or religious dispute; he was recognised so
completely as the herald of peace, under the title of
' Bard of the Isle of Britain,' that a naked weapon
was not allowed to be displayed in his presence. He
passed unmolested from one hostile country to another;
and, if he appeared in his uni-coloured robe (which
was azure, being the emblem of peace and truth)
between two contending armies, the battle was immediately suspended. One of the general titles of the

order was, ' Those who are free throughout the world,'
and their motto, ' The truth against the world.' "

The Voice of Spring, perhaps the best known and
best loved of all Mrs. Hemans's lyrics, was written
early in the year 1823; and is thus alluded to in a
letter to a friend, who had lately suffered a severe
and sudden bereavement:—" *The Voice of Spring*
expresses some peculiar feelings of my own, although
my life has yet been unvisited by any affliction so
deeply impressive, in all its circumstances, as the one
you have been called upon to sustain. Yet I cannot
but feel every year, with the return of the violet, how
much the shadows of my mind have deepened since
its last appearance ; and to me the spring, with all
its joy and beauty, is generally a time of thoughtfulness rather than mirth. I think the most delightful
poetry I know upon the subject of this season, is contained in the works of Tieck, a German poet, with
whom you are perhaps acquainted; but the feelings
he expresses are of a very different character from
those I have described to you, seeming all to proceed
from an overflowing sense of life and joy."

This indefinable feeling of languor and depression
produced by the influence of spring, will be well
understood by many a gentle heart. Never do the

> " Fond strange yearnings from the soul's deep cell,
> Gush for the faces we no more shall see,"

with such uncontrollable power, as when all external
nature breathes of life and gladness. Amidst all the
bright and joyous things around us, we are haunted
with images of death and the grave. The force of

8 *

contrast, not less strong than that of analogy, is unceasingly reminding us of the great gulph that divides us from those who are now "gone down in silence." Some unforgotten voice is ever whispering —"And I too in Arcadia." We remember how we were wont to rejoice in the soft air and pleasant sunshine; and these things can charm us no longer, "because *they* are not." The farewell sadness of autumn, on the contrary—its falling leaves, and universal imagery of decay, by bringing more home to us the sense of our own mortality, identifies us more closely with those who are gone before, and the veil of separation becomes, as it were, more transparent. We are impressed with a more pervading conviction that " we shall go to them ;" while in spring, every thing seems mournfully to echo, " they will not return to us !"

These peculiar associations may be traced in many of Mrs. Hemans's writings, deepening with the influence of years and of sorrows, and more particularly developed in the poem called *Breathings of Spring*. And when it is remembered that it was at this season her own earthly course was finished, the following passage from a letter, written in the month of May, some years after the one last quoted, cannot be read without emotion. " Poor A. H. is to be buried to-morrow. With the bright sunshine laughing around, it seems more sad to think of; yet if I could choose when I would wish to die, it should be in spring— the influence of that season is so strangely depressing to my heart and frame."

It was in 1823 that Mrs. Hemans began to be a

contributor to the *New Monthly Magazine,* then edited by Mr. Campbell; and in the summer of the same year, the volume containing *The Siege of Valencia* was published by Mr. Murray. Through some mistake of the printers, an untoward anomaly occurred in the arrangement of the contents of this volume—*The Last Constantine* taking precedence of the poem which so far exceeded it in importance and interest, and from which the work derived its name. *Belshazzar's Feast,* which appeared in the same volume, had previously been published in the *Collection of Poems from Living Authors,* edited for a benevolent purpose by Mrs. Joanna Baillie.[1]

---

[1] This work was thus referred to in one of Mrs. Hemans's letters:—"Have you seen a collection of poems by living authors, edited by Mrs. Joanna Baillie, for the benefit of a friend? She was kind enough to send me a copy, as I was one of her contributors: I mention it to you, principally to call your attention, should you meet with the book, to a very fine translation, by Sotheby, of Schiller's magnificent *Lied von der Glocke,*—a piece so very difficult to translate with effect, that I should have hardly thought it possible to give it so much spirit and grace in another language. I never, until very lately, met with a tragedy of Mrs. Baillie's, which is, I believe, less generally known than her other works—*The Family Legend.* I was much pleased with it, particularly with her delineation of the heroine. Indeed, nothing in all her writings delights me so much as her general idea of what is beautiful in the female character. There is so much gentle fortitude, and deep self-devoting affection in the women whom she portrays, and they are so perfectly different from the pretty "unidea'd girls," who seem to form the *beau idéal* of our whole sex in the works of some modern poets. Have you seen the lately published memoirs of Lady Griseld Baillie? She was an ancestress, I believe, of Joanna's, and her delightful character

After innumerable delays, uncertainties, and anxieties, the fate of the tragedy, so long in abeyance, was now drawing to a crisis. Every thing connected with its approaching representation was calculated to raise the highest hopes of success. "All is going on," writes Mrs. Hemans on the 27th November, "as well as I could possibly desire. Only a short time will yet elapse before the ordeal is over. I received a message yesterday from Mr. Kemble, informing me of the unanimous opinion of the green room conclave in favour of the piece, and exhorting me to ' be of good courage.' Murray has given me two hundred guineas for the copyright of the ' tragedy, drama, poem, composition, or book,' as it is called in the articles which I signed yesterday. The managers made exceptions to the name of *Procida*, why or wherefore I know not ; and out of several others which I proposed to them, *The Vespers of Palermo* has been finally chosen."

Under these apparently favourable auspices, the piece was produced at Covent Garden on the night of December 12, 1823, the principal characters being taken by Mr. Young, Mr. C. Kemble, Mr. Yates, Mrs. Bartley, and Miss F. H. Kelly. Two days had to elapse before the news of its reception could reach St. Asaph. Not only Mrs. Hemans's own family, but all her more immediate friends and neighbours were wrought up to a pitch of intense expectation. Various newspapers were ordered expressly for the occasion ;

seems to have been the model her descendant has copied in some of her dramas."

and the post-office was besieged at twelve o'clock at night, by some of the more zealous of her friends, eager to be the first heralds of the triumph so undoubtingly anticipated. The boys had worked themselves up into an uncontrollable state of excitement, and were all lying awake " to hear about mamma's play;" and perhaps her bitterest moment of mortification was, when she went up to their bed-sides, which she nerved herself to do almost immediately, to announce that all their bright visions were dashed to the ground, and that the performance had ended in all but a failure. The reports in the newspapers were strangely contradictory, and, in some instances, exceedingly liberal; but all which were written in any thing like an unbiassed tone, concurred entirely with the private accounts, not merely of partial friends, but of perfectly unprejudiced observers, in attributing this most unexpected result to the inefficiency of the actress who personated Constance, and who absolutely seemed to be under the influence of some infatuating spell, calling down hisses, and even laughter, on scenes the most pathetic and affecting, and, to crown all, *dying gratuitously* at the close of the piece. The acting of Young and Kemble in the two Procidi, was universally pronounced to have been beyond all praise; and their sustained exertions showed a determination to do all possible justice to the author. It was admitted, that at the fall of the curtain, applause decidedly predominated: still the marks of disapprobation were too strong to be disregarded by the managers, who immediately decided upon withdrawing the piece, till another actress should have fitted herself to under-

take the part of Constance, when they fully resolved
to reproduce it.   Mrs. Hemans herself was very far
from wishing that this fresh experiment should be
made.   " Mr. Kemble," writes she to a friend, " will
not hear of *The Vespers* being driven off the stage.
It is to be reproduced as soon as Miss Foote, who is
now unwell, shall be sufficiently recovered to learn
her part; but I cannot tell you how I shrink, after
the fiery ordeal through which I have passed, from
such another trial.   Mr. Kemble attributes the failure,
without the slightest hesitation, to what he delicately
calls "a singularity of intonation in one of the actress-
es."   I have also heard from Mr. Milman, Mr. J. S.
Coleridge, and several others, with whom there is but
one opinion as to the cause of the disaster."

Few would, perhaps, have borne so unexpected a
reverse with feelings so completely untinged with bitterness, or with greater readiness to turn for consolation to the kindness and sympathy which poured in
upon her from every side.   It would be doing her
injustice to withhold her letter to Mr. Milman, written
in the first moments of disappointment.

"Bronwylfa, Dec. 16, 1823.

" My DEAR SIR,

" It is difficult to part with the hopes of three
years, without some painful feelings; but your kind
letter has been of more service to me than I can
attempt to describe.   I will not say that it revives
my hopes of success, because I think it better that
I should file my mind to prevent those hopes from
gaining any ascendency ; but it sets in so clear a light

the causes of failure, that my disappointment has been greatly softened by its perusal. The many friends from whom I have heard on this occasion, express but one opinion. As to Miss Kelly's acting, and its fatal effect on the fortunes of the piece, I cannot help thinking that it will be impossible to counteract the unfavourable impression which this must have produced, and I almost wish, as far as relates to my own private feelings, that the attempt may not be made. I shall not, however, interfere in any way on the subject. I have not heard from Mr. Kemble; but I have written both to him and to Mr. Young, to express my grateful sense of their splendid exertions in support of the piece. As a female, I cannot help feeling rather depressed by the extreme severity with which I have been treated in the morning papers. I know not why this should be; for I am sure I should not have attached the slightest value to their praise; but I suppose it is only a proper chastisement for my temerity; for a female who shrinks from such things, has certainly no business to write tragedies.

"For your support and assistance, as well as that of my other friends, I cannot be too grateful; nor can I ever consider any transaction of my life unfortunate, which has given me the privilege of calling you a friend, and afforded me the recollection of so much long-tried kindness.—Ever believe me, my dear sir, most faithfully, your obliged

F. Hemans."

Notwithstanding the determination of the managers again to bring forward *The Vespers*, a sort of fatality seemed to attend upon it, and some fresh obstacle was continually arising to prevent the luckless Constance from obtaining an efficient representative on the London stage. Under these circumstances, Mr. Kemble at length confessed that he could not recommend the reproduction of the piece; and Mrs. Hemans acquiesced in the decision, with feelings which partook rather of relief than of disappointment. She never ceased to speak in the warmest terms of Mr. Kemble's liberal and gentlemanly conduct, both before and after the appearance of the piece, and of his surpassing exertions at the time of its representation.

It was with no small degree of surprise, that, in the course of the following February, she learned, through the medium of a letter from Mrs. Joanna Baillie,[1] that the tragedy was shortly to be represent-

---

[1] Though Mrs. Hemans had never the advantage of being personally known to this gifted and excellent lady, the occasional interchange of letters, which, from this time forward, was kept up between them, was regarded as one of the most valuable privileges she possessed. It was always delightful to her when she could love the character, as well as admire the talents, of a celebrated author; and never, surely, was there an example better fitted to call forth the willing tribute of veneration, both towards the woman and the poetess. In one of her letters to Mrs. Baillie, Mrs. Hemans thus apologized for indulging in a strain of egotism, which the nature of their acquaintance might scarcely seem to justify.—" The kindly warmth of heart which seems to breathe over all your writings, and the power of early association over my mind, make me feel, whenever I address you, as if I were writing to a friend."

It would have been very dear to her could she have foreseen how graciously that "kindly warmth of heart" would be extended to those of her children, who are more fortunate than her-ed at the Edinburgh Theatre—Mrs. Henry Siddons undertaking the part of Constance. The play was brought out on the 5th of April, and the following particulars of its reception, transmitted by one of the zealous friends who had been instrumental in this arrangement, will prove how well their kindly intentions were fulfilled:—

" The tragedy went off in a style which exceeded our most sanguine expectations, and was announced for repetition on Wednesday, amidst thunders of applause. The actors seem to have done wonders, and every one appeared to strain every nerve, as if all depended on his own exertions. Vandenhoff was the elder, and Calcraft the younger Procida. The first recognition between father and son, was acted by them to such perfection, that one of the most hearty and unanimous plaudits followed that ever was heard.

*   *   *   *   *

" Every re-appearance of the gentle Constance won the spectators more and more. The scene in the judgment hall carried off the audience into perfect illusion, and handkerchiefs were out in every quarter. Mrs. Siddons's searching the faces of the judges, which she did in a wild manner, as if to find how Raimond's father was to save him, was perfect. She flew round the circle—went, as if distracted, close up to judge after judge—paused before Procida, and fell prostrate at his feet. The effect was magical, and was manifested by three repeated bursts of applause."

---

self, in enjoying the personal intercourse she would have prized so highly.

A neatly turned and witty epilogue, surmised, though not declared, to be the production of Sir Walter Scott, was recited by Mrs. H. Siddons. When deference to a *female* was there laid claim to, loud bursts of applause ensued; but, when generosity to a *stranger* was bespoken, the house absolutely rang with huzzas.

"I knew how much you would rejoice," wrote Mrs. Hemans to a warm-hearted friend, "in the issue of my Edinburgh trial; it has, indeed, been most gratifying, and I think, amongst the pleasantest of its results, I may reckon a letter from Sir Walter Scott, of which it has put me in possession. I had written to thank him for the kindness he had shown with regard to the play, and hardly expected an answer; but it came, and you would be delighted with its frank and unaffected kindliness. He acknowledges the epilogue, "stuffed," as he says it was, " with parish jokes, and bad puns;" and courteously says, that his country folks have done more credit to themselves than to me, by their reception of *The Vespers.*

To another uncompromising champion she wrote: —" I must beg you will 'bear our faculties meekly:' you really seem to be rather in an intoxicated state; and if we indulge ourselves in this way, I am afraid we shall have something violent to sober us. I dare say I must expect some sharp criticism from Edinburgh ere all this is over; but any thing which deserves the name of *criticism* I can bear. I believe I could point out more faults in *The Vespers* myself than any one has done yet."

And then, with that endearing predominance of the

mother over the author, which formed one of the loveliest features of her character, she would turn to some nursery topic in strains such as these:—"I am just returned from a game with one of the *English* shuttlecocks (which are pronounced to be much the best flyers,) in which I have so distinguished myself by my strenuous exertions, that I feel in some danger of writing one of the three hands on which I have heard a distinguished lawyer piques himself—I mean the one which neither he himself nor any one else can read. *'Tant les forces de ma puissante vie'* (as Mademoiselle de Stael says of Corinne) *'sont épuisées.'* "

And a letter of "high discourse" on the writings of Dr. Channing, merges in the domestic mood, as follows:—"Now, lest you should forget your 'Aunt Becky's'[1] character, I have two important commissions to keep you in heart and in practice. We are in the greatest want of two humming-tops! One is to be rather a large one, but plain, and as little expensive as may be; the other of small dimensions, even such as will hum upon a table. Sundry teeth have been drawn in the household, and the tops have been promised to reward the fortitude evinced on these trying occasions."

She delighted, too, in relating little anecdotes of

---

[1] See *The Inheritance*, by Miss Ferrier. This pet name had been bestowed upon the indefatigable friend who was, for eighteen years, the purveyor of all things needful, from Italian classics to humming-tops; and, like the Countess of Pembroke and Montgomery, a reference and authority in everything, from "predestination down to slea-silk."

her children, when writing to the partial friends by
whom such "trivial fond records" were most likely
to be prized. "I must tell you," she writes, "a remark of my little George's the other day, not only as
I was much pleased with its discrimination, but as a
proof of the attention and interest with which he has
read our dear Swiss history.[1] He was reading to me
an account of the proceedings of the precious trium-
virate, Antony, Lepidus, and Octavius ; when, suddenly pausing, he exclaimed, after a moment's thought
—" Oh, mamma! what a contrast to the meeting of
the three Swiss patriots on the field of Grutli !"

Another of these " Oh, mammas," was somewhat

---

[1] A *History of Switzerland*, for young persons, published by
Darton and Harvey. This very interesting volume was written
by Mrs. Hemans's accomplished friend, the dear " Aunt Becky"
of the note above; and she took an interest in its progress, and
a pleasure in its success, which could scarcely have been exceeded had the work been her own A little volume of *Devo-
tions for Youth*, written by the same friend, and published by
Rivingtons two or three years afterwards, was one she prized
yet more highly, and frequently used with her children. " On
Christmas morning," she wrote, when they had been lent to her
in MS , " I read your prayer for that day with my boys, and I
cannot tell you the pleasure I have in associating a thought of
you with the feelings excited in such moments. I was pleased
to hear the boys say, ' Mamma, that is the nicest prayer you ever
read to us;' and could not help thinking that you, too, would
like the approbation of such accomplished critics In the lines
which I suggested as a motto to the prayers, and which are from
a birthday address to my little George, the idea of the cares of
earth lying dim on the spirit's wings, was meant to imply the
gradual fading of youthful fancy and imagination in the world's
atmosphere, just as the feathers of a bird of Paradise might be
soiled with a mist or shower."

more *piquant* in its character. " I wish you would
make the Bishop laugh with a saying of George's,
which entertained me a good deal—" Oh, mamma !
I'm in the most delightful place in my Virgil now—
I'm in Tartarus !"

She had always taken great interest in the description of the Christmas domestic festivals in Germany—
the " Christmas Tree," the mutual presents between
parents and children, and all the innocent mysteries
and pretty surprises which travellers have described
so often, but none with so much truth and nature as
Coleridge in his letter from Ratzeburg, published in
The Friend. Amongst her own little group, something of a similar celebration was always attempted.
However wearied or harassed she might be, the claims
of this joyous season were never remitted. The fate
of poetic heroes and heroines would remain in abeyance, whilst juvenile mimes and mysteries were going
on at the fireside ; and for the moment nothing seemed
so important as the invention of different devices for
the painted bags of *bonbons* destined to adorn the
boughs of the " Christmas Tree." Even in the midst
of all her dramatic vexations, she could write completely *con amore*—" The boys were very happy yesterday evening with a plain twelfth cake of their own,
when, just as it had been despatched, and the little
ones were gone to bed, there arrived a much more
splendid one from the Bishop, so we are to have a
thirteenth night this evening. Charlie lays claim to
what he calls the 'Coronation,' from the top of the
above-named cake, as he says he 'always has the
coronations from the top of the Bishop's cakes.' "

9 *

About this time, Mrs. Hemans was engaged in the composition of another tragedy, entitled *De Chatillon, or, The Crusaders;* in which, with that deference to *fair* criticism which she was always ready to avow, and to act upon, she made it her purpose to attempt a more compressed style of writing, avoiding that redundancy of poetic diction which had been censured as the prevailing fault of *The Vespers.* It may possibly be thought that in the composition in question she has fallen into the opposite extreme of want of elaboration; yet in its present state, it is, perhaps, scarcely amenable to criticism, for by some strange accident, the fair copy transcribed by herself was either destroyed or mislaid in some of her subsequent removals, and the piece was long considered as utterly lost. Nearly two years after her death, the original rough MS., with all its hieroglyphical blots and erasures, was discovered amongst a mass of forgotten papers; and it has been a task of no small difficulty to decypher it, and complete the copy now first given to the world. Allowances must, therefore, be made ,for the disadvantages under which it appears, thus deprived of her own finishing touches, and with no means of ascertaining how far it may differ from the copy so unaccountably missing.

In the autumn of 1824, she began the poem which, in point of finish and consecutiveness, if not in popularity, may be considered her principal work, and which she herself inclined to look upon as her best. "I am at present," she wrote to one always interested in her literary occupations, "engaged upon a poem of some length, the idea of which was suggested to me by some

passages in your friend Mr. Blanco White's delightful
writings.[1] It relates to the sufferings of a Spanish
Protestant, in the time of Philip the Second, and is
supposed to be narrated by the sufferer himself, who
escapes to America. I am very much interested in
my subject, and hope to complete the poem in the
course of the winter." The progress of this work was
watched with great interest in her domestic circle, and
its touching descriptions would often extract a tribute
of tears from the fireside auditors. When completed,
a family consultation was held as to its name. Various titles were proposed and rejected, till that of *The
Forest Sanctuary* was suggested by her brother, and
finally decided upon. Though finished early in 1825,
the poem was not published till the following year,
when it was brought out in conjunction with the *Lays
of Many Lands,* and a collection of miscellaneous
pieces, most of which had previously appeared in the
New Monthly Magazine, or in some of the various annuals, from whose editors Mrs. Hemans was now receiving continual overtures. The number and urgency of these applications was already beginning to be
half tormenting, half amusing, though nothing in comparison with the "Vallombrosa"-like showers of these
"autumnal leaves" which used to come pouring down
upon her in after years, when the *annual* fever had
reached its height.

It was interesting to observe the manner in which
any new idea, accidentally suggested in the course of
her reading, would take hold of her imagination,

---

[1] Letters from Spain by Don Leucadio Doblado.

awakening, as with an electric touch, a whole train
of associations and developements. Most truly, in her
case, was exemplified Mr. Wordsworth's observation
respecting poetic sensibility, in which he says, that
" the more exquisite it is, the wider will be the range
of a poet's perceptions, and the more will he be in-
cited to observe objects, both as they exist in themselves, and as reacted upon by his own mind." [1]

By her, objects were never seen simply "as they
exist in themselves." Every thing brought its own
appeals to thought and memory ; and every sight and
sound in nature awakened some distinct echo in her
heart. The very rustling of the trees spoke to her in
tones full of meaning. It was one of her favourite fancies that each tree had its peculiar language, suited
to its character for majesty, solemnity, or grace, and
that she could distinguish with closed eyes the measured tones of the oak or elm, the funereal sighs of the
cypress, or the sensitive murmurs of the willow or
poplar ! From some particular train of association,
she took great delight in seeing the waving boughs of
trees through a church window. All legends and
superstitions regarding trees and flowers, were peculiarly dear to her. When alluding to these, and similar fables, she would often quote the well-known lines
from Schiller—

" Wage du zu irren und zu traumen,
Hohen sinn liegt oft in kind'schem spiel " [2]

[1] See Preface to the First Volume of Wordsworth's Poetical
Works.
[2] " Oh! fear thou not to dream with waking eye : —
There lies deep meaning oft in childish play."
Thekla's Song—Translated by Mrs Hemans.

One of her favourites amongst the many traditions of this nature, was the Welsh legend regarding the trembling of the aspen,[1] which, with a kindred super-stition relating to the spotted arum, will be found mentioned in the Woodwalk and Hymn, in *Scenes and Hymns of Life.* And in the two sonnets, entitled " Thoughts connected with Trees," which form part of the *Records of the Spring of* 1834, she has revealed to us yet more distinctly how much " deep meaning" their " kindly whisperings" and "old sweet leaf sounds" brought home to her breast.

The howling of the wind at night had a very pecu-liar effect upon her nerves—nothing in the least approaching to the sensation of fear, as few were more exempt from that class of alarms usually called nervous; but working upon her imagination to a degree which was always succeeded by a reaction of fatigue and exhaustion. The solemn influences thus mysteriously exercised, are alluded to in many of her poems, particularly in *The Song of Night,*[2] and in *The Voice of the Wind.*

---

[1] A somewhat similar tradition appears to exist in Denmark, as shown by a poem of Ingemann's, of which a translation was given in the *Foreign Quarterly Review* for June, 1830.

[2] "Among the many congenial ideas she found in the writings of Richter, the following passage relating to Night was singu-larly in unison with her own feelings:—' The earth is every day overspread with the veil of Night, for the same reason as the cages of birds are darkened, that we may the more readily apprehend the higher harmonies of thought in the hush and quiet of darkness. Thoughts, which day turns into smoke and mist, stand about us in the night as lights and flames, even as the column which fluctuates above the crater of Vesuvius, in the day time appears a pillar of cloud, but by night a pillar of fire.' "

The sight and sound of the sea were always connected in her mind with melancholy associations; with

> " Doubt, and something dark,
> Of the old Sea some reverential fear;" [1]

with images of storm and desolation, of shipwreck and
sea-burial: the last, indeed, was so often present to
her imagination, and has so frequently been introduced
into her poetry, that any one inclined to superstitious
presentiments might also have been disposed to fancy
it a fore-shadowing of some such dark fate in store
either for herself or for some one dear to her. These
associations, like those awakened by the wind, were
perfectly distinct from any thing of personal timidity,
and were the more indefinable, as she had never suffered any calamity at all connected with the sea : none
of those she loved had been consigned to its reckless
waters, nor had she ever seen it in all its terrors, for
the coast on which her early years were passed is by
no means a rugged or dangerous one, and is seldom
visited by disaster.

In one of her later sonnets[2] on this subject, a chord
is struck, which may perhaps find an echo in other
bosoms :—

> ——" Yet, O blue deep !
> Thou that no trace of human hearts dost keep,
> Never to thee did love with silvery chain
> Draw my soul's dream, which through all nature sought
> What waves deny,—some bower of steadfast bliss,
> A home to twine with fancy, feeling, thought,
> As with sweet flowers:—But chastened Hope for this,

---

[1] Wordsworth.   [2] "A Thought of the Sea."

Now turns from earth's green valleys as from thee,
To that sole changeless world, where there is no more sea."

The same feeling is expressed in one of her letters:
—" Did you ever observe how strangely sounds and
images of waters—rushing torrents, and troubled ocean
waves, are mingled with the visionary distresses of
dreams and delirium? To me there is no more perfect emblem of peace than that expressed by the
Scriptural phrase, " there shall be no more sea."

How forcible is the contrast between the essential
womanliness of these associations, so full of " the still
sad music of humanity," and the " stern delight" with
which Lord Byron, in his magnificent apostrophe to
the sea, exults in its ministry of wrath, and recounts,
as with a fierce joy, its dealings with its victim, man!

—— " The vile strength he wields
For earth's destruction, thou dost all despise,
Spurning him from thy bosom to the skies,
And send'st him, shivering in thy playful spray,
And howling, to his Gods, where haply lies
His petty hope in some near port or bay,
And dashest him again to earth:—there let him lay !"
Childe Harold, Canto iv. Stanza clxxx.

In the spring of 1825, Mrs. Hemans, with her mother
and sister, and four of her boys, (the eldest having
been placed at school at Bangor,) removed from Bronwylfa to Rhyllon, another house belonging to her
brother, not more than a quarter of a mile from the
former place, and in full view from its windows. The
distance being so inconsiderable, this could, in fact,
scarcely be considered as a removal. The two houses,
each situated on an eminence, on opposite sides of the

river Clwyd, confronted each other so conveniently,
that a telegraphic communication was established between them (by means of a regular set of signals and
vocabulary, similar to those made use of in the navy),
and was carried on for a season with no little spirit,
greatly to the amusement of their respective inhabitants.

Nothing could be less romantic than the outward
appearance of Mrs. Hemans's new residence—a tall,
staring brick house, almost destitute of trees, and
unadorned (far, indeed, from being thus "adorned
the most") by the covering mantle of honeysuckle,
jessamine, or any such charitable drapery.[1] Bronwylfa, on the contrary, was a perfect bower of roses,
and peeped out like a bird's nest from amidst the
foliage in which it was embosomed. The contrast
between the two dwellings was thus playfully des-
canted upon by Mrs. Hemans, in her contribution to
a set of *jeux d' esprit,* called the Bronwylfa Budget
for 1825.

DRAMATIC SCENE BETWEEN BRONWYLFA AND RHYLLON [2]

BRONWYLFA, *after standing for some time in silent contemplation of* RHYLLON, *breaks out into the following vehement strain
of vituperation :* —

"You ugliest of fabrics! you horrible eye-sore!
I wish you would vanish, or put on a vizor!

---

[1] Its conspicuousness has since been a good deal modified by
the lowering of one story, and by the growth of the surrounding
plantations.

[2] Bronwylfa is pronounced as if written *Bronwilva;* and perhaps the nearest English approach to the pronunciation of Rhyllon, would be, by supposing it to be spelt *Ruthlon,* the *u* sounded
as in *but.*

In the face of the sun, without covering or rag on,
You stand and out-stare me, like any red dragon.
With your great green-eyed windows, in boldness a host,
(The only green things which, indeed, you can boast),
With your forehead as high, and as bare as the pate
Which an eagle once took for a stone or a slate,[1]
You lift yourself up, o'er the country afar,
As who should say—"Look at me!—here stands great R!'
I plant—I rear forest trees—shrubs great and small,
To wrap myself up in—*you* peer through them all!
With your lean scraggy neck o'er my poplars you rise;
You watch all my guests with your wide saucer eyes;—
    (*In a paroxysm of rage*)—
You monster! I would I could waken some morning,
And find you had taken French leave without warning;
You should never be sought like Aladdin's famed palace—
You spoil my sweet temper—you make me bear malice—
For it *is* a hard fate, I *will* say it and sing,
Which has fixed me to gaze on so frightful a thing."
    RHYLLON—(*with dignified equanimity*)—
Content thee, Bronwylfa, what means all this rage?
This sudden attack on my quiet old age?   ·
I am no *parvenu*—you and I, my good brother,
Have stood here this century facing each other;
And *I* can remember the days that are gone,
When *your* sides were no better array'd than my own.
Nay, the truth shall be told—since you flout me, restore
The tall scarlet woodbine you took from my door!
Since my baldness is mock'd, and I'm *forced* to explain,
Pray give me my large laurustinus again.
    (*With a tone of prophetic solemnity*)—
Bronwylfa! Bronwylfa! thus insolent grown,
Your pride and your poplars alike must come down!
I look through the future (and far I can see,
As St. Asaph and Denbigh will answer for me,) ·

---

[1] Bronwylfa is here supposed to allude to the pate of Æschylus, upon which an eagle dropped a tortoise to crack the shell.

Vol. I.—— 10

And in spite of thy scorn, and of all thou hast done,
From my kind heart's brick bottom, I pity thee, Bron!
The end of thy toiling and planting will be,
That thou wilt want sunshine, and ask it of me.
Thou wilt say, when thou wak'st, looking out for the light,
"I suppose it is morning, for Rhyllon looks bright."
While I—my green eyes with their tears overflow.
  (*Tenderly*)—
Come—let us be friends, as we were long ago."

In spite, however, of the unromantic exterior of her new abode, the earlier part of Mrs. Hemans's residence at Rhyllon, may, perhaps, be considered as the happiest of her life; as far, at least, as the term happiness could ever be fitly applied to any period of it later than childhood. The house, with all its ugliness, was large and convenient; the view from its windows beautiful and extensive, and its situation, on a fine green slope, terminating in a pretty woodland dingle, peculiarly healthy and cheerful. Never, perhaps, had she more thorough enjoyment of her boys than in witnessing, and often joining in, their sports, in those pleasant breezy fields, where the kites soared so triumphantly, and the hoops trundled so merrily, and where the cowslips grew as cowslips had never grown before. An atmosphere of home soon gathered round the dwelling; roses were planted, and honeysuckles trained, and the rustling of the solitary poplar near her window was taken to her heart, like the voice of a friend. The dingle became a favourite haunt, where she would pass many dream-like hours of enjoyment with her books, and her own sweet fancies, and her children playing around her. Every tree and flower, and tuft of moss that sprung

amidst its green recesses, was invested with some in
dividual charm by that rich imagination, so skilled in

> " Clothing the palpable and the familiar,
>   With golden exhalations of the dawn." [1]

Here, on what the boys would call "mamma's
sofa"—'a little grassy mound under her favourite
beech-tree—she first read *The Talisman*, and has
described the scene with a loving minuteness in her
Hour of Romance.

> " There were thick leaves above me and around,
>   And low sweet sighs, like those of childhood's sleep,
> Amidst their dimness, and a fitful sound
>   As of soft showers on water. Dark and deep
> Lay the oak shadows o'er the turf—so still,
> They seem'd but pictured glooms; a hidden rill
> Made music—such as haunts us in a dream—
> Under the fern-tufts; and a tender gleam
> Of soft green light—as by the glow-worm shed—
> Came pouring through the woven beech-boughs down."

Many years after, in the sonnet " To a Distant
Scene," she addresses, with a fond yearning, this well-
remembered haunt :—

> " Still are the cowslips from thy bosom springing,
>   O far-off grassy dell !"

How many precious memories has she hung round
the thought of the cowslip, that flower, with its "gold
coat" and "fairy favours," which is, of all others, so
associated with the "voice of happy childhood," and
was, to her, ever redolent of the hours when her

> " Heart so leapt to that sweet laughter's tone !"

---

[1] Coleridge's Translation of *Wallenstein*.

Another favourite resort was the picturesque old bridge over the Clwyd; and when her health (which was subject to continual variation, but was at this time more robust than usual) admitted of more aspiring achievements, she delighted in roaming to the hills; and the announcement of a walk to Cwm,[1] a remote little hamlet, nestled in a mountain hollow, amidst very lovely sylvan scenery, about two miles from Rhyllon, would be joyously echoed by her elated companions, to whom the recollection of these happy rambles must always be unspeakably dear. Very often, at the outset of these expeditions, the party would be reinforced by the addition of a certain little Kitty Jones, a child from a neighbouring cottage, who had taken an especial fancy to Mrs. Hemans, and was continually watching her movements. This little creature never saw her without at once attaching itself to her side, and confidingly placing its tiny hand in hers. So great was her love for children, and her repugnance to hurt the feelings of any living creature, that she never would shake off this singular appendage, but let little Kitty rejoice in her "pride of place," till the walk became too long for her capacity, and she would quietly fall behind of her own accord.

Those who only know the neighbourhood of St. Asaph, from travelling along its high-ways, can be little aware how much delightful scenery is attainable, within walks of two or three miles distance from Mrs. Hemans's residence. The placid beauty of the Clwyd, and the wilder graces of its sister stream, the Elwy,

---

[1] Pronounced *Coom.*

particularly in the vicinity of " Our Lady's Well,"
and the interesting rocks and caves at Cefn, are little
known to general tourists; though, by the lovers of
her poetry, it will be remembered how sweetly she
has apostrophised the

   " Fount of the chapel, with ages grey ;" [1]

and how tenderly, amidst far different scenes, her
thoughts reverted to the

   " Cambrian river, with slow music gliding
     By pastoral hills, old woods, and ruined towers." [2]

Every day was now bringing some fresh proof of
Mrs. Hemans's widely extending fame, and more
especially of the unprecedented favour with which
her writings were regarded in America. Many testi-
monials had reached her from various quarters, of the
high estimation in which she was held on the other
side of the Atlantic ; and she had already been engaged in a pleasant interchange of correspondence
with Dr. Bancroft, the talented author of *The History
of the United States*, who was amongst the first to
distinguish her works amongst his countrymen, by
public criticism, or rather eulogy. But, in the autumn
of this year (1825,) a still more direct communication
was opened for her with a country to which she was
thenceforward to be bound by so many ties of grateful and kindly feeling. This delightful intercourse
owed its beginning to the arrival — unexpected, as

---

[1] Our Lady's Well.
[2] Sonnet " To the River Clwyd in North Wales."
  10 *

though it had fallen from the clouds—of a packet
from Boston, containing a letter of self-introduction
from Professor Norton, of Cambridge University, New
England, informing her that a complete edition of her
works was wished for at Boston, and most liberally
offering to superintend its publication, and secure the
profits for her benefit. This packet, which also included some interesting specimens of American literature, after crossing the Atlantic in safety, had a narrow escape of being consigned to the "treasures of
the deep," by a disaster which occurred to the party
who had the charge of it, in traversing the Ulverstone Sands. But it would seem as if a missive so
fraught with genuine kindness—such as could proceed
only from the best and highest feelings of our nature
—bore within itself a spell to resist all "moving accidents by flood and field." By the courtesy of a stranger, it was singled out from a motley pile of other
flotsome and *jetsome* found drying at the kitchen fire
of a little inn on the coast of Lancashire, and carefully forwarded to the destination where it was to
impart so much gratification, and lead to such valuable results. Mrs. Hemans took infinite pleasure in
recounting the singular adventures of this memorable
packet; and the "sea change" which all its contents
had suffered, more particularly a handsomely bound
volume, *The Life of Mr. Charles Eliot,* written by
the Professor himself—made them only the more precious in her eyes. From this time forward, the arrival of such welcome tributes became of continual
occurrence, and she was supplied with all that was
most interesting in transatlantic literature, either

through the munificence of Mr. Norton, or the kindness of the respective authors, with some of whom
she was thus brought into direct communication. In
this manner she made acquaintance with the noble
writings of Dr. Channing, and entered into a correspondence with that distinguished author, for whose
lofty eloquence and fervent inculcations of truth and
morality, she entertained the highest respect, though
the religious convictions in which she differed from
him so widely, were absolutely a part of her being,
and, if possible, gained strength with every year of
her life. In her letters of this period, there is perpetual allusion to the enjoyment spread throughout
the household by every fresh arrival from Boston.
The unfolding of the various treasures was a treat to
old and young; and the peculiar odour of the pine
wood which the books used to imbibe from the cases
on their voyage, was greeted as " the American smell,"
almost as joyfully as the aromatic breezes of the New
World were first inhaled by Columbus and his companions. On one occasion, Mrs. Hemans was somewhat ludicrously disenchanted, through the medium
of a North American Review, on the subject of a
self-constituted hero, whose history (which suggested
her little poem, *The Child of the Forests*) she had
read with unquestioning faith and lively interest.
This was the redoubtable John Dunn Hunter, whose
marvellous adventures amongst the Indians—by whom
he represented himself to have been carried away in
childhood—were worked up into a plausible narrative,
admirably calculated to excite the sympathies of its
readers. But how far it was really deserving of them,

may be judged by the following extract from a letter
to a friend who had been similarly mystified :—" I
send you a North American Review, which will
mortify C. and you with the sad intelligence that John
Hunter—even our own John Dunn—the man of the
panther's skin—the adopted of the Kansas—the
shooter with the rifle—no, with the long bow—is, I
blush to say it, neither more nor less than an impostor ;
no better than Psalmanazar ; no, no better than Car-
raboo herself. After this, what are we to believe
again ?   Are there any Loo Choo Islands ?   Was there
ever any Robinson Crusoe ?   Is there any Rammohun
Roy ?   All one's faith and trust is shaken to its foun-
dations.   No one here sympathises with me properly
on this annoying occasion ; but you, I think, will know
how to feel, who have been quite as much devoted to
that vile John Dunn as myself."

Thus pleasantly passed the first year of Mrs. Hemans's residence at Rhyllon ; enlivened by so many
tokens of good will from afar, and blessed by health,
sustaining love, and social enjoyment at home, where
the family circle had lately been increased by the
welcome return of her second brother[1] and his wife,
after an absence of several years in Canada.   In this
kindly atmosphere of household affection, she cou-
rageously persevered in her daily routine of duties,
accomplishing them with a facility astonishing even
to those who best knew her powers ; and after long
mornings of application,—hours spent first of all in
the instruction of her children, then in answering

---

[1] Now Major Browne, Commissioner of Police in Dublin.

countless letters, and satisfying the pressing claims of impatient editors,—she would shake off the burthen of care, "like dew-drops from a lion's mane," and emerge into the fresh air with all the glad buoyancy of a school-boy released from his tasks, and with that pure, child-like enjoyment of the world out of doors, which made

"The common air, the earth, the skies,
To her an opening Paradise."

" Soft winds and bright blue skies" (to quote from one of her own letters) " make me, or dispose me to be, a sad idler; and it is only by an effort, and a strong feeling of necessity, that I can fix my mind steadily to any sedentary pursuit when the sun is shining over the mountains, and the birds singing 'at heaven's gate;' but I find frost and snow most salutary monitors, and always make exertion my enjoyment during their continuance. For this reason I must say I delight in the utmost rigour of winter, which almost seems to render it necessary that the mind should become fully acquainted with its own resources, and find means, in drawing them forth, to cheer ' with mental light the melancholy day.'"

The tranquil cheerfulness of this period of Mrs. Hemans's life, was destined to be but too soon over-shadowed by the sorrow and sickness of some of the dearest objects of her affections. The spring of 1826 was clouded by severe affliction in the house of her eldest brother, whose once joyous hearth was now left lonely and deserted; and this visitation was speedily followed by an alarming change in the health of that admirable mother, whose unwearied spirit of active self-forgetting, hopeful exertion, had ever been the mainspring of happiness to all around her. So accustomed were her children to her all-pervading superintendence—so indispensable seemed her patient counsels, her ready sympathy, her unfailing love, that the idea of her ever being taken away from them, seemed a thing impossible to contemplate: they would have thought the world (their own little world at least) could not go on without her. And when, after the fluctuating symptoms of a tedious illness of eight months, and all those melancholy gradations which mark from day to day the increasing weakness of the sufferer—whose dear companionship is first missed from the daily walk, then from the household meal and the family prayer, and lastly, to be found only in the chamber of sickness itself—when after a sorrowful familiarity with all these indications of failing strength, the rapid increase of her danger could no longer be hid from their eyes—there was still, even to the very end, an obstinacy of hope within their hearts. Her own extraordinary mental energy and unsubdued cheerfulness—for her death, like her life, was an exemplification of the beautiful maxim, that

"True piety is cheerful as the day"—

were, indeed, almost sufficient to excuse this fond delusion. Her warm-hearted interest in all that was passing around her, was never extinguished by weariness or suffering; and that pure flame of maternal pride which burnt steadiest to the last, was brightened within a very few days of her death, by the arrival of a treasure-store of fresh tributes from the "far West"—tributes, not merely of homage to the genius

of the poet, but of veneration for the high moral purposes to which that genius was directed. Such records
were fitted to excite feelings far too deep for vanity
in her to whom they were addressed, and were meet
offerings to be laid on the dying bed of the mother,
from whom had been imbibed her love for " whatsoever things are true, whatsoever things are holy," and
whose fading eyes lighted up with exulting fondness
at these proofs of distant fame, which seemed to her,
as she emphatically declared, " like a bright star in
the West."[1]

At length the solemn moment came, when those
kind eyes were sealed for ever. With what feelings
this stroke had been anticipated, may be seen in the
" Hymn by a bed of sickness," written almost at the
last; how deeply it was felt, yet how meekly borne,
is best shown in Mrs. Hemans's own words, taken from
a letter—one of the first she wrote after her bereavement, to an old and much valued friend.

" I cannot suffer you to remain in anxiety about
me, which I know is painful. My soul is indeed
' exceeding sorrowful," dear friend; but, thank God!

---

[1] One of the last things on which she looked, was a little view
of " Bronwylfa, the residence of Mrs. Hemans," which had been
lithographed in America; and the last poem she listened to was
the " Domestic Scene," afterwards published with the *Hymns
for Childhood.* In alluding to these lines some months afterwards, Mrs. Hemans wrote—" I read them to her by her bed-
side, about three weeks before I was deprived of her, and the
tender pleasure with which she heard them, has rendered them
to me a ' thing set apart.' " And the holy scene they record (a
picture from real life) was worthy of being enshrined in recollections so sacred.

I can tell you that composure is returning to me, and
that I am enabled to resume those duties which so
imperiously call me back to life. What I have lost,
none better knows than yourself. I have lost the
faithful, watchful, patient love, which for years had
been devoted to me and mine ; and I feel that the void
it has left behind, must cause me to bear ' a yearning
heart within me to the grave ;' but I have her example before me, and I must not allow myself to sink.

" You have, I know, been told of the wonderful
collectedness she displayed to the last. Sickness and
suffering, and sorrowful affection we have witnessed ;
but no despondence, no perplexity, nothing which can
in any way connect horror with the awfulness of death.
I was almost in a stupor for a few days after, but it
is past, and I do not think my health will suffer, though
I now feel wearied and worn, and longing, as she did,
for rest. That rest was almost, indeed, perfect in her
last hours, so deep and still was the slumber into which
she had sunk, and which our selfish hearts almost
longed to hear broken even by the renewed sickness
of the preceding night ; for the utter separation from
us implied by such a state of solemn tranquillity,
seemed almost 'greater than we could bear.' Oh!
this earthly weakness, when we should praise God for
one ' departed this life in His faith and fear."

In a subsequent letter she thus alluded to her
mother's room. " I have frequently entered it since
its privation, and, indeed, am in the habit of going
there when my heart is more than usually oppressed.
It seems to me almost a place of refuge from care

and fear, which too often weigh down my spirit heavily."

This passage brings involuntarily to remembrance the beautiful lines of Young—

"The chamber where the good man meets his fate,
Is privileged beyond the common walk
Of virtuous life;—quite in the verge of Heaven."

The following letter, addressed to the same friend (then suffering from sorrows of her own), though not written till some months later, belongs so completely to the same train of feeling, as to claim an introduction in this place.

"I have been haunted, since the arrival of your last sad letter, by an anxiety to write to you, which it has not, until to-day, been in my power to fulfil. The intelligence startled us most painfully; I almost felt as if I had known the amiable and beloved friend who is lost to you; and words are inadequate to express what one feels for her sister, who had so much interested us. So sudden a shock, too!—and yet they talk of preparation;—alas! we are ever unprepared for the stroke which deprives us of those we love; it is impossible to believe it at hand; I suppose from the impossibility of conceiving that we can and must live without them. I think first, naturally, of her who is most bereaved; but I well know what you too must have felt upon this breaking of a tie of many years; and wish I were near you to give you such comfort as I could. I have received a letter of consolation from Mr. Norton, on my own affliction, from which I must copy you a part. If any human

comfort could avail, it would surely be a view so pure
and elevating as this. I think, when the poor mourner
may be supposed to have regained a little calmness, I
shall write and send it to her. 'When one so dear is
taken away, an object of constant reference, respect,
and affection, a principal part of all our enjoyments,
a support in all affliction, one in whom we had lived,
one through whom the Spirit of God had powerfully
operated to produce all that is good within us; the
whole aspect of things is changed, and the world
becomes a different place from what it was before.
It must ever remain so. But in time perhaps it may
become even a better and a brighter spot. The thick
veil which separates it from the World of Life and
Light, has been broken through for us by the friend
who is gone before; and beams of glory may find their
way where it has been rent. Between us and that
world, a new and most affecting connection has been
formed; for one whom we most loved is there. A deep
feeling of the reality and certainty of all which in
truth *is* real and certain, thus becomes permanent in
our minds, blending itself with all our best affections.
Blessed beyond all our conceptions of happiness are
the Dead who die in the Lord. They have rested
from the labours which we still must bear. They
have gone before us to prepare our place and our
welcome, and are waiting to receive us again, with
more than human love. Amid the trials of life, he
who feels his own weakness, must sometimes almost
wish that he, too, were as secure.'

  "This is surely the language of real consolation;
how different from that which attempts to soothe us

by general remarks on the common lot, the course of
nature, or even by dwelling on the release of the
departed from pain and trial. Alas! I know by sad
experience, that the very allusion to those pains and
trials only adds tenfold to the inexpressible yearnings
of the heart when all is over, when Love can do no
more."

There was one little trait which Mrs. Hemans loved
to dwell upon, as having afforded her a bright gleam
of comfort in the darkest hour of her affliction. On
the evening of her mother's death,[1] after long watching in the solemn stillness of the sick-chamber, she
went down for a while to solace her oppressed spirit
with the looks and voices of her children. She found
them all sitting hushed and awe-struck, round the fire.
They looked at her sad face with sorrowful wonder,
and her "little George" entreated to be allowed to
read her a chapter in the Bible—"he was sure it
would do her good." May he never lose the remembrance of that holy hour! tenderly as it was recorded
in the heart of his mother, who thus saw fulfilled her
birthday exhortation to him—

> " Yet ere the cares of life lie dim
>   On thy young spirit's wings,
> Now in thy morn, forget not Him
>   From whom each pure thought springs.
>
> " So, in the onward vale of tears,
>   Where'er thy path may be,
> When strength hath bow'd to evil years,
>   He will remember thee.'

[1] 11th January, 1827.

It is affecting to remember how soon, with a heart so deeply wounded, she resumed the daily routine of her maternal duties, not indulging in the "luxury of grief," but returning to her appointed tasks with all her wonted perseverance. In a letter relating to some French books, which she wished to procure for one of her boys, she goes on to say,—"He has done with fables, the old *Veillées du Chateau*, &c., and I have not really the heart to venture upon *Télémaque*, which was always a particular aversion of mine. I think some parts of the *Chateaux Suisses* would cheer him on a little, if you could spare them for a time. I want to excite such an interest in the language, or rather to make him feel so much at home in it, that he may seek his amusement or information in it as readily as in English. It is well for me, and I ought to be thankful, that I have these objects of strong and permanent interest, to win me from thoughts too deeply tinged with sorrow. No less important duties could have called me back to exertion with a voice at once so sweet and so powerful."

To say that the loss of her mother was an irreparable one to Mrs. Hemans, is saying little. From henceforth she was to be a stranger to any thing like an equal flow of quiet, steadfast happiness. Fugitive enjoyments—entrancing excitements—adulation the most intoxicating—society the most brilliant—all these, and more than these, were hers in after years; but the old home feeling of shelter and security was gone for ever—"removed like a shepherd's tent"—and how many mournful allusions to this "aching void" were henceforth to be found in her poetry; how

many, still more affecting, were poured forth in her
letters!¹   Her health, too, which for many years had

---

¹ There is a very touching analogy between the effects of her
mother's loss upon Mrs. Hemans, and those produced by a similar cause upon another poetic nature, differing, indeed, from hers
as darkness from light, in all else save this one pure feeling.
The heart-piercing eloquence of the following letter (taken
from an article on the *Life and Writings of Werner*, in the
Foreign Quarterly Review, for January, 1838,) must find an
echo in so many bosoms, that any excuse for its introduction
seems unnecessary.

"Extract of a letter from Werner to his friend Hitzig: — ' I
know not whether thou hast heard that on the 24th of February,
my mother departed here in my arms.   My friend! God knocks
with an iron hammer at our hearts; and we are duller than
stone if we do not feel it, and madder than mad if we think it
shame to cast ourselves into the dust before the All-powerful,
and let our whole so highly miserable self be annihilated in the
sentiment of His infinite greatness and long-suffering.

*   *   *   *   *   *

"This death of my mother — the pure, royal, poet and martyr
spirit, who, for eight years, had lain continually on a sick-bed,
and suffered unspeakable things, affected me (much as for her
sake I could not but wish it) with altogether agonizing feelings.
Ah! friend, how heavy do my youthful faults lie on me.   How
much would I give to have my mother back to me but one week,
that I might disburthen my heavy-laden heart with tears of re-
pentance.   My beloved friend! give thou no grief to thy parents!
Ah! no earthly voice can wake the dead.   God and parents —
that is the first concern—all else is secondary.'

The Reviewer then goes on to observe — "This affection for
his mother forms, as it were, a little island of light and verdure
in Werner's history, where, amid so much that is dark and desolate, one feels it pleasant to linger.

*   *   *   *   *   *

"His poor mother, while alive, was the haven of all his earthly
wanderings; and in after years, from amid far scenes and crush-

11 *

been so delicate, and at all times required innumerable precautions, of which she was painfully regardless, now began to give token of alarming fragility. The inflammatory symptoms to which she had always had a tendency, recurred with unwonted frequency, and she became liable to attacks of palpitation of the heart, and distressing pain at the chest. These would cause for a time complete and rapid prostration of strength; and then, with that natural elasticity for which her constitution was so remarkable, there would be an equally sudden reaction, and she would seem, for a season, to have shaken off all disquieting symptoms. This tremulous state of health was naturally accompanied by corresponding fluctuations of spirits; and their fitful gaiety, through which an under cur-

---

ing perplexities, he often looks back to her grave with a feeling to which all bosoms must respond. See, for example, the preface to his *Mutter der Makkabaer,* written at Vienna in 1819. The tone of still, but deep and heartfelt sadness, which runs through the whole of this piece, cannot be communicated in extracts. We quote only a half stanza, which, except in prose, we shall not venture to translate.

> 'Ich, dem der Liebe Kosen,
> Und alle Frendenrosen,
> Beym ersten Schaufeltosen
> Am Muttergrab entflohn.'

'I, for whom the caresses of love, and all roses of joy withered away, as the first shovel with its mould sounded on the coffin of my mother.'

"The date of her decease became a memorable era in his mind, as may appear from the title which he gave long afterwards to one of his most popular and tragical productions—*Die vier-und-zwanzigste Februar.*"

rent of sadness might always be traced, was almost
more melancholy than their frequent depression. " My
spirits"—thus she wrote of herself—" are as variable
as the lights and shadows now flitting with the wind
over the high grass, and sometimes the tears gush
into my eyes when I can scarcely define the cause."
And in another letter of the same period—" My health
is quite renewed, and my spirits, though variable, are
often all that they used to be. I am a strange being,
I think. I put myself in mind of an Irish melody,
sometimes, with its quick and wild transitions from
sadness to gaiety." This comparison was from her a
very expressive one, as she had always a peculiar
feeling for Irish music. " There breathes through it"
(she once wrote, and would often say,) " or perhaps I
imagine all this—a mingling of exultation and despondence, like funeral strains with revelry, a something
unconquerable, yet mournful, which interests me
deeply." Even yet more applicable to these " mental lights and shades" are the similes in that well-
known passage from the works of Mrs. Joanna Baillie,
which she loved no less for its beauty, than from feeling how appropriately it might have been written for
herself.

" Didst thou ne'er see the swallow's veering breast,
   Winging the air beneath some murky cloud,
   In the sunn'd glimpses of a stormy day,
   ·Shiver in silver brightness?
   Or boatman's oar as vivid lightning flash
   In the faint gleam, that like a spirit's path
   Tracks the still water of some sullen lake?
   Or lonely tower, from its brown mass of woods,
   Give to the parting of a wintry sun

One hasty glance, in mockery of the night,
Closing in darkness round it? Gentle friend!
Chide not her mirth who was sad yesterday,
And may be so to-morrow."[1]

A few original fragments found after Mrs. Hemans's death in one of her MS. books, may here be given as belonging to this date.

" Oh, that we could but fix upon one eternal and unchangeable Being, the affections which here we pour forth, a wasted treasure, upon the dust! But they are ' of the earth, earthy ;' they cling with vain devotedness to mortal idols; how often to be thrown back upon our own hearts, and to press them down with a weight of ' voiceless thoughts,' and of feelings which find no answer in the world !"

" Oh, that the mind could throw from it the burthen of the past for ever! Why is it that voices and tones and looks, which have passed away, come over us with a suddenness and intenseness of remembrance which make the heart die within us, and the eyes overflow with fruitless tears? Who shall explain the mysteries of the world within ?"

" 'As the hart panteth for the water-brooks,' or as the captive for the free air of Heaven, so does the ardent spirit for the mingling of thought with thought, —for the full and deep communion of kindred natures. The common, every-day intercourse of human beings —how poor it is—how heartless!—how much more

---

[1] From the Tragedy of *Orra*.

does it oppress the mind with a sense of loneliness, than the deepest solitude of majestic nature! Can it indeed be, that this world has nothing higher, nobler, more thrilling? and the thousands of minds that seem to dwell contented within this narrow circle do they dream of nothing beyond? I often ask myself this question in what we call society, and what should be the answering thought? '*I thank thee that I am not as this man ;*' or, '*Surely this man is happier than I!*' Yet, when a sudden spark of congenial thought or feeling seems to be struck from the mind of another by our own, is not the joy so great as almost to compensate for hours and days of weariness? Is it not like the swift breaking in of sunshine through the glades of a forest, sending gladness to their very depths? Yes;—but 'few and far between' are such moments; widely severed the fresh fountains at which we drink strength and hope, to bear us on through the desert beyond."

"How the name of love is profaned in this world! Truly does Lord Byron call 'circumstance' an 'unspiritual God.' What strange coarse ties,—coarse but not strong,—one daily sees him forming!—not of the "silver cords" of the heart, but of the homely housewifely worsted of interest—convenience—economical consideration. One wonders how they are to resist the wear and tear of life, or how those whom they link together are to be held side by side through sorrow, difficulty, disappointment, without the strong affection which 'overcometh all things,' and ennobles all things — even the humblest offices performed in attendance at the sick-bed of one we love. What work, what sacrifice is there which a deep, true, powerful feeling cannot dignify ?"

" Is not the propensity of ardent and affectionate natures to love and trust, though disappointed again and again, as a perpetual spring in the heart, ever throwing out fresh buds and flowers, though but to be nipped by the ' killing frost ?'—Far better thus, than to be bound in the lifelessness of winter."

" What is fame to a heart yearning for affection, and finding it not ?   Is it not as a triumphal crown to the brow of one parched with fever, and asking for one fresh healthful draught — the ' cup of cold water ?' "

" Is it real affliction—ill health—disappointment— or the ' craving void that aches within the breast' for sympathies which perhaps earth does not afford—that weans us most from life ?—I think the latter. If we could only lie down to die as to sleep, how few would not willingly throw off what Wordsworth calls

——' The weight
Of all this unintelligible world !'
and ' flee away, and be at rest.' "

" ' The ancients feared death ;— we, thanks to Christianity, fear only *dying ;'* so says the author of the *Guesses at Truth,* and surely it is even so. I, that have seen a spirit pass away in sleep, in soft and solemn repose that almost melted into death, should

scarcely fear even the latter; and yet, the very stillness of such a parting is almost too awful for human
nature to sustain. It seems as if there should be last
words of love, and tears, and blessings, when the
strong ties that bound soul to soul are broken;—but
to call and not to be answered by the voice that ever
before spoke kindness and comfort!—who can sound
the deep gulf of separation that must be ' set between,'
when that moment arrives?"

———

" Our home!—what images are brought before us
by that one word! The meeting of cordial smiles,
and the gathering round the evening hearth, and the
interchange of thoughts in kindly words, and the
glance of eyes to which our hearts lie open as the
day;—there is the true ' City of Refuge;'—where are
we to turn when it is shut from us or changed? Who
ever thought his home could change? And yet those
calm, and deep, and still delights, over which the
world seems to have no breath of power, they too are
like the beautiful summer clouds, tranquil as if fixed
to sleep for ever in the pure azure of the skies, yet
all the while melting from us, though imperceptibly
' passing away!' "

*　　*　　*　　*　　*　　*　　*

Innumerable are the projects contained in these
MS. volumes, where ideas were written down at the
moment they occurred, to be worked out at future
leisure. Sometimes the whole outline of a long poem
is drawn out; then follows a list of subjects for lyrics;
or some suddenly awakened association, or newly suggested simile is recorded in hasty and unstudied phrase.

It may be interesting to give a few specimens of these memoranda. The following was the plan of " The Picture Gallery," designed to be a connected series of poems, of which the only one ever completed was that called " The Lady of the Castle."

"A young Bride leads her husband through the castle of her ancestors, an ancient chateau in Provence or Languedoc. Her favourite haunt is the Picture Gallery, where she passes hours with him every day, relating to him the stories of the sons and daughters of her house. These tales are:—

" That of the celebrated Countess of Tripoli, for whom a troubadour died of love.

" Of the haughty Lady of Montemar, who will not weep at the death of her son, but falls down dead upon his bier.

" Of a youth of that house, who dies for his king, like Herbert de St. Clair. He had been brought up with a young king as his friend and companion;—they come down together on a visit to the father of the youth; the castle is besieged by rebels, and the youth receives in his own heart an arrow aimed at that of his king. The king laments him bitterly, and visiting his tomb many years after, on his return from a great victory, weeps over it like a child.

" Story of ' The Lady of the Castle.'

" Of two brothers, who are represented in the same picture. After living together in the greatest harmony, they become attached to the same lady, who returns the affection of the younger. Their marriage-day is fixed, and she, after apparently languishing in sickness a few days previously, falls dead at the altar.

not without suspicions of poison, which attach to the elder brother, who has disappeared, and is not heard of for years. The younger, in despair, retires to a Carthusian monastery, the regulations of which are most severe. Here, after several years' seclusion, he finds himself dying, and implores the abbot, if ever the brother on whom so dreadful a suspicion has fallen, should visit that abode, to assure him that he had died in charity with him. The abbot, moved with compassion, introduces his brother, who had been some time in the convent unknown to him. They are reconciled—the younger dies.

" Of a beautiful Saracen female, who comes to the castle as the bride of the eldest son, by whom she has been brought home from the East. Her being a Saracen, though converted, causes discord between the father and son; and one day, during the absence of the latter, she throws herself at the old man's feet, with her infant daughter, and entreats him to dispose of her at his will, and send her back to her own land, so that she may no longer be the cause of dissension between him and his son. This softens his heart; he takes her to his bosom — blesses her as his daughter —is tended by her in his last illness, and expires in her arms.

" Of a fair girl, who watches from the battlements the combat in which her brother is engaged. She sees him fall, and left deserted as the army are charging onward. She rushes down to his assistance, and is killed herself whilst binding up his wounds.

" Of Constance, a daughter of the house, who being left motherless at an early age, devotes herself to the

care of her infant sisters, and refuses to marry, though
tenderly attached to a noble youth, worthy of her
affection.   Her lover falls in a distant land, and after
all her duties are fulfilled, she goes on a pilgrimage
to his grave, returns, and closes her days in peace.
She possesses a gift of sacred song, and the young
bride, Azalais, concludes her tales with an evening
hymn of Constance's.   She then bids the portraits of
her ancestors farewell, as the day is come on which
she is to leave the dwelling of her father for that of
her husband."

"*Plan of a Poem to be called ' The Death-bed of
St. Louis.'*

" Encampment of St. Louis in Carthage under prosperous auspices.   The Oriflamme.   The plague, which
is most dreadful when all nature is smiling, attacks
his army.   Death of warriors in a foreign land while
the troubadours and minstrels are singing in their
distant homes.   The mysterious power of Africa in
repelling all invaders—thousands buried beneath the
sands.   Marius—Scipio—Dido—Sophonisba—Wife
of Asdrubal—Cato.   Evocation of the gods of Carthage.   Those shores had still another and a nobler
lesson to learn.   Morning of the death of St. Louis—
stillness of the camp—warlike and triumphant sounds
upon the sea during his last moments.   Address to the
Mediterranean.   Disembarkation of Charles of Anjou.
Bitter feelings occasioned by turning from the bed of
death to the duties of active life.   Mournfulness of
the victory gained over the infidels, after the death
of St. Louis.   Departure of the Crusaders."

" *Fountain superstitions.*—Different marvellous properties anciently attributed to the waters of fountains. Those are lovely spots of earth where they rise, whether amongst the laurel groves of Greece, or the citrons of Italy. It is no marvel if man, in darker ages, has bestowed a presiding genius on each of them."

" *A Norwegian Legend.*—A traveller in Norway, standing amongst some *Hünengräber* (ancient northern tombs,) and gigantic stone altars, is told the legend of the scene. That during a time of great public calamity, the Priests of Odin had declared it to be necessary for the king of the country to offer up the treasure he most valued. They had accordingly seized upon his son, a gallant boy of eight years old. He was about to be bound upon the stone of sacrifice, when his mother, a Scandinavian princess, rushed in, declaring that she was the being whom the king loved best, and must therefore be sacrificed instead of her son. The King having darted forward to drag her away, she appealed to this as a proof, gave her son into his arms, and rushed upon the sacrificial knife of the Priests."

" A traveller, sleeping on the banks of the Oronoco, has heard the mysterious sounds of the *Laxas de musica.*[1] He wakens his Indian guide, who congratulates him on having heard them, and tells him they are the voices of his departed friends from the regions

---

[1] Rocks which are said to emit musical tones at sunrise.

of the dead, giving him assurance that they are happy, and that they watch over him : that he need not now fear the paw of the tiger, nor the bite of the serpent, for he is thus protected; but far happier are they who so guard him."

_____

" A scene of surpassing beauty in Switzerland, with a cottage, inhabited by the wife of a chamois hunter. Soliloquy of a wanderer, who imagines that no human passions can ever have disturbed the repose of that sublime solitude. The chamois hunter is brought in dead."

_____

" The maid before the wizard's glass — her mind, wearied with the excitement of its scenes, turns in joy to the green fields and the skies."

_____

" On leaving a church full of sculpture, and coming into the open air. — The blessing of those feelings which withdraw us occasionally from thoughts too high and awful."

_____

"THOUGHTS AND SIMILES.

" Distance — to be dreaded by those who love, as so completely dividing the current of their thoughts and sympathies. One may be revelling at a banquet, whilst the other lies on a bed of pain, — one walking at evening in the summer woods, whilst the other is tossing on the stormy wave, at the moment of ship-wreck."

_____

" Our search into the futurity of the grave, after the excitements of life, compared to the first going forth into the darkness, after leaving a brilliant hall, with lights and music; but, by degrees, we become accustomed to the obscurity; star after star looks through it, and the objects begin to clear."

"Virtues and powers concealed in the mind, compared to the landscapes and beautiful forms sometimes found in the heart of a block of marble."

"Ruins of a magnificent city seen under the waves, (as those of Tyre are said to be), like the traces of man's lofty original, obscured and faintly discernible through the shadows of mortality."

"Water thrown upon ancient paintings and reviving their forms and colours, like any sound or circumstance reviving images of the past."

"Strong passions, discernible under a cold exterior, like the working of water, seen under a crust of ice."

Such are a few specimens, selected from amongst hundreds thus recorded, of the "struggling harmonies" which filled that ever peopled and ever busy imagination. Various as are these themes of song, it will be seen how completely they are all attuned to the keynote of her own woman's heart;—affection—pure, holy, self-sacrificing—ennobling life, surviving death, and sending back "a token and a tone" even from the world of spirits.[1]

---

[1] Amongst the many subjects of a graver cast are the following:—

A Jewish funeral at midnight in the valley of Ajalon,

12 *

Mrs. Hemans's literary correspondence was now continually on the increase. Scarcely a day passed without bringing some new communication, interesting either from its own originality, or from the distinguished name of the writer. It was with no less truth than kindliness that Mrs. Grant of Laggan thus wrote to her :—" Shenstone complains of his hard fate, in wasting a lonely existence, ' not loved, not praised, not known.' How very different is your case ! Praised by all that read you,—loved by all that praise you,— and known, in some degree, wherever our language is spoken."

It is pleasing to dwell upon the generous apprecia-

Maronite procession round the Cedars of Lebanon.

These " Cedar Saints" had always a great hold upon her imagination, and she eagerly sought out all the descriptions of them given by Eastern travellers. How truly after her own heart, would have been the reverential spirit and poetic feeling with which the sublime scenery of Lebanon has been described by Lord Lindsay, whose graphic touches,—"the stately bearing and graceful repose of the young cedars," contrasted with " the wild aspect and *frantic attitude* of the old ones, flinging abroad their knotted and muscular limbs like so many Laocoons," [1] bring the impressive scene so completely before the mind's eye ! And how she would at once have transferred to some one of her " Books of Gems," that lovely picture, which haunts one like a dream,— the " view of the Red Sea from the plain where the children of Israel encamped after leaving Elim ;" and where the rocks, " now so silent, must have re-echoed the song of Moses, and its ever returning chorus,—' Sing ye to the Lord, for he hath triumphed gloriously ; the horse and his rider hath he thrown into the sea !' " [2]

[1] Lord Lindsay's Letters, Vol. I p 212   [2] Idem, Vol. I. p. 315.

tion with which she was regarded by the gifted of her
own sex, and the frank, confiding spirit which always
marked her intercourse with them.   She would rejoice
in their success with true sisterly disinterestedness;
and the versatility of her tastes, to which every thing
really good in its kind was sure to be acceptable
(always excepting science and statistics, from which
she stood aloof in silent awe), gave her a capacity for
enjoying with equal zest, the noble simplicity of Mrs.
Joanna Baillie, the graphic reality of Miss Mitford,
the true-hearted originality of Mary Howitt, or the
exquisite tenderness of Miss Bowles.   The *Sunday
Evening* of the latter — that pure and pious little
poem, which, in its own sweet language,

> " Falls on the heart like dew
> On the drooping heather-bell,"

was first introduced to Mrs. Hemans through a
strangely circuitous medium, having been sent to her
from Canada by her brother, in a Montreal gazette.
Long before they knew even the name of its author,
it had gained for itself the love and favour of the
whole household.   It was copied by the elders, learnt
by the children, and is now consecrated by recollections far dearer than belong to the finest monuments
of genius; and which involuntarily excite a feeling
of affectionate intimacy with the writer.   Miss Bowles's
Solitary Hours were often made by Mrs. Hemans the
companions of her own; and had she lived to read
The Birthday, its simple pathos and deep tenderness
would have awakened many an answering tone in her
heart.

The letter in which she introduced herself to Miss

Mitford, describes what she would have expressed to others even yet more warmly — the thorough relish with which she enjoyed the unrivalled powers of description and fine old English feelings of that delightful writer, who is as completely identified with " the greenwood tree," and all the fresh, free thoughts belonging to it, as Robin Hood himself.

"Rhyllon, St. Asaph, June 6th, 1827.

" MADAM,

"I can hardly feel that I am addressing an entire stranger in the author of *Our Village*, and yet I know it is right and proper that I should apologize for the liberty I am taking. But really, after having accompanied you again and again, as I have done, in ' violetting' and seeking for wood-sorrel; after having been with you to call upon Mrs. Allen in ' the dell,' and becoming thoroughly acquainted with May and Lizzy, I cannot but hope that you will kindly pardon my intrusion, and that my name may be sufficiently known to you to plead my cause. There are some writers whose works we cannot read without feeling as if we really had looked with them upon the scenes they bring before us, and as if such communion had almost given us a claim to something more than the mere intercourse between author and 'gentle reader.' Will you allow me to say that your writings have this effect upon me, and that you have taught me, in making me know and love your *Village* so well, to wish for further knowledge, also, of her who has so vividly impressed its dingles and coppices upon my imagination, and peopled them so cheerily with healthful and

happy beings? I believe, if I could be personally
introduced to you, that I should, in less than five minutes, begin to enquire about Lucy and the lilies of the
valley, and whether you had succeeded in peopling
that shady border in your own territories 'with those
shy flowers.' My boys, the constant companion of my
walks about *our* village, and along our two pretty
rivers, the Elwy and Clwyd, are not less interested in
your gipsies young and old, your heroes of the cricket-
ground, and, above all—Jack Hatch!—woeful and
amazed did they all look, when it was found that Jack
Hatch could die! But I really must come to the aim
and object of this letter, which I fear you may almost
begin to look upon as 'prose run mad.' I dare say
you laugh sometimes, as I am inclined to do myself, at
the prevailing mania for autographs: but a very kind
friend of mine in a distant country does no such thing,
and I am making a collection for him, which I should
think (and he too, I am sure) very much enriched by
your name. If you do me the favour to comply with
this request, it will give me great pleasure to hear
from you, under cover to the Bishop of St. Asaph.—
With sincere esteem, I beg you to believe me, Madam,
your faithful servant,

" FELICIA HEMANS."

This application was answered by Miss Mitford in
just the kind and cordial tone which might have been
expected from her; and Mrs. Hemans had the pleasure
of transmitting to Mr. Norton, the friend for whom
she was making the collection of autographs, "that
pretty and joyous song" (as she called it in her letter

of acknowledgment), " The Welcome Home," in Miss Mitford's own hand-writing. " Your autograph," she wrote some months later, " which I transmitted to my American friends, was very gratefully received, and is enshrined in a book amidst I know not how many other ' bright names:' for aught I know, Washington himself may be there, side by side with you; and not improbably is, for they are going to send me an original letter of his, which I shall prize much."

Several years after, when this song was published in the fifth volume of *Our Village*, the following note was appended to it by the warm-hearted writer. " I have a kindness for this little song quite unconnected with any merit of its own—if merit it have—since it formed one of the earliest links in my correspondence with the richly gifted poetess, the admirable and delightful woman, Mrs. Hemans. She will remember the circumstance. Our correspondence has sometimes languished since, but the friendship that sprang from it I humbly hope can never alter."

The correspondence had indeed " languished," with many others not less valued ; for by that time (1833) the delicacy of Mrs. Hemans's health had obliged her in a great measure to give up letter writing, her reclining posture making it necessary to adopt the use of the pencil instead of the pen. But the warmth of her feelings towards those she loved and admired continued undiminished, and when this affectionate little notice was unexpectedly brought before her, she described herself as having been moved almost to tears by the genuine cordiality of its tone, while it gladdened her heart like a sudden meeting with a friend. It was one of her many projects at that period to write a volume of prose sketches—Recollections of a Poet's Childhood, and descriptions of scenes which had most interested and struck her in after years—and this she intended to dedicate to Miss Mitford.[1]

But this is anticipating. To return to the year 1827, and to a letter to Mrs. Joanna Baillie, in which she writes—"You say, my dear madam, that you wish you had something to send me. May I, thus emboldened, ask you for something which I have long wished to possess, but have not been able to procure, as I believe it is at present out of print,—your delightful little drama of *The Beacon?*—or perhaps you can guide me as to where I may meet with it. I have an edition of your works, containing the Plays

---

[1] That little song, with its name of happy omen, "The Welcome Home," does not cease to be identified with the pleasantest recollections. Mr. Norton will forgive the liberty that is taken in making the following extract from one of his letters, for the sake of showing how such remembrances are cherished in a far-distant land. "Most of my autographs have a peculiar value to me from their associations with the donors as well as the writers; and as I shall record the names of the former in the volume (the first) which I am just about completing, it will be to me a book full of deeply interesting recollections. I have a particular value for some pieces in my collection, but for none more than a song sent by Miss Mitford to Mrs. Hemans, and given by the latter to me, which Miss Mitford mentions in the last volume of *Our Village* in a manner to make it an object of curiosity and feeling as long as *Our Village* or Mrs. Hemans's poetry is read; that is, as long as English literature exists."—Cambridge, N. E. 24th May, 1835.

on the Passions (with the exception of *Orra*), *Ethwald*, *Rayner*, and *Constantine*, and I have *The Family Legend* separate; but *The Beacon* I have not met with since I read it almost in childhood, and made some extracts from it which would amuse you if you could see them in the school-girl hand of fourteen or fifteen. That heart-cheering song,

'The absent will return—the long, long lost be found,'

I remember being more especially pleased with—it breathes such a spirit of hope and joy; and I am by nature inclined to both, though early cares have chastened and subdued a mind, perhaps but too ardent originally.

"I have another favour to request; it is the permission to dedicate to you, of whom my whole sex may be proud, a work which I shall probably publish in the course of this present year, and which is to be called *Records of Woman*. If you do not object to this, I will promise that the inscription shall be as simple as you could desire.

"My children were much pleased by your kind mention of them; the one who had been reading *Ethwald* with such interest, was not a little amused to find himself designated as a girl: I have none but boys, a circumstance I often am inclined to regret; for I married so young that they are even now beginning to spring from childhood into youth themselves, and, in the course of a few years I must expect that they will long for, and be launched into, another world than the green fields in which they are now contented to play around me. Let me, however, be thankful for the happiness I at present enjoy, and for the privilege which peculiar circumstances have afforded me, and which is granted to so few mothers, of being able myself to superintend their education, and give what I hope will be enduring impressions to their minds. Now that I am upon this subject, dear madam, I am strongly tempted to relate a little anecdote which I think will interest you — (mammas are always prone to believe their children *must* be interesting) — of one of them at eleven years old. I had been reading to him Lord Byron's magnificent address to the sea —

'Roll on, thou deep and dark-blue ocean,—roll!'

He listened in almost breathless attention, and exclaimed, the moment I had finished it — 'It is very grand indeed! — but how much finer it would have been, mamma, if he had said at the close, that God had measured out all those waters with the hollow of his hand!' I could not help being struck with the true wisdom thus embodied in the simplicity of childhood."

The same remark may be applied to an anecdote related in a letter to another friend, about this time. "Charles" (then eight years old) "is sitting by me, reading Warton's *Death-bed Scenes*, with which he is greatly delighted. One of the stories is called 'The Atheist,' and on my explaining to him what the word meant, which he did not know, he exclaimed, with the greatest astonishment — "Not believe in a God, mamma!—Who does he *expect* made the world and his own body?'"

These little traits call to mind the concluding **verse** of Wordsworth's " Anecdote for Fathers;"—

> " O dearest, dearest boy! my heart
> For better lore would seldom yearn,
> Could I but teach the hundredth part
> Of what from thee I learn."

In the autumn of 1827, at the urgent request of Mr. Alaric Watts, who was then forming a gallery of portraits of the living authors of Great Britain, Mrs. Hemans was prevailed upon to sit for her picture. The artist selected on this occasion was Mr. W. E. West, an American by birth, who had passed some time in Italy, and painted the last likeness ever taken of Lord Byron, and also one of Madame Guiccioli, which was engraved in one of the annuals. During his stay at Rhyllon, where he remained for some weeks, he finished three several portraits of Mrs. Hemans; one for Mr. Alaric Watts, one which is now in the possession of Professor Norton, and a third, which he most courteously presented to Mrs. Hemans's sister, to whom it was even then a treasure, and is now become one of inestimable value. This likeness, considered by her family as the best ever taken of her, is the one which suggested Mrs. Hemans's affecting lines, " To my own portrait." The first-named of these pictures has now, it is understood, passed into the hands of Mr. Fisher, the proprietor of *The Drawing-room Scrap-Book*. Engravings from it have appeared in that work and in *The Christian Keepsake;* but they are any thing but satisfactory; and give the idea of a sallowness of complexion and stern-

ness of countenance, as different from the original as
possible. It is, however, only fair to repeat the remark already made, and in which all those who were
accustomed to study the play of her features must
concur—that there never was a countenance more
difficult to transfer to canvas; so varying were its
expressions, and so impossible is it to be satisfied with
the *one* which can alone be perpetuated by the artist.
The great charm of Mr. West's picture is its perfect
freedom from any thing set or constrained in the air;
and the sweet, serious expression, so accordant with
her maternal character, which recalls her own lines,—

> " Mother! with thine earnest eye
> Ever following silently," [1]

and which made one of her children remark, in glancing from it to the bust, executed some years after by
Mr. Angus Fletcher, " The bust is the poetess, but the
picture is *all mother*."

Even yet more difficult than to depict the animation of her countenance, would it be to give any adequate idea of the brilliant versatility of her conversation; its delicate wit, its engaging playfulness, and
that perpetual flow of allusion and illustration, which
proved her possession of inexhaustible stores of knowledge, far more general than her writings, from the
individuality of their character, ever brought into
evidence. Many people, who had prepared themselves to see in the author of *The Sceptic*, and *The
Forest Sanctuary*, a " potent, grave, and reverend"

---

[1] From *The Hour of Prayer.*

personage, whom it would be necessary to approach
with a solemn air, and a formal complimentary address, were as much astonished by her frankness and
vivacity, as by her thorough freedom from pretension, and everything approaching to the technicalities
of a "learned lady." All these she held as much in
detestation as she did the *duty compliments* and conventional homage of those by whom every intellectual woman is indiscriminately treated as a *bas bleu,*
and saluted in some such strain of hyperbole as used
to prevail in the Della Cruscan coteries of Hayley
and Miss Seward; whilst no one could be more alive
to the delight of being really understood and appreciated, or of knowing that anything she had written
had found its way into the depths of any kind, and
true, and loving heart.

She had that quick sense of the ludicrous, which is
the frequent concomitant of an intense perception of
the beautiful, and few could have wielded the shafts
of ridicule more effectually; yet it has been truly
said, that "no sharp or scornful speech is on record
against her." Sarcasm she deprecated as unwomanly
and unamiable; personalities were ever distasteful to
her, and, from the sensitiveness of her own nature,
she instinctively learned a "thoughtful tenderness" for
others. Sincerity, in however grotesque a guise,
always insured her respect; and its contrary, though
clothed in "*paroles d'or et de soie,*" was, of all others,
the thing of which she was most intolerant. The
blended loftiness and simplicity of her nature—a union
so little to be understood by the commonplace and the
worldly—exposed her to perpetual misconstructions.

None but her most intimate friends could fully appreciate her varied powers, and frank, deep affections. Amongst those chosen few, her endearing guilelessness —her uncomplaining sorrows—her susceptibility to kindness, on which her peculiar position made her lean so trustingly—her high aspirations and gentle charities—her very self-forgetfulness, which seemed to require the presence of some ever watchful and tenderly ministering spirit—all these awakened a mingled feeling of admiration, honour, anxiety, and protecting care, which amounted to absolute enthusiasm.   In this spirit, one who knew her long and well, wrote of her, with an honest warmth at which few could have the heart to cavil.—" Nothing but ignorance or ill-nature *could* point out a marring trait in a woman's nature, in which there were no faults that were not better in themselves, and more engaging, than the virtues or merits, whatever people choose to call them, of most others."   When amongst those she loved and trusted (and with her, indeed, these terms were synonymous), she would give herself up, with childlike *abandon*, to the mood of the moment, whatever it might be.   Her first impulse was to impart to her friends whatever had delighted or amused herself; and in this way, she would good-humouredly enjoy with them the strange proofs of celebrity—the whimsical tributes, the adulatory letters, the overstrained compliments, which were showering down upon her daily.   Yet nothing would have distressed her more than the idea of any of these communications ever being held up to public ridicule—nothing could be more repugnant to her feelings than to give pain to
13*

any one who had wished to give *her* pleasure, or to incur the charge of requiting with ingratitude anything meant in kindness.

During the winter of 1827, her health was very variable, and the inflammatory attacks to which she was always subject, were unfortunately increased both in frequency and violence, by her personal carelessness, which no warnings or entreaties could control, and by her unconquerable dislike to the adoption of the necessary remedies, and the being laid up as an acknowledged invalid. This made her unwilling to confess what she suffered, as long as it was possible to bear on in silence. "*Entre nous*," she wrote to a friend, " my chest and side have begun to burn again fiercely. I have not yet mentioned the recurrence of this pain at home, because they would make me put blisters on, and I am in hopes, if I keep quiet, that I shall get rid of it without such abominations."

    *   *   *   *   *   *   *

"Do not be uneasy about this fiery pain of mine; I am told that it is not from the lungs, but only nervous, and in this opinion I am inclined to agree, because it generally attacks me after I have been thinking intently, or after any agitation of mind."

All this time, her imagination was at work more busily than ever; new thoughts and fresh fancies seemed to spring up "as willows by the water-courses," and the facility with which her lyrics were poured forth, approached, in many instances, to actual improvisation. When confined to her bed, and unable to use a pen, she would often employ the services of those about her, to write down what she had com-

posed. " Felicia has just sent for me," wrote her
amanuensis on one of these occasions, " with pencil
and paper, to put down a little song,¹ which, she said,
had come to her like a strain of music, whilst lying in
the twilight under the infliction of a blister; and as I
really think, ' a scrap' (as our late eccentric visiter
would call it) composed under such circumstances, is,
to use the words of Coleridge, a ' psychological curiosity,' I cannot resist copying it for you. It was suggested by a story she somewhere read lately, of a
Greek islander, carried off to the Vale of Tempe, and
pining amidst all its beauties, for the sight and sound
of his native sea."

One of the pieces of this date is thus mentioned by
herself. " I am so glad you liked ' Fairy Favours.'
It is, indeed, filled with my own true and ever yearning feeling; that longing for more affection, more confidence, more entire interchange of thought, than I
am ever likely to meet with. However, I will not
repine, whilst I have friends who love me as you do."

To Mrs. Joanna Baillie, she wrote, " with the return
of the violet,"—" It seems very long since I have had
any communication with you; but this privation has
been my own fault, or rather my misfortune; for a
good deal of illness during the winter compelled me to
give up all other occupation, for that particularly
uninteresting one—taking care of myself, or rather
allowing others to take care of me. I know not how
it is, but I always feel so ashamed of the apparent
egotism and selfishness attendant on indisposition—

---

¹ " Where is the Sea?"

the muffling one's self up, taking the warmest place, shrinking from the mirthful noises of those who are in full health, &c. &c., that I believe I am apt to fall into the contrary extreme, and so, in the end, to occasion ten times more trouble than I should have done with a little proper submission. But a truce to the remembrances of indisposition, now that the Spring is really come forth with all her singing-birds and violets. It seems as if sadness had no right to a place amongst the bright and fair things of the season.

" Dr. Channing has lately published a very noble essay on the character of Napoleon, occasioned by Sir Walter Scott's Life of that dazzling but most unheroic personage. I wish you may meet with it; I am sure that the lofty thoughts embodied by its writer, in his own fervid eloquence, could not fail to delight you; and his high views of moral beauty are really freshening to the heart, which longs to pour itself forth in love and admiration, and finds so little in the every-day world whereon such feelings may repose.

" The little volume, *Records of Woman*, which you kindly gave me permission to inscribe to you, is now in the press, and I hope I shall soon be able to send you a copy; and that the dedication, which is in the simplest form, will be honoured by your approval. Mr. Blackwood is its publisher."

Mrs. Hemans always spoke with pleasure of her literary intercourse with Mr. Blackwood, in whose dealings she recognised all that uprightness and liberality which belonged to the sterling worth of his character. The *Records of Woman*, the first of her works published by him, was brought out in May,

1828. This volume was, to use the words of its author, the one in which " she had put her heart and individual feelings more than in anything else she had written;" and it is also, and perhaps consequently, the one which has held its ground the most steadily in public favour.

The following extract is from a letter of this date, to Mrs. Howitt, who had lately had to mourn the loss of one of her children :—

" I can feel deeply for the sorrow you communicate to me; it is one which Heaven has yet graciously spared me; but the imagination within us is a fearful and mysterious power, and has often brought all the sufferings of that particular bereavement before me, with a vividness from which I have shrunk almost in foreboding terror. And I have felt, too (though not through the breaking of *that* tie,) those sick and weary yearnings for the dead, that feverish thirst for the sound of a departed voice or step, in which the heart seems to die away, and literally to become ' a fountain of tears.' Who can sound its depths?—One alone, and may He comfort you!

" When you write to Mr. Bernard Barton, with whom, most probably, you are in frequent communication, will you mention, with my kind regards. that many months of languishing health have caused the interruption in my correspondence with him, but that I am now reviving, and hope shortly to resume it. I sent a copy of your delightful little volume, *The Desolation of Eyam*, a short time since, to some very intelligent friends, whom I am fortunate enough to possess.

in America; they will, I know, be able to appreciate all its feeling and beauty."

Early in the summer of this year, Mrs. Hemans accomplished a long-projected visit to her old friends at Wavertree Lodge, under whose hospitable roof, and more than affectionate care, she remained for several weeks. The state of her health appeared to them so serious, that she was at last persuaded to resign herself to medical discipline; and amongst many other precautionary measures, the almost entire adoption of a reclining posture was prescribed to her. One of her objects in this visit, besides the pleasure of being once more in the society of those she valued so truly, was, to make the necessary arrangements for engaging a residence in that neighbourhood, to which she was inclined to remove, on the approaching dispersion of the family circle at Rhyllon, occasioned by the marriage of her sister, and the appointment of her second brother to an official situation in Ireland. The possession of such attached friends in that vicinity (amongst whom she already numbered Mrs. Lawrence of Wavertree Hall, in herself a host), with the anticipation of superior advantages for the education of her boys, and of more literary communion for herself, combined to influence her in selecting this spot for her new abode; and the eager delight with which her project was hailed by those who were ready with open arms to receive her amongst them, contributed not a little to confirm her in the decision. She was not long in fixing upon a suitable house, situated in the village of Wavertree, but a little apart from the road; and arrangements were accordingly made for her removal in the following September. During her present visit, notwithstanding the medical restrictions she had to submit to, her spirits were refreshed and cheered by much enlivening society, and the formation of many new acquaintances; one of which, that with the Chorley family, soon ripened into friendship. Some of its members were, at that time, interested in the superintendence of that pretty Annual, *The Winter's Wreath*, for which Mrs. Hemans's contributions had been solicited; and the correspondence which had begun on editorial subjects, led first of all to personal communication, and then to the discovery of so many congenial tastes and pursuits (more especially with reference to music and German literature), that a cordial intimacy was speedily established, and Mrs. Hemans looked forward to its cultivation as one of the pleasant features of her new perspective. This anticipation was well borne out by the reality; many of her happiest hours of intellectual and social enjoyment during the next two years, were passed at Mrs. Chorley's friendly fireside, where the zealous and considerate kindness that always awaited her, made a little bright realm of home-like sunshine, which was just the atmosphere in which she shone " brightest and best"—in which her mind expanded like a bower, and her conversation flowed forth like a gushing stream. Though the intercourse thus mutually enjoyed was afterwards dissolved by her final change of residence, she always reverted to it with undiminished pleasure. To the thoughtful, steady, indefatigable friendship of Mr. W. B. Chorley, more particularly, shown in a thousand acts of service to herself and her children, she would often allude during her last illness, and desire he might be assured how gratefully she cherished the remembrance of it.

Amongst other interesting acquaintances made by her at this time, was that of Mary Howitt, best known by her own sweet and simple designation, of whose writings she had long been a sincere admirer, and whose society derived an additional charm from her being the first member of the Society of Friends whom Mrs. Hemans had ever known personally, though she had been in correspondence with more than one of the fraternity. A still brighter smile of good fortune awaited her, in the unexpected arrival in Liverpool of her kind New England friends, Mr. and Mrs. Norton. They had written to announce their coming, but the letter had not been received, so that their appearance was quite unlooked for. " I assure you," wrote Mrs. Hemans, in detailing the lucky coincidences which led to this meeting, "the delightful surprise was almost too much for me. I had the greatest difficulty in refraining from tears when I first met them."

The short personal intercourse she was permitted to enjoy with these interesting friends, was a source of the truest gratification to her both in the reality and the retrospect. She had the pleasure of renewing it for a few days on her return into Wales, as, after making a tour through the most remarkable parts of Great Britain, they paid a visit to St. Asaph before re-embarking for America.

This period, so rich in friendships and recollections, was also the one which brought Mrs. Hemans into immediate communication with another bright spirit, now, like her own, passed away from earth. This was the late Miss Jewsbury, afterwards Mrs. Fletcher —whose extraordinary mental powers, and lofty, ardent nature, have never been appreciated as they deserved—were never, in fact, fully manifested except to the few who knew her intimately. She had long admired the writings of Mrs. Hemans with all the enthusiasm which characterised her temperament; and having been for some time in correspondence with her, she eagerly sought for an opportunity of knowing her more nearly, and with this view, determined upon passing a part of the summer and autumn of 1828 in the neighbourhood of St. Asaph. No better accommodation could be found for her than a very small dwelling called Primrose Cottage, a corruption (meant, perhaps, for a refining) of its original appellation of *Pumrhos* (The Five Commons). The place in itself was as little attractive as a cottage in Wales could well be, and its closeness to the road took away even from its rurality; but it possessed the advantage of being not more than half a mile from Rhyllon; and it had its little garden, and its roses, and its green turf, and pure air; and these to an inhabitant of Manchester, which Miss Jewsbury then was, were things of health and enjoyment. Thither then she repaired, with the young sister and brothers to whom she had long and well performed the duties of a mother; and there Mrs. Hemans found her established on her own return from Wavertree at the end of July. It may well be conceived how soon a feeling of warm interest and thorough understanding sprang up between two minds so rarely gifted, and both so intent upon consecrating their gifts to the highest and holiest purposes.

Vol. I.——14

Yet it was scarcely possible to imagine two individual natures more strikingly contrasted—the one so intensely feminine, so susceptible and imaginative, so devoted to the tender and the beautiful; the other endowed with masculine energies, with a spirit that seemed born for ascendency, with strong powers of reasoning, fathomless profundity of thought, and feelings, like those of her own Julia,[1] "flashing forth at intervals with sudden and Vesuvian splendour, making the beholder aware of depths beyond his vision." No less an authority than Mr. Wordsworth has said of her, that "in one quality, viz., quickness in the motions of the mind, she had, within the range of his acquaintance, no equal."[2] With all this, she possessed warm and generous affections, a peculiar faculty for identifying herself with the tastes and predilections of those she loved, and in conversation, when embodying the conceptions of her own " ever salient mind" (to quote an expression from Bishop Jebb), a singular talent for eliciting thoughts from others, which reminded one of the magic properties of the divining rod. From early years she had had to contend with that precarious and suffering state of health, so often the accompaniment of the restless, ardent spirit, which

"O'er-informs its tenements of clay."

She came into Wales, indeed, completely as an invalid, but was soon sufficiently recruited to enter

---

[1] In *The Three Histories.*

[2] See the Note to the Poem of " Liberty," in the fifth vol. of Wordsworth's *Poetical Works.*

with full enjoyment into all the novelties around her, to pass long mornings in the dingle, to take distant rides on her donkey, surrounded by a troop of juvenile knights-errant, and to hold levees in the tent she had contrived as a temporary addition to her tiny dwelling, whose wicket gate can now never be passed, by those still left to remember the converse of those bright hours, without a gush of mournful recollections.

Many of the poems in her *Lays of Leisure Hours,* which she dedicated to Mrs. Hemans " in remembrance of the summer passed in her society," were written in this little cottage. Some of them were immediately addressed to her, particularly that " To an absent one ;" and the first of the series of " Poetical Portraits," in the same volume, was meant to describe her. The picture of " Egeria," in *The Three Histories,* written by Miss Jewsbury some time afterwards, was avowedly taken from the same original; and allowing for a certain degree of idealization, is drawn with no less truth than delicacy, and may well claim an introduction in this place. " Egeria was totally different from any other woman I had ever seen, either in Italy or England. She did not dazzle, she subdued me. Other women might be more commanding, more versatile, more acute; but I never saw one so exquisitely feminine."

  *   *   *   *   *

" Her birth, her education, but above all, the genius with which she was gifted, combined to inspire a passion for the ethereal, the tender, the imaginative, the heroic,—in one word, the beautiful. It was in

her a faculty divine, and yet of daily life—it touched
all things, but, like a sun-beam, touched them with a
'golden finger.'   Any thing abstract or scientific was
unintelligible and distasteful to her; her knowledge
was extensive and various, but, true to the first principle of her nature, it was poetry that she sought in
history, scenery, character, and religious belief,—
poetry, that guided all her studies, governed all her
thoughts, coloured all her conversation.   Her nature
was at once simple and profound; there was no room
in her mind for philosophy, nor in her heart for am-
bition;—the one was filled by imagination, the other
engrossed by tenderness.   She had a passive temper,
but decided tastes; any one might influence, but very
few impressed her.   Her strength and her weakness
alike lay in her affections; these would sometimes
make her weep at a word, at others, imbue her with
courage; so that she was alternately ' a falcon-hearted
dove,' and 'a reed shaken with the wind.'   Her voice
was a sad, sweet melody, and her spirits reminded me
of an old poet's description of the orange tree, with its

"Golden lamps hid in a night of green;"

or of those Spanish gardens where the pomegranate
grows beside the cypress.   Her gladness was like a
burst of sun-light; and if, in her depression, she resembled night, it was night bearing her stars.   I
might describe and describe for ever, but I should
never succeed in portraying Egeria; she was a muse,
a grace, a variable child, a dependent woman, the
Italy of human beings."

Miss Jewsbury's enthusiasm for the poetry of Mr.

Wordsworth, whose friendship she regarded, and with reason, as one of the highest privileges she possessed, was the means of leading Mrs. Hemans to a more close and intimate acquaintance with the treasures she had hitherto reverenced rather with vague and general admiration than with earnest and individual study. How readily this obligation was acknowledged, appears in a letter, the date of which was considerably prior to that of Miss Jewsbury's visit to Wales.

"The inclosed lines,¹ an effusion of deep and sincere admiration, will give you some idea of the enjoyment, and I hope I may say advantage, which you have been the means of imparting, by so kindly entrusting me with your precious copy of Wordsworth's Miscellaneous Poems. It has opened to me such a treasure of thought and feeling, that I shall always associate your name with some of my pleasantest recollections, as having introduced me to the knowledge of what I can only regret should have been so long a ' Yarrow unvisited.' I would not write to you sooner, because I wished to tell you that I had really *studied* these poems, and they have been the daily food of my mind ever since I borrowed them. There is hardly any scene of a happy, though serious, domestic life, or any mood of a reflective mind, with the spirit of which some one or other of them does not beautifully harmonize. This author is the true poet of home, and of all the lofty feelings which have their root in the soil of home affections. His fine sonnets to Liberty, and indeed all his pieces which have

---

¹ Those addressed " To the Poet Wordsworth."
14 *

any reference to political interest, remind me of the
spirit in which Schiller has conceived the character
of William Tell, a calm, single-hearted herdsman of
the hills, breaking forth into fiery and indignant eloquence, when the sanctity of his hearth is invaded.
Then what power Wordsworth condenses into single
lines, like Lord Byron's ' curdling a long life into one
hour !'

'The still, sad music of humanity'—
'The river glideth at his own sweet will'—
'Over his own sweet voice the stock-dove broods'—

and a thousand others, which we must some time (and
I hope not a very distant one), talk over together.
Many of these lines quite haunt me; and I have a
strange feeling, as if I must have known them in my
childhood; they come over me so like old melodies. I
can hardly speak of favourites among so many things
that delight me; but I think ' The Narrow Glen,' the
' Lines on Corra Linn,' the ' Song for the Feast of
Brougham Castle,' ' Yarrow Visited,' and ' The Cuc-
koo,' are among those which take hold of imagination
the soonest, and recur most frequently to memory.

*   *   *   *   *   *

" I know not how I can have so long omitted to
mention the *Ecclesiastical Sketches*, which I have read
and do constantly read, with deep interest. Their
beauty grows upon you and developes as you study it,
like that of the old pictures by the Italian masters."

In one of her letters of this autumn, Mrs. Hemans
makes mention of an interesting visit she had received
from the Poet Montgomery (not the new aspirant to
that name, but the " real Peter Bell"), who had just

come from Snowdon, full of animation and enthusiasm. "He complained much in the course of conversation," she writes, "and I heartily joined with him, of the fancy which wise people have in the present times, for *setting one right;* cheating one, that is, out of all the pretty old legends and stories, in the place of which they want to establish dull facts. We mutually grumbled about Fair Rosamond, Queen Eleanòr and the poisoned wound, Richard the Third and his hump back; but agreed most resolutely that nothing *should* ever induce us to give up William Tell."

There was nothing she disliked more than the disturbance of any old associations, or the reasoning away of any ancient belief, endeared to our hearts by the childish recollections with which it is interwoven. "I admire your resolute spirit of faith," she once wrote to a friend who had been visiting some scenes consecrated by tradition; "for my part, so determined is mine, that if I went to Rushin Castle, I should certainly look for the giant, said to be chained and slumbering in the dark vaults of that pile."

She would often speak with delight of the taste she had discovered in Bishop Heber for fairy tales and fantastic legends; and it is needless to say how heartily she entered into the congenial predilections of Sir Walter Scott. Her own enjoyment of such fanciful creations was fresh and childlike. The "Irish Fairy Legends" were always high in her favour, and the "German popular Stories" were as familiar to her young auditors at the fireside readings, as to those of Mr. Crabbe.[1]

---

[1] See the "Life of Crabbe," p. 304.

> " Alice my wife,
> The plague of my life,"

was in quite as bad repute amongst them, as she could
have been at Pucklechurch, and little voices would
make the hearth ring with manly threats of " what *I*
would do, if I had such a wife !"

" I am very much enjoying myself," she wrote in
one of her notes from Wavertree, " in the society of
certain *Luft und Feuergeister, Wasser und Wald-
geister*, and *Feen und Feldgeister*,[1] introduced to me
by the worthy Herr Dobeneck, in a book of *Deutschen
Volksglauben*.[2] These *geister* of his, are, to be sure,
a little wild and capricious in their modes of proceeding ; but even this is a relief, after the macadamized
mortality in which one has to pass all the days of one's
life. I like your superstition about good wishes, and
am very much inclined to agree with him who says
' *Es ist alles wahr wodurch du besser wirst*.' "[3]

There was one German tradition in particular,
" *Die Sage vom Wolfsbrunnen*" (The Legend of the
Wolf's Well,) which had made a deep impression
upon her imagination, and at one time she had
thought of making it the subject of a poem of some
length ; but the train of feeling it suggested was too
painfully exciting, and she wisely decided upon laying
it aside.[4]

---

[1] Air and Fire Spirits, Water and Wood Spirits, and Fairies
and Field Spirits.

[2] German Popular Superstitions.

[3] Every thing is true by which thou art made better.

[4] The Wolfsbrunnen, a place of real existence, is situated in
a romantic little valley near Heidelberg. The secluded and

The time had now arrived for Mrs. Hemans's leaving Wales, and this removal, which had been contemplated at a distance with more of hope than of dread, proved in the reality a heart-rending trial, increased in bitterness, too, by the additional sorrow of parting with her two eldest boys, who were sent at this time to join their father at Rome. " I am suffering deeply," she wrote to her late kind hosts, " more than I could have dreamt or imagined, from the ' farewell sadness.' My heart seems as if a night-mare weighed

---

somewhat melancholy air of the spot accords well with the tradition belonging to it, which relates, that in ancient days, long before the building of the present Castle of Heidelberg, there existed, on the mountain where the ruins called the *Jetthe Bühl* are still to be seen, an enchanted Castle, which was inhabited by a maiden of surpassing beauty, generally regarded as a sorceress. A young hunter, named Ferrand, famed alike for his daring deeds and manly beauty, had one day the hardihood to penetrate into the magic precincts of the Castle. He became enamoured of the fair Enchantress, by whom his love was in time returned. Yielding to his incessant importunities that she would reveal to him the secret of her supernatural powers, she at last disclosed to him that she was not a fairy, but the daughter of a Northern King, and that it had been predicted at her birth that she was to become the prey of a wolf. Her mother, who was of Southern origin, had consigned her, when on her own deathbed, to the care of an enchanter, who had promised to transport her far from the rugged regions of the North. He had placed her in this Castle, and invested her with Talismans to ward off the approach of evil. These were the white bird which perpetually hovered round her, the girdle of gems which she always wore, and the golden Tiara which encircled her beautiful hair. But the imperious Ferrand insisted upon her throwing aside all these appendages, which he regarded as the spells of some malignant spirit, and making an assignation with

it down.   Seriously and truly, I *am* most careful of myself, though too many conflicting thoughts and feelings are at work upon me now,—and I have to say too many of those 'words which must be and have been,' to admit of my making the progress I otherwise might.' You know it is impossible I should be better till all these billows have passed over me.   The improvisatore talent has scarcely deserted me yet, but it is gushing from a fountain of tears — Oh ! that I could but lift up my heart, and sustain it at that height where alone the calm sunshine is !"

The description of her feelings, when the actual parting took place, proves that there was no exaggeration in the affectionate sadness of her " Farewell

---

him to show herself to his parents as a simple mortal, divested of all supernatural attributes   The gentle Welleda consented, though dark inward forebodings whispered but too plainly of the fatal consequences that would ensue : these warnings she imparted to her ungenerous lover, but without shaking his purpose. She promised, therefore, to meet him in the evening, by the side of this fountain, under the shade of its overarching lime trees. Thither she repaired at the appointed hour, and Ferrand, hastening to the rendezvous, arrived at the very moment when the fang of a ravenous wolf had inflicted a mortal wound on his hapless Welleda   Frantic with horror and remorse, he annihilated the ferocious animal on the spot, and then turned to receive the last sighs of the fond being who had sacrificed herself to his exacting tyranny.   He buried her beside the fountain, and quitted the spot no more till his own death, which followed erelong.   A kind shepherd then laid him beside his Welleda, and planted a Linden tree on the mound of turf which covered the remains of these unfortunate lovers.

This legend has been worked up into a pretty little prose romance in German by Madame Von Helwig.

to Wales," and the blessing she thus fondly left with it : —

"The sound of thy streams in my spirit I bear—
Farewell! and a blessing be with thee, green land!
On thy hearths, on thy halls, on thy pure mountain air,
On the chords of the harp, and the minstrel's free hand!
From the love of my soul with my tears it is shed,
As I leave thee, green land of my home and my dead."

"Oh! that Tuesday morning!" (thus she wrote in her first letter to St. Asaph.) " I literally covered my face all the way from Bronwylfa until the boys told me we had passed the Clwyd range of hills. Then something of the bitterness was over.

"Miss P. met me at Bagillt, and on board the packet we found Mr. D., who was kinder to me than I can possibly tell you. He really watched over me all the way with a care I shall not soon forget; and notwithstanding all you may say of *female* protection, I felt that of a gentleman to be a great comfort, for we had a difficult and disagreeable landing. As we entered the port, a vessel coming out, struck against ours, and caused a great concussion; there was no danger, I imagine, but it gave one a faint notion of what the meeting must have been between the Comet and the Aire. We had a pretty sight on the Water; another packet, loaded, clustered all over with blue-coat boys, sailed past. It was their annual holiday, on which they have a water excursion; and as they went by, all the little fellows waved their hats, and sent forth three cheers, which made our vessel ring again. Only imagine a ship-load of happiness! That word reminds me of my own boys, who are enjoying

themselves greatly. Of myself, what can I say to
you? . . . . . . When I look back on the short time
that has elapsed since I left this place, I am astonished; I seem in it to have lived an age of deep, strong,
vain feeling."

After remaining for a time with her ever considerate friends at Wavertree Lodge, Mrs. Hemans at
length took possession of her own little domicile,
where she was surrounded by all that the most sedu-
lous kindness could devise, to foster and shelter, and
reconcile her to the new soil in which she was now
to take root. Not only by the old friends on whose
regard she had a claim, but by numbers hitherto
strangers, she was overwhelmed with offers of service
and marks of courtesy. From the overtures of the
latter, however, she was, in a great measure, obliged
to withdraw, as her habits, her health, the urgency
of her literary occupations, and the indescribable
pressure of correspondence, of which words can
scarcely give any adequate idea — for of letters and
notes it might really be said that

     "Each minute teems a new one"—

made it absolutely impossible for her to keep up the
conventional forms and etiquettes of an extensive general acquaintance. Nothing could be further from her
nature than ungraciousness or incivility; yet, from
circumstances quite beyond her own control, for which
few were disposed to make sufficient allowances, she
often incurred the charge of both, through an utter
want both of leisure and physical energy, to cope with
all the bewildering claims upon her attention.

A few extracts from notes written soon after her -establishment at Wavertree, will best express her own views and feelings.

" I have no taste, no health, for the enjoyment of extensive society. I have been all my life a creature of hearth and home, 'and now that ' the mother that looked on my childhood' is gone, and that my brothers and sisters are scattered far and wide, I have no wish, but to gather around me the few friends who will love me and enter into my pursuits. I wish I could give you the least idea of what kindness is to me—how much more, how far dearer than Fame. I trust we may pass many pleasant evenings together this winter at my little dwelling, which I hope to see often cheered and lit up by happy and familiar faces."

" Generally speaking, I cannot tell you how painful going out is to me now. I know it is a weakness which I must conquer, but I feel so alone, so unprotected, and this weary celebrity makes such things, I believe, press the more bitterly."

" I can well imagine the weariness and disgust with which a mind of intellectual tastes must be oppressed by the long days of ' work-day world' cares, so utterly at variance with such tastes ; and yet, perhaps, the opposite extreme is scarcely more to be desired. Mine, I believe, has been too much a life of thought and feeling for health and peace. I *can* certainly quit this little world of my own for active duties ; for, however I may at times playfully advocate the cause of weak-

Vol. I.——15

ness, there is no one who has, with deeper need for strength, a fuller conviction of its necessity; but it is often by an effort, and a painful one, that I am enabled to obtain it."

The following letters will equally speak for themselves:—

"Nov. 10th, 1828.

"My dear Miss Mitford,

"Accept my late, though sincere and cordial congratulations on the brilliant success of *Rienzi*, of which I have read with unfeigned gratification. I thought of your father and mother, and could not help imagining that your feelings must be like those of the Greek general, who declared that his greatest delight in victory arose from the thought of his parents. I have no doubt that your enjoyment of your triumph has been of a similar nature. I ought to have acknowledged long, long since, your kind present of the little volume of plays, valued both for your sake and theirs, for they are indeed full of beauty; but I have been a drooping creature for months,—ill, and suffering much from the dispersion of a little band of brothers and sisters, among whom I had lived, and who are now all scattered; and, strange as it may seem to say, I am now, for the first time in my life, holding the reins of government, independent, managing a household myself; and I never liked anything less than ' ce triste empire de soi-même.' It really suits me as ill as the *southron* climate did your wild Orkney school-girls, whom perhaps you, the creator of so many fair forms and images, may have forgotten, but I have not. I have changed my residence since I last wrote to you, and my address is now at Wavertree, near Liverpool, where I shall, as the Welsh country-people say, ' take it very kind' if you write to me ; and I really cannot help venturing to hope that you will. I have yet only read of *Rienzi* a few noble passages given by the newspapers and magazines, but in a few days I hope to be acquainted with the whole. Every woman ought to be proud of your triumph—in. this age, too, when dramatic triumph seems of all others the most difficult. How are May, and Mossy, and Lucy, and Jack Hatch?—no, Jack Hatch actually died, to the astonishment of myself and my boys, who thought, I believe, he had been ' painted for eternity'—and Mrs. Allen, and the rest of the dear villagers? I trust they are well. Your mother, I believe, is always an invalid, but I hope she is able fully to enjoy the success of her daughter, as only a mother can enjoy it. How hollow sounds the voice of Fame to an orphan![1] Farewell, my dear Miss Mitford—long may you have the delight of gladdening a father and mother !"

"Wavertree, Dec. 11th, 1828.
" My dear Mrs. Howitt,

" You will not, I trust, have thought me very ungrateful for your delightful letter, though it has been left so long unanswered. I am sure I shall give

---

[1] In one of Mrs. Hemans's MS. books is an extract from Richter, of which she must have felt the full force. " O thou who hast still a father and a mother, thank God for it in the day when thy soul is full of joyful tears, and needs a bosom whereon to shed them !"

your heart greater pleasure by writing now, than I
could have done by an immediate reply; for I had
suffered so deeply, so much more than I had imagined
possible, from leaving Wales, and many kind and ' old
familiar faces' there, as well as from the breaking up
of my family on the occasion of my sister's marriage,
that my spirits were, long after my arrival here, over-
shadowed by constant depression. My health, also,
had been much affected by mental struggles, and I
thought within myself, ' I will not write what I know
will only sadden so kind a heart; I will wait till the
sunshine breaks in.'   And now, I can tell you that it
begins to dawn ; for my health and spirits are decidedly
improving, and I am reconciling myself to many things
in my changed situation, which, at first, pressed upon
my heart with all the weight of a Switzer's home
sickness. Among these, is *the want of hills.* Oh ! this
waveless horizon !—how it wearies the eye accustomed
to the sweeping outline of mountain scenery ! I would
wish that there were, at least, woodlands, like those
so delightfully pictured in your husband's *Chapter on
Woods,* to supply their place; but it is a dull, unin-
ventive nature all around here, though there *must* be
somewhere little fairy nooks, which I hope, by degrees,
to discover. I must recur to the before-mentioned
Chapter, it delighted me so particularly by the freshness of its spirit, deep feeling, and minute observation
of nature. ' The fading of the leaf, which ought
rather to be called the *kindling* of the leaf,'—how
truly and how poetically was that said ! That I might
become better acquainted with his writings, I have
lately borrowed some volumes of *Time's Telescope,* in

which I believed I could not fail to discover the same characteristics; and I anticipate much enjoyment from *The Book of the Seasons,* which, I am sure, will be a rich treasury of natural imagery and pure feeling.[1]

" I hear, with great pleasure, my dear friend, that the place of your lost one is to be supplied, ' the hollow of his absence' filled up. All the kindly wishes of a woman's and a mother's heart attend you on the occasion !

       *   *   *   *   *

" I trust your dear little girl is well. Has she quite forgotten ' Felicia Hemans?' I cannot tell you with how much pleasure I read your praises in the *Noctes Ambrosianæ.* They were bestowed, too, in language so delicate and appropriate, that I think you must have felt gratified, especially as you have one to gratify by your success."

A remarkable instance of Mrs. Hemans's powers of memory, is recorded about this time, in the fact of her having repeated, and even written down, with extraordinary accuracy, the beautiful stanzas address-

---

[1] In this anticipation she was not disappointed; for she wrote of it two years after as "a little book which has quite charmed me. Do you know," she continued, "I think that the rumours of political strife and convulsion now ringing round us on all sides, make the spirit long more intensely for the freshness, and purity, and stillness of nature, and take deeper delight in everything that recalls these lovely images. I am sure I shall forget all sadness, and feel as happy as a child or a fawn, when I can be free again amongst hills and woods. I long for them ' as the hart for the water brooks.' "

15 *

ed by Lord Byron to his sister, after hearing them
only twice read aloud in manuscript.

A few extracts, bearing more particularly on literary subjects, will give some idea of her predominant
tastes at this period.

" I send Herder's beautiful ballads of *The Cid*, and
I wish you may take as much pleasure as I have always done in their proud *clarion music*. I often
think what a dull, faded thing life — such life as we
lead in this later age — would appear to one of those
fiery knights of old. Only imagine *my Cid*, spurring
the good steed Bavieca through the streets of Liverpool, or coming to pass an evening with me at Wavertree !"

" I owe you many thanks for so kindly introducing
me to all those noble thoughts of Richter's. I think
the vision in the church magnificent both in purpose
and conception : it is scarcely possible to stop for the
contemplation of occasional extravagances, when
borne along so rapidly and triumphantly, as by 'a
mighty rushing wind,' some of the detached thoughts
are so exquisite."

*   *   *   *   *

" Now, let me introduce you to a dear friend of
mine, Tieck's *Sternbald*, in whose *Wanderungen*,
which I now send — if you know them not already —
I cannot but hope that you will take almost as much
delight as I have done amidst my own free hills and
streams, where his favourite book has again and again
been my companion."

" We have been talking much of French poetry lately. Do you know the *Dernier Chant de Corinne?* I sent it, marked in the third volume of the book, and you shall have the others if you wish. If the soul, without the form, be enough to constitute poetry, then it surely is poetry of the very highest order.

·*   * .   *   *   *

" That book (*Corinne*), in particular towards its close, has a power over me which is quite indescribable. Some passages seem to give me back my own thoughts and feelings, my whole inner being, with a mirror more true than ever friend could hold up."

" How very beautiful are those letters of Lord Collingwood to his family! — there is something in all those thoughts of hearth and home, and of the garden trees and of the ' old summer-seat,' which, breathing as they do from amidst the far and lonely seas, affect us like an exile's song of his fatherland. The letters to his wife brought strongly to my mind the poor Queen of Prussia's joyous exclamations in the midst of her last sufferings—' Oh ! how blessed is she who receives such a letter as this !' "

" I send my copy of *Iphigenia*, because I shall like to know whether you are as much struck with all that I have marked in it as I have been. Do you remember all we were saying on the obscurity of *female* suffering in such stormy days of the lance and spear, as the good Fray Agapida describes so vividly ? Has not Goethe beautifully developed the idea in the lines which I inclose ? They occur in Iphigenia's supplication to Thoas for her brother."

" I have been delighted with the paper on Burns,[1] which you were kind enough to lend me. I think that the writer has gone further into 'the heart of the mystery' than any other, because he, almost the first of all, has approached the subject with a deep reverence for genius, but a still deeper for truth: all the rest have seemed only anxious to make good the attack or the defence. And there is a feeling, too, of 'the still sad music of humanity' throughout, which bears upon the heart a conviction full of power, that it is listening to the voice of a brother. I wonder who the writer is: he certainly gives us a great deal of what Boswell, I think, calls ' bark and steel for the mind.' I, at least, found it in several passages; but I fear that a woman's mind never can be able, and never was formed to attain that power of sufficiency to itself, which seems to lie somewhere or other amongst the *rocks* of a man's."

———

" I send you the Moravian air ; and this is the old Swedish tradition of which I was speaking to you last night. There is a dark lake somewhere among the Swedish mountains, and in the lake there is an island of pines, and on the island an old castle, and there is a spirit-keeper, who lives far down in the lake, and when any evil is going to befall the inhabitants of the castle, he rises to the surface, and plays a most mournful ditty on his shadowy harp, and they know that it is a music of warning. I met with it in *Olaus Magnus*—such a strange wild book !"

---

[1] That by Carlyle in the *Edinburgh Review.*

"Did it ever strike you how much lighter sorrow's 'pining cares' become, out in the free air, and under the blue sky, than 'beneath a smoky roof,' as the sea-kings of old used to say? For my part, I am never the least surprised to hear of people becoming fasci-nated with Indian life, and giving up all our boasted refinements for the range of the tameless forests. This reminds me of some American books, which I send you; in one of them, *New England's Memorial*, I wish to call your attention to the beautiful map at the beginning, with all those gallant ships, and groups of armed men, and wolves and bears wandering about, to express, I suppose, the dangers which the pilgrim fathers so bravely encountered. The other, *Made-moiselle Riedesel's Memoirs*, I send for Mrs. C., whom, I think, it will interest: the heroine goes through many trials, but, sustained as she is by 'the strong affection which overcometh all things,' who can look upon her with pity?"

"I am quite surprised at your liking my 'Storm-Painter' so much: as an expression of strong and per-turbed feeling, I could not satisfy myself with it in the least;—it seemed all done in pale *water-colours*."

"Will you tell your brother, I regretted, after you and he had left me the other evening, that, instead of Werner's *Luther*, which I do not think will interest him much, I had not lent him one of my greatest favourites, Grillparzer's *Sappho*. I therefore send it him now. It is, in my opinion, full of beauty, which I am sure he will appreciate, and of truth, developing itself clearly and sorrowfully through the colouring mists of imagination."

———

" I have been thinking much of the German scenes for translation, respecting which you paid me the compliment of wishing for my opinion. The interview between Philip the Second and Posa[1] is certainly very powerful, but to me its interest is always destroyed by a sense of utter impossibility, which haunts me throughout. Not even Schiller's mighty spells can, I think, win the most ' unquestioning spirit' to suppose that such a voice of truth and freedom could have been lifted up, and endured, in the presence of the cold, stern Philip the Second—that he would, even for a moment, have listened to the language thus fearlessly bursting from a noble heart. Three of the most impressive scenes towards the close of the play, might, I think, be linked together, leaving out the intervening ones, with much effect;—the one in which Carlos, standing by the body of his friend, forces his father to the contemplation of the dead: the one in which the king comes forward, with his fearful, dreamy remorse, alone amidst his court,

Gieb diesen todten mir heraus, &c.[2]

and the subsequent interview between Philip and the Grand Inquisitor, in which the whole spirit of those fanatic days seems embodied.

" There is a scene in one of Oehlenschlager's dramas, *Der Hirtenknabe*,[3] which has always affected me

———

[1] In Schiller's *Don Carlos.*   [2] " Give me this dead one back."
[3] The Shepherd Boy.

strongly. It has also the recommendation of telling its own tale at once, without need of any preliminaries. An aged priest wishes by degrees, and with tenderness, to reveal to a father the death of his only child. The father, represented as a bold and joyous character, full of hope, and strength, and *muth des lebens,*[1] attributes all the ' dark sayings,' and mournful allusions of his visitant, to the natural despondency of age, and attempts to cheer him by descriptions of *his* bright domestic happiness. " Starke dich," he says, " *in meinen sonnenschein !*"[2] The very exultation of his spirit makes you tremble for him, and feel that fate is approaching : at last, the old man uncovers the body of the child, and then the passionate burst of the father's grief is indeed overpowering :— then the mother enters, and even amidst all her anguish, the meekness of a more subdued and chastened being is felt, and beautifully contrasted with her husband's despair.

" In Goethe's *Egmont,* the scenes in which Clarchen endeavours to rouse the spirit of the bewildered citizens, and in which Brackenburg communicates to her the preparations for Egmont's execution, seem to stand out from the rest in the bold relief of their power and passion ; and the interview between Egmont in prison and Ferdinand, the son of his enemy, who soothes even the anguish of those moments by the free-will offering of his young heart's affection and reverence, I have always thought most deeply touching."

---

[1] Spirit of life.   [2] Strengthen thyself in my sunshine.

It may here not be out of place to introduce a few
recollections regarding Mrs. Hemans's progressive
tastes, supplied by the friend already described, as
having been for so many years her indefatigable literary purveyor.

"My book *beckifications* in the days of old were
multifarious enough; in English, French, German,
Italian, and Spanish poetry; or prose (not *prosy* prose),
grave or gay, lively or severe, history or fiction (the
history chiefly of feudal ages), essay or criticism; only
nothing in the service of science ever found a place in
them.[1] At a later period, during her Wavertree residence, I was often struck with the change of her
tastes, which then seemed to have retreated from the
outer world, and devoted themselves exclusively to the
passionate and imaginative. The German poets were
always on her table, especially Goethe. Wordsworth
was ever growing in her favour, yet I think at that
time she oftener quoted Byron, Shelley, and Madame
de Stael, than any other. This was aliment too
stimulating for an organization that so much needed

---

[1] All the works of Sismondi, particularly the *Litterature du
Midi*, and *Republiques Italiennes*, held a high place in her estimation; perhaps she prized them all the more from their having
been especial favourites of her mother. Fauriel's *Chants Popu-
laires de la Grèce Moderne*, opened out to her a world of new
ideas and feelings, and suggested, as the books she loved always
did, some of her sweetest lyrics.

Amongst the old household favourites, none was more popular
than the *Narrative of a Ten Years' Residence in Tripoli*, by
the sister-in-law of Mr. Tully; and in one of Mrs. Hemans's
letters, she says—"What will you think of our wanting to bor-
row, for the sixth time, the dear old letters from Tripoli?"

more sedative influences—and while her poetry at
that period was deeper, tenderer, more touching than
ever, it was like the pelican's heart-blood, poured
forth (if naturalists would let these pretty stories pass)
to feed her brood."

One of the peculiar features of the increased sensitiveness of her temperament at this time, was an
awakened enthusiasm for music, which amounted to
an absolute passion. "I do not think," she wrote,
"that I can bear the burthen of my life without
music for more than two or three days." Yet, with
sensibilities so exquisite as hers, this melomania was
a source of far more pain than pleasure; it was so
impossible for any earthly strains to approach that
ideal and unattainable standard of perfection which
existed within her mind, and which she has shadowed
forth with a mournful energy in " Mozart's Requiem."

> Like perfumes on the wind,
> Which none may stay or bind,
> The beautiful comes rushing through my soul;
> I strive, with yearnings vain,
> The spirit to detain,
> Of the deep harmonies that past me roll.
> Therefore disturbing dreams
> Trouble the secret streams
> And founts of music that o'erflow my breast;
> Something far more divine
> Than may on earth be mine,
> Haunts my worn heart, and will not let me rest.

From time to time, however, she had enjoyment of
music of a very high character, for much of which
she was indebted to her acquaintance with Mr. Lodge,
the distinguished amateur, by whom so many of her

songs have been set to melodies of infinite beauty and feeling. At a somewhat later period she derived much delight from the talents of Mr. James Zengheer Herrmann, from whom, for a time, she took lessons, for the express purpose of studying, and fully understanding, the *Stabat Mater* of Pergolesi, which had taken an extraordinary hold of her imagination. This fine composition was first brought to her notice by Mr. Lodge, to whom she thus expressed her appreciation of it:—"It is quite impossible for me to tell you the impression I have received from that most spiritual music of Pergolesi's, which really haunted me the whole night. How much I have to thank you for introducing me, in such a manner, to so new and glorious a world of musical thought and feeling!"

And she wrote of it again, some time after, with no less deep a feeling. "I am learning Pergolesi's *Stabat Mater*, which realizes all that I could dream of religious music, and which derives additional interest from its being the last work in which the master-spirit breathed forth its enthusiasm."

The state of her health had long obliged her to discontinue the practice of her harp, but the same friend whose recollections have been already quoted from, recalls a singular instance of sudden and transient return to it. "I remember," she writes, " her stringing and tuning it one day, just after she settled at Wavertree, and pouring forth a full tide of music all without notes, and with as much facility of execution as if she had had the instrument daily under her hand for years. Having listened and wondered for about half an hour. I said, ' Really. Felicia, it seems to me that there is something not quite *canny* in this; so, especially as it is beginning to be twilight, I shall think it prudent to take my departure.' The harp, however, required more physical exertion than she could well afford, and it soon fell into neglect again."

The " brightly associated hours" she passed with Mrs. Lawrence, have been alluded to by Mrs. Hemans, in the dedication to the *National Lyrics*, and recorded by " her friend, and the sister of her friend, Colonel D'Aguilar," in her own affectionate *Recollections*. The " Books and Flowers" of Wavertree Hall, were ever fondly identified with their dear mistress; and years after the enjoyment of them had passed away from all senses but memory, she who was then herself, too, " passing away," thus tenderly alluded to them from her sick couch at Redesdale. " When I write to you, my imagination always brightens, and pleasant thoughts of lovely flowers, and dear old books, and strains of antique Italian melody, come floating over me, as Bacon says, the rich scents go ' to and fro like music in the air.' "

The reviving influences of these intellectual enjoyments were, however, but too powerfully counterbalanced by the constant pressure of inward sorrows, and daily anxieties. The experience of a first winter, moreover, occasioned Mrs. Hemans many misgivings as to the healthiness of her new residence; and the illness of her three boys, who were seized with the hooping cough, very soon after their establishment at Wavertree, was anything but an encouraging inauguration to one so new to the cares of household management. The fatigue she endured in nursing them,

was far more than she was equal to; and at length it
proved, by way of climax, that she had actually
caught this harassing and tedious complaint herself.
Change of air was, of course, recommended; and
early in the spring, the whole party of invalids repaired for a short time to Seacombe, a small bathing-
place on the Cheshire side of the Mersey. Here they
speedily derived all the benefits anticipated from the
sea air; and the cheerful tone of some of the following extracts, exhibits once more the naturally elastic
spirits of the writer.

"You will rejoice to hear that we are going on
extremely well, and are able to be out a great deal.
It is very strange to me to be here. You know how
rapidly my thoughts and feelings chase each other,
like shadows of clouds over the mountains; sometimes
I feel quite forlorn—at others, and those, I think, the
most frequent, enjoying with child-like pleasure, the
moving picture of the waters, the thousand sails and
streamers glancing and gleaming past 'like things of
life.' I can hardly leave this animated sea-beach,
when once I have reached it; and at this distance

'The city's voice itself
Is soft as Solitude's.' "

"The boys and I passed a most comic yesterday,
sitting in a sort of verdant twilight, as we were
obliged to have the outworks of green blinds fastened
over the windows, to keep them from blowing in.
Then the wind kept lifting the knocker, and perform-
ing such human knocks all day, that we thought
friends must be coming to see us in the shape of

meteoric stones—for certainly in no other could they have approached us. However, Charles cut out and painted what he pleases to call the Weird Sisters from *Macbeth*; and Henry set to music ' The Homes of England,' in a style only to be paralleled by Charles's painting; and I read *The Robbers*; and the knocks at the door were thought so full of happy humour, that they made us laugh *aux eclats*.'

———

" Last Sunday I visited a very interesting scene— the Mariners' Church, on the Liverpool side of the water. It is the hulk of a ship of war, now fitted up for divine service, which is performed by Mr. Scoresby. The earnest attention of the hardy, wea- ther-beaten countenances, all steadfastly fixed upon the preacher, connected with the images of past danger by flood and fire, which such a scene would naturally call up — these things were very deeply impressive, and I am glad to have borne away a recollection of them. I had a good deal of conversa- tion with Mr. Scoresby, in the vestry (the ci-devant *powder-room*, I suppose) of his church.

" We are very dissipated indeed, as far as receiving visiters can make us so, for we have only been alone two evenings since we came here. Our guests, to be sure, are obliged to depart at most patriarchal hours, having to set off with the speed of Harold Harefoot, at eight o'clock in the evening, in order to be in time for the steam-boat which is to convey them back, and which they do not always overtake. Charlie's despatch, which I have left open for your amusement, will, I think, rather entertain you. His

16 *

consternation on seeing the advertisement of the rival work on Dogs, was most comic. I am thankful to say that he looks better, and can now take exercise again without ' *sick knees.* ' "

" I really know nothing that so tempts one into idleness as a beach like this, with all its gay pictures. I am sure you will rejoice that I am able to derive so much pleasure from it, and to be out a good deal in the open air, after the long weary confinement of the winter. I shall quite regret leaving Seacombe; the *broad river* between me and Liverpool, gives me so comfortable a feeling of security in the morning; and in the evening, those whom I really like to see think nothing of crossing it to visit me.

" I meet with so many offers of service, that the boys sometimes laugh and say, ' Mamma, you are like the young lady who could not dance with the King of Prussia, because she was engaged to the Emperor of Russia.'[1] Yesterday I had an American gentleman here, introduced by Mr. Norton, a clergyman of Boston, very mild and pleasing, with a highly intellectual countenance. Do you know he had never seen a primrose, and upon my desiring Charles to bring me some from the hedges, as we were walking down to the beach, he asked if that was the flower so often celebrated by English poets.

" Mr. Blackwood has just sent me a delightful book by one of his contributors, Miss Bowles; it is

---

[1] This actually happened to the burgomaster's daughter at Berlin, on the occasion of a ball given by the municipal authorities of that city, to the Emperor Alexander.

published without her name, and only called *Chapters on Churchyards*. Pray read the work: I know you will enjoy its depth of feeling and playfulness of wit. . . . . . I *must* return home next Monday, having now been here a month. I certainly have derived benefit from the change, and Charlie, about whom I was getting very anxious, is wonderfully improved; able to be out almost all day, and coming in with a bright, clear, brown complexion, instead of the sickly transparency it had begun to assume."

———

The following extracts, from letters written in a far different and deeper tone, will need no comment, excepting the explanation that they were severally addressed to the two friends to whom she was most wont to lay open her heart, in all its strength and weakness : —

"You speak 'high words' to me, dear friend! I gratefully feel them, and own their power. They remind me of Wordsworth's beautiful expression—

> 'To teach us how divine a thing
> A woman may be made.'

And I, too, have high views, doubt it not. My very suffering proves it—for how much of this is occasioned by quenchless aspirations after intellectual and moral beauty, never to be found on earth! they seem to sever me from others, and make my lot more lonely than life has made it. Can you think that any fervent and aspiring mind ever passed through this world without suffering from that void which has been the complaint of all? 'Les âmes dont l'imagination tient

à la puissance d'aimer et de souffrir, ne sont-ils pas
les bannis d'une autre region ?'   I know that it must
be so; that nothing earthly can fill it, and that it cannot be filled with the infinite, until infinity shall have
opened upon it:—for these intense affections are
human : they were given us to meet and answer
human love; and though they may be 'raised and
solemnized' even here, yet I do believe that it is only
in the 'Better Land' they ever did, or will approxi-
mate to what is divine.   Fear not any danger for me
in the adulation which surrounds me.   A moment's
transient entertainment—scarcely even that at times,
is the utmost effect of things that 'come like shadows,
so depart.'   Of all things, never may I become that
despicable thing, a woman living upon admiration!
The village matron, *tidying up* for her husband and
children at evening, is far, far more enviable and
respectable."

———————

" Why should you try to wean yourself from me,
my dear friend, because our paths are divided, and
because the burthen of fragile health and over-occu-
pation laid upon me, prevents my giving more time in
return for all your affectionate anxiety.   Be assured
that, in the midst of constant excitement, homage,
ideal wanderings, and real cares, which so strangely
'weave the warp and weave the woof' of my 'mystic
thread of life,' my heart is ever true to the past—a
heart of home, though no home be for it here; and
never to forget all your love and care for me and mine.
So think of me still, and often as ever, and in some
points (strangely as I am placed, and surrounded with

things that might, I frankly confess, a little turn my
head, but for the deep remembrances of my heart)
think of me with less anxiety; for I do feel, notwithstanding all this, my mind in a more healthful state,
and more open to happy influences than it has been—
the fever of the mental nerves is subsiding."

"'Safe in the grave,'—what deep meaning there is
in those words, and how often does the feeling they
convey come over me amidst the varied excitements
of my strange, unconnected life! How I look back
upon the comparative peace and repose of Bronwylfa
and Rhyllon—a walk in the hay-field—the children
playing round me—my dear mother coming to call
me in from the dew—and you, perhaps, making your
appearance just in the ' gloaming,' with a great bunch
of flowers in your kind hand! How have these things
passed away from me, and how much more was I
formed for their quiet happiness, than for the weary
part of *femme célèbre*, which I am now enacting! But
my heart is with those home enjoyments, and there,
however tried, excited, and wrung, it will ever
remain."

In the month of July, 1829, Mrs. Hemans was prevailed upon to make the very unwonted exertion of
undertaking a journey, or rather a voyage, to Scotland. To this she had a thousand inducements, in the
attractive invitations continually pressed upon her by
her friends and admirers in that hospitable country,
where her name had long enjoyed an extraordinary
degree of popularity, mingled with strong and affec-

tionate personal interest. She had, for some time, numbered amongst her most valued correspondents, Mr. Hamilton, the accomplished author of *Cyril Thornton,* then residing with his lady at Chiefswood, near Abbotsford; and the visit they had for many months been kindly urging her to make them, with the peculiar allurements it held out, was the primary object of what, to a person of her usually quiescent habits, was somewhat of an adventurous enterprise.

"Now, I am going to excite a sensation," wrote she, in announcing this wonderful project to her friend at St. Asaph—"I am actually about to visit Scotland —going to Mr. Hamilton's at Chiefswood. Charles has been longing to communicate the important intelligence, as he and Henry are to accompany me; but I could not possibly afford the pleasure of the surprise to any one but myself. And you *are* about as much surprised at this moment, I am sure, as if I had written you word I was going to the North Pole. The cause of this marvellous exertion on my part, is, that Mr. and Mrs. Hamilton are going to Italy in the autumn, and are very anxious that I should visit Scotland before they set out. Altogether, I thought the occasion quite worthy of rousing my energies."

In her first letter from Chiefswood, Mrs. Hemans speaks of having had a good deal of illness on the road, visiting her chiefly in-the form of faintness and violent beating of the heart; "but I do not feel," she continues, "as if my general health would be at all the worse for the journey, as I have had very refreshing sleep since I reached this still and lovely place."

The next affords a proof of that rapid accession of

vigour and energy, which, under happy and kindly
influences, was yet a characteristic of her buoyant
temperament.

"You will be pleased to think of me, as I now am,
in constant, almost daily, intercourse with Sir Walter
Scott, who has greeted me to this mountain land in
the kindest manner, and with whom I talk freely and
happily, as to an old familiar friend. I have taken
several long walks with him over moor and *brae,* and
it is indeed delightful to see him thus, and to hear him
pour forth, from the fulness of his rich mind and peopled memory, song, and legend, and tale of old, until
I could almost fancy I heard the gathering-cry of
some chieftain of the hills, so completely does his spirit
carry me back to the days of the slogan and the fire-
cross. The other day, he most kindly made a party
to take me to the banks of Yarrow, about ten miles
from hence. I went with him in an open carriage.
We forded Ettrick river, passed Carterhaugh (the
scene of the wild fairy legend of ' Tam o' Linn'), and
many a cairn and field of old combat, the heroes of
which seemed to start up before me, in answer to the
' mighty master's' voice, which related their deeds as
we went by. And he is, indeed, a fitting narrator:
his whole countenance—the predominant expression
of which is generally a sort of arch benevolence—
changes at the slightest allusion to any ' bold emprize.'
It is

'As the stream late conceal'd
  By the fringe of its willows,
When it flashes, reveal'd
  In the light of its billows;'

or like the war-horse at the sound of the trumpet.

Sometimes, in reciting a verse of old martial song, he will suddenly spring up, and one feels ready to exclaim—

'Charge, Chester, charge!—on, Stanley, on!'

so completely is the electric chain struck by his own high emotion. But Yarrow! beautiful Yarrow! we wound along its banks, through some stately ground belonging to the Duke of Buccleuch; and was it not like a dream to be walking there with Sir Walter Scott by my side, reciting, every now and then, some verse of the fine old ballad? We visited Newark Tower, and returned to Abbotsford through the Tweed. The rest of the day was passed at that glorious place, the hall of which, in particular, is a scene to dream of, with the rich, purple light streaming in through its coloured windows, and mantling its stately suits of armour and heraldic blazonries. We had a great deal of music in the evening—Sir Walter is particularly fond of national airs — and I played many of my waltzes, and mazurkas, and Spanish melodies, for which I wish you could have heard how kindly and gracefully he thanked me.[1] I am fortunate in seeing him, as I do, surrounded only by his children and grandchildren, wandering through his own woods, taking the fresh delight of an unquenchably youthful spirit in the creations of his own hands. It is all so healthful to see and feel! The boys, too, are quite at home with him, and he sometimes sings to Charlie—

---

[1] His words, treasured up by her boys, were,—"I should say you had *too many* gifts, Mrs. Hemans, were they not all made to give pleasure to those around you."

‘Charlie is my darling, my darling, my darling,.
Charlie is my darling, the young Chevalier.’[1]

"We are going to Abbotsford on Saturday, to pass some days, and then I return to Edinburgh.

*   *   *   *   *   *   *

"I have said nothing of the Dominie—even the original Dominie Sampson, with whom I have lately become acquainted—nor of my American friends, the Wares, who dined at Chiefswood the other day (I having been introduced to Mrs. Ware on the very pinnacle of Melrose Abbey, by moonlight) — nor of Mr. Hamilton himself, whose mind developes so delightfully —but all these will be amongst the bright recollections I shall bring away with me."

A few days later Mrs. Hemans wrote:—"I have now had the gratification of seeing Sir Walter in

---

[1] One day, when he had taken them both out to walk with him, they were so emboldened by his condescending good-nature, that one of them, thinking it an excellent opportunity to settle a question which he had often heard speculated upon at home, daringly inquired—"Sir Walter, what *did* you mean by those two lines in *The Lady of the Lake* —

‘Fox-glove and nightshade, side by side,
Emblems of punishment and pride?’

Mamma has always been dying to know, and aunt Harriet has been puzzling about it all her life."

"Why, my dear little fellow," answered the benignant bard, "I can only hope when *you* write poetry, that you will make much better sense of it; for those emblems, in fact, are very bad ones. I merely chose the fox-glove to exemplify pride, from its being so tall and stately; and nightshade, you know, is poisonous, and so might be made the means of punishment; but I believe *hemlock* would have been more to the purpose."

Vol. I.——17

every point of view I could desire : we had one of the
French princes here yesterday, with his suite—the
Duc de Chartres, son of the Duc d'Orleans, and there
was naturally some little excitement diffused through
the household by the arrival of a royal guest. Sir
Walter was, however, exactly the same, in his own
manly simplicity—kind, courteous, unaffected—' *his
foot upon his native heath ;*' and his attention even
to Henry and Charles, and their little indulgencies,
considerate and watchful as ever. I must say a few
words of the duke, who is a very elegant young man,
possessing a finished and really noble grace of manner, which conveys at once the idea of Sir Philip Sidney's high thoughts, seated ' in a heart of courtesy,'
and which one likes to consider as an *appanage* of
royal blood. I was a little nervous when Sir Walter
handed me to the piano, on which I was the sole per-
former, for the delectation of the courtly party."

One of the things which particularly struck her
imagination, amongst the thousand relics at Abbotsford, was the "sad, *fearful* picture of Queen Mary
in the dining-room."[1] And " Oh! the bright swords !"
—she breaks forth in one of her letters—" I must not
forget to tell you how I sat, like Minna in *The Pirate*
(though *she* stood or moved, I believe), the very ' queen
of swords.' I have the strongest love for the flash of
glittering steel—and Sir Walter brought out I know
not how many gallant blades to show me ; one which

---

[1] Fearful, indeed—representing her head in a charger, like
John the Baptist's ; and painted the day after her execution at
Fotheringay, by Amias Canrood.

had fought at Killiecrankie, and one which had belonged to the young Prince Henry, James the First's son, and one which looked of as noble race and temper as that with which Cœur de Lion severed the block of steel in Saladin's tent."

This visit to Abbotsford was a bright passage in her life, never referred to without a rekindling of chivalrous and affectionate enthusiasm. She had contemplated recording her recollections of it in the little volume of prose sketches already alluded to, as one of the many projects she was not permitted to accomplish. With this view, she wrote down the slight notes which follow (and which have never been hitherto in any way made use of), intending to amplify them at some future opportunity.

"July, 1829. — I walked with Sir Walter Scott through the Rhymour's Glen. He showed me the site of a little hamlet, which had been deserted on account of the supposed visits of a spirit. He described to me some extraordinary cavern scenes he had explored in his voyage round the northern coasts and isles of Scotland; mentioned his having sometimes heard the low, rolling murmur of storms in the air along those dreary coasts, for hours before the bursting of the tempest; told me of a friend of his, a man of by no means an imaginative mind, who had heard the Wild Huntsman in the air at night, at Valenciennes. So persuaded was this gentleman that a real chase was sweeping past him through the streets, that he turned aside into the porch of a church in order to make way for it. Nothing, however, was visible; and he at last became affected with feelings

of supernatural fear. On mentioning the circumstance to the people with whom he lodged, they were
much awe-struck, and told him it was fortunate that,
heretic as he was, he had sheltered within the shadow
of a Catholic church. Sir Walter repeated, with
much animation, part of the Spanish ballad of ' Dra-
gut'—(see Lockhart's Collection)—

> Row, row, my slaves, quoth Dragut,' &c.

" He gave me a thrilling description of a scene
which had been witnessed by a friend of his at
Ehrenbreitstein — the German army of liberators
crossing the Rhine after their victories. Upon the
first gleam of the noble river, they burst forth into
the song of ' Am Rhein, am Rhein !' They were two
days crossing, during which the rock and the castle
rang out to the peal of this gallant strain ; and even
the Cossacks, as they passed over, caught the national
enthusiasm, and, with the clash, and clang, and the
roar of their stormy war-music, swelled out the
chorus of ' Am Rhein, am Rhein !'[1]

---

[1] This anecdote (on which was founded her own " Rhine
Song"), and the look and tone with which it was related, made
an impression on her memory which nothing could efface. The
very name of the " Father Rhine," the " exulting and abounding
river" (how often would she quote that magnificent line of Lord
Byron's !) had always worked upon her like a spell, conjuring up
a thousand visions of romance and beauty; and Haydn's inspiring *Rheinweinlied*, with its fine, rich tide of flowing harmony,
was one of the airs she most delighted in. " You are quite
right," she wrote to a friend who had echoed her enthusiasm,
" it *was* the description of that noble Rhine scene which interested me more than any part of Sir Walter's conversation ; and

"I was much struck with a spot, where we paused a few moments, and where Huntley burn — the little stream running through the Rhymour's Glen — falls down a steep bank into a sort of natural basin, over-hung with mountain ash. Sir Walter said he liked to associate the names of his friends with objects of interest in natural scenery, and, turning to an old countryman who walked with us, desired him to make a seat there, and to call it by my name. I repeated to him the image employed by a Welsh poet (Aneurin) to describe the advance of an army — ' the sound of their march was like the *surly laughter* of ocean before a storm.' He seemed much impressed by it. He told me that Cattraeth's Vale, the scene of Aneu-rin's poem, was supposed to be in the Ettrick country.

"A few days afterwards, I walked with him through the *Hexel's Cleugh ;* a name which he derives from the German *Hexe,* a witch. He repeated some curi-ous anecdotes of animals, of the habits of which he is very observant. He mentioned that sheep always choose for their sleeping-place in the pasture, a quar-ter analogous to the one whence they came; for instance, that sheep from a western country will always sleep towards the west, and so on. He spoke of dogs, and of the poor Indian, who thinks —

> ' Admitted to that equal sky,
> His faithful dog shall bear him company !'

He laughed, and said, ' What a train I should have in the other world ! there would be Maida and Nim-

---

I wished more that you could have heard it than all the high legends and solemn scenes of which we spoke that day."

17 *

rod, and Spicy and Ginger; 'black spirits and white, blue spirits and grey.' He told me that so completely did his occasional songs and pieces of poetry pass from his mind, that one day, hearing a lady sing, 'Farewell, farewell, the voice you hear' (from *The Pirate*), he admired the music exceedingly, and, after bestowing due praise upon it, bethought himself, to the great amusement of the company, of also highly complimenting the words. His love of music appears to me entirely the result of association; he is much interested in any air which possesses a national character, or has a story, or strong feeling connected with it. I played for him 'O Richard, O mon Roi!' — the 'Rhine Song' — the 'Tragala Perro' of the Spanish Liberals — a Swiss Ranz des Vaches — and other music of similar character, to which he listened with earnest attention; but I should not say he had naturally any strong feeling of music, merely *as* such, though he describes, with thrilling power, its effects in peculiar scenes and hours of public excitement.[1] He took me to see the Yarrow. On our way, he spoke with much interest and respect of the high and proud feeling of ancestry sometimes manifested by peasant men; and told an affecting story of two brothers, descended from some noble family, but so reduced in circumstances as to be labouring for daily bread. One of these brothers died, and a gentleman,

---

[1] Sir Walter's own admissions on this head went still further; for, in a letter written in 1828, to Mrs. Hemans's sister, he compared himself to Jeremy in *Love for Love* — "having a reasonable good ear for a jig, though solos and sonatas give me the spleen."

much interested in them, said to the survivor — ' You are, I know, obliged to struggle for your maintenance; leave the care of your brother's funeral to me.'—' No, sir,' was the answer; ' I feel your kindness gratefully; but we are of the house of ——, and, though poor and forlorn, my brother must sleep amongst his kindred, and it must be at the charge of their last descendant that he is conveyed there.' Sir Walter described an amusing rencontre between himself and Platoff. They met on the Boulevards at Paris; Platoff was riding, attended by several Cossacks; he immediately dismounted, ran up to Sir Walter, threw his arms round his neck, and kissed him.

"On the banks of Yarrow, I was shown the house where Mungo Park was born. Sir Walter, in walking along the stream, one day came suddenly upon Park, who was employed, and apparently absorbed, in throwing stones into the water, and watching the bubbles that followed their descent. ' Park, what is it that thus engages your attention ?' asked Sir Walter. —' I was thinking,' was the reply, ' how often I had thus tried to sound the rivers in Africa, by calculating how long a time had elapsed before the bubbles rose to the surface.'—' Then,' said Scott, ' I know you think of returning to Africa.'—' I do, indeed,' was the answer; ' but it is yet a secret.' We saw Park's name, inscribed by himself, in Newark tower, to which we ascended, after winding along the Yarrow through the beautiful grounds of the Duke of Buccleuch.[1]

---

[1] Here, as "little Charlie" recollects, on seeing two tourists make a precipitate retreat when the Abbotsford party approached

"On the way back, we talked a good deal of trees. I asked Sir Walter if he had not observed that every tree gives out its own peculiar sound to the wind. He said he had, and suggested to me that something might be done by the union of music and poetry, to imitate those voices of trees, giving a different measure and style to the oak, the pine, the willow, &c. He mentioned a Highland air of somewhat similar character, called ' The Notes of the Sea-birds.'

"Lord Napier, at dinner, made some observations upon a recent history of the Peninsular War, in which the defence of Saragossa had been spoken of as a vain and lavish waste of life. I was delighted with the kindling animation of Sir Walter's look and tone, as he replied—" Never let me hear that brave blood has been shed in vain! It sends a roaring voice down through all time!" In the evening we had music. Not being able to sing, I read to him the words of a Béarnaise song, on the captivity of Louis XVI. and Marie Antoinette in the Temple; though simple even to homeliness, they affected him to tears, and he begged me not to finish them.[1] I think the feeling of loy-

the tower, Sir Walter said, smiling—" Ah! Mrs. Hemans, they little know what two Lions they are running away from!"

[1] This song will now, perhaps, be read with interest. It is called " La Complainte Béarnaise."

1.

"Un Troubadour Béarnais,
  Les yeux inondés de larmes,
  A ses montagnards chantait
  Ce refrain, source d'alarmes,—
  Louis, le fils d'Henri,
  Est prisonnier dans Paris.

alty—chivalrous loyalty—such as must have existed
amongst the Paladins and *preux chevaliers* of old—
seems the truest and deepest in his character; he

2.

"Il a vu couler le sang
De cette garde fidèle
Qui vient donner en mourant
Aux Français un beau modèle—
Mais Louis, le fils d'Henri,
Est prisonnier dans Paris.

3.

"Il a tremblé pour les jours
De sa compagne chérie,
Qui n'a trouvée de resource
Que dans sa propre energie;
Elle sait Louis, fils d'Henri,
Dans les prisons de Paris.

4.

"Quel crime donc ont-ils commis,
Pour être enchaînés de même?
Du peuple ils sont amis;
Le peuple veut-il qu'on l'aime,
Quand il met le fils d'Henri,
Dans les prisons de Paris?

5.

"Le Dauphin, ce fils chéri,
Qui fait seul notre espérance,
De pleurs sera donc nourri!
Le berceau qu'on donne en France,
Aux fils de notre Henri,
Est la prison de Paris.

6.

"Français, trop ingrats Français!
Rendez au Roi sa compagne!
C'est l'amour des Béarnais,
C'est l'enfant de la montagne—

gives me the idea of being born an age too late for its free scope. This day has been—I was going to say, one of the happiest, but I am too isolated a being to use that word—at least, one of the pleasantest and most cheerfully exciting of my life. I shall think again and again of that walk under the old solemn trees that hang over the mountain-stream of Yarrow, with Sir Walter Scott beside me; his voice frequently breaking out, as if half unconsciously, into some verse of the antique ballads, which he repeats with a deep and homely pathos. One stanza, in particular, will linger in my memory like music.

'His mother through the window look'd,
With all the longing of a mother,
His little sister, weeping, walk'd
The greenwood path to find her brother.

Le bonheur qu' avait Henri
Nous l'assurons à Louis.

7.

"Au pied de ce monument,
Où le bon Henri respire,
Pourquoi l'airain foudroyant?[1]
On veut que Henri conspire
Lui-même contre ses fils,
Dans les prisons de Paris.

8.

"Sèches tes pleurs, O Troubadour!—
Béarnais, séchez vos larmes—
Entrainés par leur amour,
Tous les Français courent aux armes,
Pour tirer le fils d'Henri
De sa prison à Paris."

[1]Canon placé au pied du monument d'Henri Quatre à Paris.

They sought him east, they sought him west,
They sought him far with moan and sorrow —
They only saw the cloud of night,
They only heard the roar of Yarrow !'

" Before we retired for the night, he took me into
the hall, and showed me the spot where the imagined
form of Byron had stood before him. This hall, with
the rich gloom shed by its deeply-coloured windows,
and with its antique suits of armour, and inscriptions,
all breathing of 'the olden time,' is truly a fitting scene
for the appearance of so stately a shadow.

" The next morning I left Abbotsford; and who can
leave. a spot so brightened and animated by the life,
the *happy* life of genius, without regret? I shall not
forget the kindness of Sir Walter's farewell—so frank,
and simple, and heartfelt, as he said to me—'There
are some whom we meet, and should like ever after
to claim as kith and kin; and *you* are one of those.'
It is delightful to take away with me so unmingled an
impression of what I may now call almost affectionate
admiration."

Amongst the numerous friends Mrs. Hemans was
fortunate enough to possess in Scotland, there was
one to whom she was linked by so peculiar a bond
of union, and whose unwearied kindness is so precious
an inheritance to her children, that it is hoped the
owner of a name so dear to them (though it be a part
of her nature to shrink from publicity), will forgive its
being introduced into these pages.

This invaluable friend was Lady Wedderburn,[1] the

---

[1] The Lady of Sir David Wedderburn, Bart , and sister of the
late Viscountess Hampden. The monument on which the lines
are inscribed, is at Glynde, in Sussex, near Lord Hampden's seat.

mother of those "two brothers, a child and a youth," for whose monument Mrs. Hemans had written an inscription, which, with its simple pathos, has doubtless sunk deep into the heart of many a mourner, as well as of many a yet rejoicing parent, there called upon to remember that for them, too,

―― "Speaks the grave,
Where God hath sealed the fount of hope He gave."

Into the gentle heart, which has found relief for its own sorrows in soothing the griefs and promoting the enjoyments of others, the author of this sacred tribute was taken with a warmth and loving-kindness which extended its genial influence to all belonging to her; and during their stay in Edinburgh, whither they proceeded from Abbotsford, Mrs. Hemans and her children were cherished with a true home welcome at the house of Sir David Wedderburn. Her impressions of that queen-like city, and the generous cordiality of her reception amongst some of the most distinguished of its inhabitants, will best appear in her own words.

"I am quite delighted with Edinburgh — it is a gallant city to behold, full of picture at every turn of the streets; and I have been greeted with such attention here, that truly I might begin to fancy myself a queen in good earnest, if I remained much longer. I never can forget the cordial kindness I have received, and all the impressions I shall carry hence will be bright and pleasant. I am very glad to have seen it at this time of the year, when it was represented to me as a perfect desert. A person must be of most gregarious habits indeed, who cannot find more than enough of society even in these desolate months. I have made some very interesting acquaintance—Mrs. Grant of Laggan, Captain Basil Hall, and, above all, Mr. Jeffrey, at whose house in the country I dined yesterday. His conversation is such *mental champagne* as I never tasted before—rich, full of imagery, playful, energetic; certainly one of the most delightful days I have passed in Scotland, has been the one at Craig Crook, as his seat is called. To-day we are going to dine with Mrs. Grant. The boys are well, and are delighted to see their *heroine* 'mamma' so kindly welcomed by every one."

The next extract is from a letter to her son Claude, who was staying, during her absence, at Wavertree Lodge. " I have just returned from visiting Edinburgh Castle (the citadel, you know, of this noble town), and looking at the Scottish regalia, which are kept in one of the rooms. There is something impressive in the sight of a crown, sword, and sceptre, which have been the object of so many gallant struggles; and I could have looked at them long with increasing interest. They are shown by the light of lamps, though at noonday, in a small room, hung with dark crimson. Last Sunday I attended the preaching of Mr. Alison: he has a countenance of most venerable beauty, a deep mellow voice, and an earnest gentleness of manner, which goes at once to the heart, and wins a feeling of almost filial affection. After the service was ended, he came forward very kindly to be introduced to me, and took me, with Charles and Henry, into the vestry-room, where I had a good deal of conversation with

him.   He gave me an account of his having seen the
body of James V. (father to Mary Queen of Scots),
several years ago, in such perfect preservation, that
the resemblance of the features to the portraits of that
king, was quite distinct.

"Nothing in Edinburgh delights me so much as
the Calton Hill, which I visit whenever I have an
opportunity, and on which stands the unfinished Par-
thenon, with its graceful pillars. The view from the
summit, of the strange gloomy Old Town, 'piled deep
and massy, close and high,' and all the classic buildings and columns of the New, is quite unparalleled.
All this, too, lies set in a frame of hills of the boldest
outline.   I have not yet felt strong enough to ascend
Arthur's Seat, and almost fear that I must not think
of it, as I have violent palpitations of the heart when
over fatigued.   Charlie goes out every morning, to
draw *from nature,* as he calls it, some of the fine public buildings of Edinburgh, and has now quite a series
of these sketches, which I am sure you will like to see."

"I have just returned from paying the visit I mentioned to Mr. Mackenzie, the 'Man of Feeling,' and
have been exceedingly interested.   He is now very
infirm, and his powers of mind are often much affected
by the fitfulness of nervous indisposition, so that his
daughter, who introduced me to his sitting-room, said
very mournfully as we entered, 'You will see but the
wreck of my father.'   However, on my making some
allusion, after his first kind and gentle reception of me,
to the 'men of other times,' with whom he had lived
in such brilliant association, it was really like the
effect produced on the 'Last Minstrel'—

——'when he caught the measure wild ;
The old man raised his face, and smiled,
And lighted up his faded eye ;'

for he became immediately excited, and all his furrowed countenance seemed kindling with recollections of a race gone by. It was singular to hear anecdotes of Hume, and Robertson, and Gibbon, and the other intellectual 'giants of old,' from one who had mingled with their minds in familiar converse. I felt as if carried back at least a century.

" 'Ah!' said he, half playfully, half sadly, ' there were men in Scotland then!' I could not help thinking of the story of ' Ogier the Dane'—do you recollect his grasping the iron crow of the peasant who broke into his sepulchre, and exclaiming, ' It is well, there are *men* in Denmark still?' Poor Miss Mackenzie was so much affected by the sudden and almost unexpected awakening of her father's mind, that, on leaving the room with me, she burst into tears, and was some time before she could conquer her strong emotion. I hope to have another interview with this delightful old man before I leave Edinburgh.

" Yesterday I went to visit a fine colossal group of sculpture, Ajax bearing away the body of Patroclus, which has just been completed by an Edinburgh artist, and is exciting much interest here. Its effect, standing as it does, quite alone, in the midst of a large hall hung with dark crimson, is exceedingly imposing ; and the contrast of life and death in the forms of the combating and the departed warrior, struck me as full of power and thought.

" A few nights ago, I made a party to walk through
some of the most beautiful streets by moonlight. We
went along Prince's Street, to the foot of the Calton
Hill, and gazed down upon Holyrood, lying so dark
and still in its desolateness, and forming so strong a
contrast to the fair pillars of the Hill, which looked
more pure and aerial than ever, as they rose against
the moonlight sky. ' *Mais qu'ils se passent des orages
au fond du cœur !*' and how little can those around
one form an idea, from outward signs, of what may
be overshadowing the inner world of the heart. Such
a sense of strangeness and loneliness came suddenly
over me, surrounded as I was, amidst all this dusky
magnificence, by acquaintance of yesterday. I felt as
if all I loved were so far, far removed from me, that
I could have burst into tears from the rush of this
unaccountable emotion."

The adulation and excitement with which she was
surrounded, however animating and amusing at the
moment, could not but be followed, to a heart and
frame constituted like hers, by a reaction of inward
depression and physical languor. Amidst all her lively
details, there are continual allusions to " the pure and
home-feeling—the cup of water—to which I turn from
all else that is offered me, as I would to a place of
shelter from the noon-day ;" and she gratefully wrote
of finding Lady Wedderburn's " *maternal* kindness, as
a ' soft green to the soul' amidst all this excitement."
She was singularly impressed by the picture at Holyrood House, shown as that of Rizzio. The authenti-
city of this designation is said to be more than doubt-

ful; but hers was not a mind for question or cavil on points of this nature. The "local habitation and the name" were in themselves sufficient to awaken her fancy and to satisfy her faith. As Rizzio's portrait, it took its place in her imagination; and the train of deep and mournful thoughts it suggested, imbued, as was her wont, with the colouring of her own individual feelings, was embodied in the lines " To a remembered Picture :"—

"They haunt me still—those calm, pure, holy eyes!
Their piercing sweetness wanders through my dreams;
The soul of music that within them lies,
Comes o'er my soul in soft and sudden gleams:
Life—spirit—life immortal and divine
Is there—and yet how dark a death was thine!"

In a very different strain was a *jeu d'esprit* produced at this time, which owed its origin to a simple remark on the unseasonableness of the weather; made by Mrs. Hemans to Mr. Charles Kirkpatrick Sharpe, whom she was in the habit of seeing at Sir David Wedderburn's. " It is so little like summer," she said, "that I have not even seen a butterfly." "A butterfly!" retorted Mr. Sharpe—"I have not even seen a wasp!" The next morning, as if in confutation of this calumny, a wasp made its appearance at Lady Wedderburn's breakfast table. Mrs. Hemans immediately proposed that it should be made a prisoner, inclosed in a bottle, and sent to Mr. Sharpe: this was accordingly done, and the piquant missive was acknowledged by him as follows:—

18 *

"SONNET TO A WASP, IN THE MANNER OF MILTON, &c., BUT
MUCH SUPERIOR.

Poor insect! rash as rare!—Thy sovereign,[1] sure,
Hath driven thee to Siberia in disgrace—
Else what delusion could thy sense allure,
To buzz and sting in this unwholesome place,
Where e'en the hornet's hoarser, and the race
Of filmy wing are feeble [1]—Honey here
(Scarce as its rhyme) thou findest not.—Ah! beware
Thy golden mail, to starved Arachne dear;[2]
Though fingers famed, that thrill th' immortal lyre,
Have pent thee up, a second Asmodeus,
I wail thy doom—I warm thee by the fire,
And blab our secrets—do not thou betray us!
I give thee liberty, I give thee breath,
To fly from Athens, Eurus, Doctors, Death!!"

To this Mrs. Hemans returned the following re-
joinder:—

"THE LAST WORDS OF THE LAST WASP OF SCOTLAND.

Sooth'd by the strain, the Wasp thus made reply—
(The first, last time he spoke not waspishly)—
"Too late, kind Poet! comes thine aid, thy song,
To aught first starved, then bottled up so long.
Yet, for the warmth of this thy genial fire,
Take a Wasp's blessing ere his race expire.
Never may provost's foot find entrance here!   •
Never may bailie's voice invade thine ear!
Never may housemaid wipe the verd antique
From coin of thine—Assyrian, Celt, or Greek!
Never may Eurus cross thy path!—to thee
May winds and wynds[3] alike propitious be!

---

[1] Beelzebub is the king of flies.
[2] A beautiful allusion to our starving weavers.
[3] Alluding to antiquarian visits to these renowned closes.

And when thou diest—(live a thousand years!)—
May friends fill classic bottles¹ with their tears!
I can no more—receive my parting gasp!—
Bid Scotland mourn the last, last lingering Wasp!"

In the families of the late revered Baron Hume
and Mr. Alison, Mrs. Hemans formed friendships which
were most affectionately maintained throughout her
life, and of which a grateful remembrance was be-
queathed to her children. Another name, associated
with a thousand pleasant recollections of courteous
services to herself, and indefatigable good-nature to
her boys, was that of the late Dr. James Gregory,
that "bright-minded and most amiable being" (to use
her own words), whose early death, which, only three
years afterwards, removed him from a circle of which
he was the delight and ornament, filled her with sorrow and sympathy.

She would often playfully boast of the great favour
she had all her life enjoyed with "very old gentle-
men," to whom, indeed, her winning and filial manner
was always peculiarly endearing. This was especially
instanced in the case of the venerable Sir Robert
Liston, who, at that time, though already an octo-
genarian, was yet in the fullest exercise of all his
refined tastes and courtly hospitalities. Nothing could
exceed the enthusiasm of his admiration for Mrs.
Hemans, nor the kindliness of his interest in her children. It was at the earnest request of her chivalrous old friend, that, when on the point of returning

---

¹ Referring to certain precious lachrymatories in the possession of Mr. Sharpe.

to Wavertree, she was persuaded to adjourn for a short time to Milburn Tower, his beautiful retreat near Edinburgh, for the purpose of sitting for her bust to Mr. Angus Fletcher. " How happy I shall be," she wrote, " to breathe in the green shades of Milburn! It is a lovely place, and I delight in the thoughts of its comparative repose, for I cannot tell you how I am yearning for quiet."

" Sitting for a bust," she wrote in a subsequent letter, " awful as it may sound, is by no means an infliction so terrible as sitting for a picture: the sculptor allows much greater liberty of action, as every part of the head and form is necessary to his work. My effigy is now nearly completed, and is thought to be a performance of much talent."

It is indeed very graceful as a work of art, and though the likeness is not satisfying *at first* to homely and household eyes, it wins its way by degrees into the heart, and from certain accidents of light or position, a resemblance may sometimes unexpectedly be caught, which is almost startling.

After her visit to Milburn Tower, Mrs. Hemans returned to her own little dwelling, rich in recollections, and eager, as usual, to share them with her friends. She had, soon afterwards, a cheerful visit from Miss Jewsbury, who was struck with her improved spirits, and liked her house, and gave a pleasant sketch of the evening group. — " When night comes," she wrote, " and the darling boys are arrived from school, and candles are lighted, and the doors shut, our cabinet room would make a charming cabinet picture."

In the *Edinburgh Review*, for October, 1829,[1] was an article on the poetry of Mrs. Hemans, from the master-hand of Mr. Jeffrey. The peculiar characteristics of her style are there touched upon with a delicacy and discrimination worthy of the mighty critic, who had in this instance laid aside his terrors, and may well be said to have "done his spiriting gently." Her writings are treated throughout as a fine exemplification of "female poetry;" and he brings into beautiful relief "that fine accord she has established between the world of sense and of soul — that delicate blending of our deep inward emotions with their splendid symbols and emblems without."

"Almost all her poems," writes this high authority, "are rich with fine descriptions, and studded over with images of visible beauty. But these are never idle ornaments: all her pomps have a meaning; and her flowers and her gems are arranged, as they are said to be among Eastern lovers, so as to speak the language of truth and of passion. This is peculiarly remarkable in some little pieces, which seem at first sight to be purely descriptive — but are soon found to tell upon the heart, with a deep moral and pathetic impression. But it is a truth nearly as conspicuous in the greater part of her productions; where we scarcely meet with any striking sentiment that is not ushered in by some such symphony of external nature,

---

[1] It should have been mentioned in the proper order of date, that a very favourable critique on Mrs. Hemans's earlier poems (including all her publications, from the "Restoration of the Works of Art," to the "Stanzas to the Memory of the late King,") appeared in the *Quarterly Review*, for October, 1820.

and scarcely a lovely picture that does not serve as a foreground to some deep or lofty emotion."

Mrs. Hemans's productions, during this winter, were chiefly lyrics belonging to the series of *Songs of the Affections*, and other short miscellaneous pieces. The principal one of these, " The Spirit's Return," was at that time preferred by herself to any thing else she had written. Still it was far from satisfying her, and she was worn and excited during its composition, by what she was wont to call " that weary striving after ideal beauty which one never can grasp," and yet more by those awful contemplations of the visionary world, on which it led her to dwell with an interest too intense, a curiosity too disquieting.

" Sometimes I think," she wrote of this poem to a friend, " that I have sacrificed too much in the apparition scene, to the idea that sweetness and beauty might be combined with supernatural effect. The character of the Greek sculpture, which has so singular a hold upon my imagination, was much in my thoughts at the time." And, referring to the same piece two years after, she wrote:—" If there be, as my friends say, a greater power in it than I had before evinced, I paid dearly for the discovery, and it almost made me tremble as I sounded ' the deep places of my soul.' "

The following extracts belong to this period :—

" I have found the Spanish ballad on the death of Aliatar, since you were here, and have been surprised, notwithstanding all the proud music of the original language, by the superior beauty of Southey's translation. The *refrain* of

"Tristes marchando,
   Las trompas roncas,"

has certainly a more stately tone of sorrow, than

"Sad and slow,
   Home they go;"

and yet the latter is to me a thousand times more touching. Is it that word home which makes it so, with all that it breathes of tenderness and sadness?"

"On calling up and reconsidering my impressions of Martin's picture,[1] it seems to me that something more of gloomy grandeur might have been thrown about the funeral pyre; that it should have looked more like a thing apart, almost suggesting of itself the idea of an awful sacrifice. Perhaps it was not in the resources of the painter to do all this; but the imagination, *mine* at least, seems to require it."

"Have you read Manzone's noble ode on the death-day of Napoleon,[2] translated by Archdeacon Wrangham? It has just been sent me by Signor Grimaldi, and I know not when I have met with Italian poetry so rich in deep thought and powerful expression."

"I send you part of the conversation which so much delighted me in Tieck's *Phantasien*. I think you will recognise all the high tone of the thoughts, and be pleased with the glimpse — a bright though transient one — of the dreaming-land — that strange

---

[1] The Fall of Nineveh.   [2] The *Cinque Maggio*.

world, which, were I to designate it by my own experience, I should call a wilderness of beauty and of sorrow."

" I believe it is only where the feelings are deeply interested, that the imagination causes such perpetual bitterness of disappointment. Do you remember St. Leon's dissatisfaction at the manner in which his daughters receive the tidings of his death? I begin to think that all imaginative persons are, to a certain degree, St. Leons, and that they expect what human nature is very seldom rich enough to afford."

" I have been reading Godwin's *Cloudesley*. It does not, I think, carry away the imagination with anything like the mighty spirit of his earlier works; but it is beautifully written, with an occasional flow of rich and fervent eloquence, reminding me of the effects he attributes to the conversation of his own old alchemist in St. Leon."

Early in the summer of 1830, Mrs. Hemans published her volume of *Songs of the Affections*, which was dedicated to her revered friend, Sir Robert Liston. In the month of June, of the same year, she accomplished a project which she had long had at heart, of making a visit to the Lakes of Westmoreland. Her tremulous health, which had undergone many vicissitudes during the winter, needed repose and refreshment; her spirit was wearied out with the 'glare and dust of celebrity,' and she longed to 'flee away and be at rest,' for a season amongst the green hills, and beside the still waters. More than all, she

was attracted to that lovely land by the yet stronger
spell exercised over her mind, by the prospect of immediate communion with Mr. Wordsworth, of whom
she was daily becoming a more zealous disciple, and
whose invitations had been kind and reiterated. Her
son Charles wàs her companion on the journey to
Rydal Mount; and the two other boys joined her as
soon as she was established in a temporary abode of
her own.

No words but those of her own letters can do justice to her impressions of society and scenery, which,
by those who have once enjoyed them, can never be
forgotten.

" My nervous fear at the idea of presenting myself
to Mr. Wordsworth, grew upon me so rapidly, that it
was more than seven o'clock before I took courage to
'leave the inn at Ambleside. I had, indeed, little
cause for such trepidation. I was driven to a lovely
cottage-like building, almost hidden by a profusion of
roses and ivy; and a most benignant-looking old man
greeted me in the porch. This was Mr. Wordsworth
himself; and when I tell you that, having rather a
large party of visiters in the house, he led me to a
room apart from them, and brought in his family by
degrees, I am sure that little trait will give you an
idea of considerate kindness which you will both like
and appreciate."

*　　*　　*　　*　　*　　*　　*

" There is an almost patriarchal simplicity about
him—an absence of all pretension. All is free, unstudied —   .

" The river winding at its own sweet will"—

in his manner and conversation. There is more of impulse about them than I had expected; but in other respects I see much that I should have looked for in the poet of meditative life: frequently his head droops, his eyes half close, and he seems buried in quiet depths of thought. I have passed a delightful morning to-day in walking with him about his own richly shaded grounds, and hearing him speak of the old English writers, particularly Spenser, whom he loves, as he himself expresses it, for his " earnestness and devotedness."

* * * * * * *

" I must not forget to tell you that he not only admired our exploit in crossing the Ulverstone Sands, as a deed of " derring do," but as a decided proof of taste: the Lake scenery, he says, is never seen to such advantage as after the passage of what he calls its majestic barrier."

" I have been making you a little drawing of Mr. Wordsworth's house, which, though it has no other merit than that of fidelity, will, I know, find favour in your sight. The steps up the front lead to a little grassy mound, commanding a view always so rich, and sometimes so brightly solemn, that one can well imagine its influence traceable in many of the Poet's writings. On this mount he frequently sits all evening, and sometimes seems borne away in thought."

" I seem to be writing to you almost from the spirit-land; all is here so brightly still, so remote from every-day cares and tumults, that sometimes I can hardly persuade myself I am not dreaming. It scarcely seems to be 'the light of common day' that is clothing the woody mountains before me; there is something almost visionary in its soft gleams and ever-changing shadows. I am charmed with Mr. Wordsworth, whose kindness to me has quite a soothing influence over my spirits. Oh! what relief, what blessing there is in the feeling of admiration, when it can be freely poured forth! 'There is a daily beauty in his life,' which is in such lovely harmony with his poetry, that I am thankful to have witnessed and *felt* it. He gives me a good deal of his society, reads to me, walks with me, leads my pony when I ride; and I begin to talk with him as with a sort of paternal friend. The whole of this morning, he kindly passed in reading to me a great deal from Spenser, and afterwards his own *Laodamia*, my favourite *Tintern Abbey*, and many of his noble sonnets. His reading is very peculiar, but, to my ear, delightful; slow, solemn, earnest in expression more than any I have ever heard: when he reads or recites in the open air, his deep rich tones seem to proceed from a spirit-voice, and belong to the religion of the place; they harmonize so fitly with the thrilling tones of woods and waterfalls. His expressions are often strikingly poetical; such as—' I would not give up the mists that spiritualize our mountains, for all the blue skies of Italy.' Yesterday evening he walked beside me as I rode on a long and lovely mountain-path, high above Grasmere Lake. I was much interested by his showing me, carved deep into the rock, as we passed, the initials of his wife's name, inscribed there many years ago by himself; and the dear old man, like ' Old

Mortality,' renews them from time to time.   I could scarcely help exclaiming ' Esto perpetua !' "

" It is delightful to see a life in such perfect harmony with all that his writings express—

'True to the kindred points of Heaven and home!'

You may remember how much I disliked, and I think you agreed with me in reprobating, that shallow theory of Mr. Moore's with regard to the unfitness of genius for domestic happiness.   I was speaking of it yesterday to Mr. Wordsworth, and was pleased by his remark, ' It is not because they possess genius that they make unhappy homes, but because they do not possess genius enough ; a higher order of mind would enable them to see and feel all the beauty of domestic ties.'   His mind, indeed, may well inhabit an untroubled atmosphere, for, as he himself declares, no wounded affections, no embittered feelings, have ever been his lot ; the current of his domestic life has flowed on, bright, and pure, and unbroken.   Hence, I think, much of the high, sculpture-like repose which invests both his character and writings with so tranquil a dignity."

" Mr. Wordsworth's kindness has inspired me with a feeling of confidence which it is delightful to associate with those of admiration and respect, before excited by his writings ;—and he has treated me with so much consideration, and gentleness, and care !— they have been like balm to my spirit after all the *fades* flatteries with which I am *blasée*.   I wish I had time to tell you of mornings which he has passed in reading to me, and of evenings when he has walked beside me, whilst I rode through the lovely vales of Grasmere and Rydal; and of his beautiful, sometimes half-unconscious recitation, in a voice so deep and solemn, that it has often brought tears into my eyes. One little incident I *must* describe. We had been listening, during one of these evening rides, to various sounds and notes of birds, which broke upon the stillness, and at last I said—'Perhaps there may be a deeper and richer music pervading all Nature, than we are permitted, in this state, to hear.' He answered by reciting those glorious lines of Milton's,

'Millions of spiritual creatures walk the earth,
  Unseen, both when we wake and when we sleep,' &c.

and this in tones that seemed rising from such depths of veneration! I cannot describe the thrill with which I listened; it was like the feeling which Lord Byron has embodied in one of his best and purest moments, when he so beautifully says,—

'And not a breath crept through the rosy air,
  And yet the forest leaves seemed stirred with prayer.'

Mr. Wordsworth's daily life in the bosom of his family, is delightful—so affectionate and confiding. I cannot but mournfully feel, in the midst of their happiness, 'Still, still, I am a stranger here!'—but where am I not a stranger *now?*"

———

" Yesterday I rode round Grasmere and Rydal Lake. It was a glorious evening, and the imaged heaven in the waters more completely filled my mind, even to

19 *

overflowing, than I think any object in nature ever did before. I could have stood in silence before the magnificent vision for an hour, as it flushed and faded, and darkened at last into the deep sky of a summer's night. I thought of the scriptural expression, ' A sea of glass mingled with fire:' no other words are fervid enough to convey the least impression of what lay burning before me."[1]

In the midst of all these enjoyments, a slight acci-dent, or rather an accident *manqué*, a little interfered with the improvement in her health, which had before been so apparent. " I have been very nearly thrown," she wrote, " from a spirited palfrey; and though I flatter myself that Di. Vernon herself could scarcely have displayed more self-possession in the actual mo-ment of danger, still the shock and surprise, which were so great as to deprive me of my voice for several minutes, have brought on severe beating of the heart, and left me as tremulous as an aspen leaf. They

---

[1] This sweet vale of Grasmere, with its secluded beauty, par-taking almost of an air of consecration, was one of the visions she best loved to call up; and her sonnet, " A Remembrance of Grasmere," written four years afterwards, describes the peculiar colouring with which her imagination invested it.

> "O vale and lake, within your mountain urn,
> Smiling so tranquilly, and set so deep!
> Oft doth your dreamy loveliness return,
> Colouring the tender shadows of my sleep
> With light Elysian:—for the hues that steep
> Your shores in melting lustre, seem to float
> On golden clouds from spirit-lands remote —
> Isles of the blest;—and in our memory keep
> Their place with holiest harmonies."——

have not, however, startled my courage from its ' pride
of place,' as I am going to mount the same steed this
evening."

After continuing for more than a fortnight the
inmate of Rydal Mount,[1] Mrs. Hemans took up her

---

[1] The description of this lovely spot, in a little poem called
"The Poet's Home," written by Miss Jewsbury, and published
in the *Literary Magnet* for 1826, is so true and graphic, that it
cannot but add to the interest of these details, and must be
echoed by all who can personally vouch for its fidelity.

> " Low and white, yet scarcely seen
>   Are its walls, for mantling green,
>   Not a window lets in light,
>   But through flowers clustering bright;
>   Not a glance may wander there,
>   But it falls on something fair;
>   Garden choice, and fairy mound,
>   Only that no elves are found;
>   Winding walk, and sheltered nook,
>   For student grave, and graver book:
>   Or a bird-like bower, perchance,
>   ·Fit for maiden and romance.
>   Then, far off, a glorious sheen
>   Of wide and sun-lit waters seen;
>   Hills, that in the distance lie,
>   Blue and yielding as the sky;
>   And nearer, closing round the nest,
>   The home, — of all, the ' living crest,'
>   Other rocks and mountains stand,
>   Rugged, yet a guardian band,
>   Like those that did, in fable old.
>   Elysium from the world infold.
>
>   Poet! though such dower be thine,
>   Deem it not as yet divine;

abode at a sweet little retired cottage called Dove
Nest, which had so taken her fancy when she first

What shall outward sign avail,
 If the answering spirit fail?
What this beauteous dwelling be,
If it hold not *hearts* for thee?
If thou call its charms thine own,
Yet survey those charms alone?
— List again: — companions meet
Thou shalt have in thy retreat.

One, of long tried love and truth,
Thine in age, as thine in youth;
One whose locks of partial grey
Whisper somewhat of decay;
Yet whose bright and beaming eye
Tells of more, that cannot die.
Then a second form beyond,
Thine too, by another bond;
Sportive, tender, graceful, wild,
Scarcely woman, more than child —
One who doth thy heart entwine,
Like the ever clinging vine;
One to whom thou art a stay,
As the oak, that, scarred and grey,
Standeth on, and standeth fast,
Strong and stately to the last.

Poet's lot like this hath been;
Such perchance may I have seen;
Or in fancy's fairy land,
Or in truth, and near at hand:
If in fancy, then, forsooth,
Fancy had the force of truth;
If again a truth it were,
Then was truth as fancy fair;
But whichever it might be,
'T was a paradise to me!"   M. J. J.

saw it from the lake, that it seemed quite a gleam of
good fortune to find that it was to be let, and that she
could engage rooms there for a few weeks' sojourn.
Here she was joined by the rest of her little group,
and it might have been difficult to say which of the
party was most alive to the "sweet influences" around
them. "Henry out with his fishing-rod, and Charles
sketching, and Claude climbing the hill above the
Nest. I cannot follow," she continued, "for I have
not strength yet; but I think in feeling I am more a
child than any of them."

"How shall I tell you," she wrote from this deli-
cious retirement, "of all the loveliness by which I
am surrounded—of all the soothing and holy influence
it seems shedding down into my inmost heart. I have
sometimes feared, within the last two years, that the
effect of suffering and adulation, and feelings too
highly wrought and too severely tried, would have
been to dry up within me the fountains of such pure
and simple enjoyment; but *now* I know that

> ——'Nature never did betray
> The heart that loved her.'

I can think of nothing but what is pure, and true,
and kind; and my eyes are filled with grateful tears
even whilst I am writing to you.

"I must try to describe my little nest, since I cannot 'call spirits from the vasty Lake,' to bring you
hither through the air. The house was originally
meant for a small villa, though it has long passed into
the hands of farmers, and there is in consequence an
air of neglect about the little demesne, which does not

at all approach desolation, and yet gives it something
of touching interest. You see every where traces of
love and care beginning to be effaced—rose trees
spreading into wildness—laurels darkening the windows with too luxuriant branches; and I cannot help
saying to myself, 'Perhaps some heart like my own in
its feelings and sufferings has here sought refuge and
found repose.' The ground is laid out in rather an
antiquated style, which, now that nature is beginning
to reclaim it from art, I do not at all dislike. There
is a little grassy terrace immediately under the window, descending to a small court with a circular grass
plot, on which grows one tall white rose tree. You
cannot imagine how I delight in that fair, solitary,
neglected-looking tree. I am writing to you from an
old-fashioned alcove in the little garden, round which
the sweet briar and moss rose tree have completely
run wild; and I look down from it upon lovely Winandermere, which seems at this moment even like another
sky, so truly is every summer cloud and tint of azure
pictured in its transparent mirror."

"I am so much delighted with the spot, that I
scarcely know how I shall leave it. The situation
is one of the deepest retirement; but the bright lake
before me, with all its fairy barks and sails, glancing
like 'things of life,' over its blue water, prevents the
solitude from being overshadowed by any thing like
sadness."

"I visited Elleray, Professor Wilson's house¹ (though

¹ Now the residence of Thomas Hamilton, Esq.

he is not now at home), a few days since.   The scene, around it is in itself a festival.   I never saw any land-scape bearing so triumphant a character.   The house, which is beautiful, seems built as if to overlook some fairy pageant, something like the Venetian splendour of old, on the glorious lake beneath."

"I should have thanked you sooner for all those spirit-stirring tales from the early annals of England: they will afford me food for thought some future day: but I think my spirit is too much lulled by these sweet scenes, to breathe one song of sword and spear until I have bid Winandermere farewell."

* * * * * * *

"There is balm in the very stillness of the spot I have chosen.[1]   The majestic silence of these lakes, perfectly soundless and waveless as they are, except when troubled by the wind, is to me most impressive. Oh! what a poor thing is society in the presence of skies and waters and everlasting hills!   You may be sure I do not allude to the dear intercourse of friend with friend;—that would be dearer tenfold—more precious, more hallowed in scenes like this."

In dwelling upon these records of pure and health-ful enjoyment, poured forth so freshly and freely from, the ever-gushing fountain of her heart, it is difficult to repress the natural pangs that arise, of sorrowful yearning and tender pity, for one who, with feelings

---

[1] "Where even the motion of an angel's wing
Would interrupt the intense tranquillity
Of silent hills, and more than silent sky."
                              Wordsworth.

so attuned to the sweetest and holiest harmonies of life, was, by her troubled and bewildering lot, shut out from all but transient breathings, "few and far between," of "an ampler ether, a diviner air." Such instances are fraught with regrets to human hearts,— with sad and strange mysteries to mortal vision; regrets and mysteries which can alone be soothed and solved by unquestioning faith, and serene reliance on the good providence of God. A passage from the works of the late John Bowdler, bearing upon this subject, and quoted in one of her own letters, was appropriated by her with no less happy effect than fitting application. It is as follows:—"Could the veil which now separates us from futurity be drawn aside, and those regions of everlasting happiness and sorrow, which strike so faintly on the imagination, be presented fully to our eyes, it would occasion, I doubt not, a sudden and strange revolution in our estimate of things. Many are the distresses for which we now weep in suffering or sympathy, that would awaken us to songs of thanksgiving; many the dispensations which now seem dreary and inexplicable, that would fill our adoring hearts with thanksgiving and joy."

The soothing and healthful repose which had been so thoroughly and thankfully appreciated, was, alas! not destined to be of long continuance. Subsequent letters speak of the irruption of parties "hunting for lions in dove's nests"—of a renewal of the "Album persecution"—of an absolute Maelstrom of letters and papers threatening "to boil over the drawer to which they were consigned;" till at last the despairing conclusion is come to, that "one might as well hope for peace in the character of a shadowless man as of a literary woman." How heartily could Mrs. Hemans now have repeated what she had written some months before, under the pressure of peculiar irritation — "Do you know the song — 'Where shall we bury our *shame?'* Change the last word into *fame*, and it will express all my present perplexities."

On quitting her pretty Dove Nest[1] about the middle of August, Mrs. Hemans was prevailed upon to make a second visit to Scotland, chiefly in compliance with the urgent invitations of her kind old friend Sir Robert Liston, whose advanced age made it so improbable that she should have any other chance of ever seeing him again. On this occasion, she and her little "Carlo dolce," as some of her friends would affectionately call him, were every where received with the same gratifying distinction, and still more

---

[1] Her residence at this fairy dwelling was pleasingly recorded by the magic pen of Christopher North, in the paper called, a "Day at Winandermere," in *Blackwood's Magazine*, for September, 1830. He is describing the principal features of the landscape from one favourite point — "On the nearer side of these hills is seen stretching far off to other lofty regions—Hillbell and High Street conspicuous over the rest—the long vale of Troutbreck, with its picturesque cottages, 'in numbers without number, numberless,' and all its sable pines and sycamores; on the farther side, that most sylvan of all sylvan mountains, where lately the Hemans warbled her native woodnotes wild in her poetic bower, fitly called Dove Nest; — and beyond, Kirkstone Fells and Rydal Head, magnificent giants, looking westward to the Langdale Pikes,

'The last that parley with the setting sun'

gratifying kindness, which had marked their sojourn
in the North. Several of the visits were now accomplished which she had, at that time, been obliged
to decline; particularly to those "stately homes of
Scotland," Hopetoun House and Kinfauns Castle.
During her stay at Milburn Tower, she formed a
friendship with the family of the late J. C. Graves,
Esq. of Dublin, who were Sir Robert Liston's guests
at the same time; and having in view a visit to
Wales in the course of the autumn, she was induced
by them to carry this into effect by way of Dublin
and Holyhead, instead of proceeding from Glasgow to
Liverpool.

Mrs. Hemans had been for some time possessed with
the conviction that her situation at Wavertree was
neither suitable to her own health, nor half so favourable a one as she had been led to hope, for the education of her sons. She had therefore found it necessary to contemplate another change of residence, and
had once serious thoughts of establishing herself in
Edinburgh; a plan which would have been, in many
respects, most desirable; but the opinion of her medical friends was uniform and decided, that her constitution was totally unfit to brave the severity of a
northern climate, and that, in fact, one winter, or
rather spring, in Edinburgh, might be fatal to her.

Having formed very agreeable impressions of Dublin on her present visit, and being much influenced
by the encouraging reports she heard of its climate
and educational advantages, as well as by the circumstance of her brother, Major Browne, being settled in
Ireland, she now came to the determination of remov

ing there in the following spring.   Late in the autumn,
on her way back to Wavertree, she paid her last visit
to Bronwylfa, and bade a second, and now an unconsciously final, adieu to the

"Green land of her childhood, her home, and her dead."

The following extracts are chiefly from letters addressed to her new friends in Dublin :—

    "I thought Anglesey, through which I travelled,
without exception, the most dreary, culinary looking
land of prose I ever beheld.   I strove in vain to conjure up the ghost of a Druid, or even of a tree, on
its wide, monotonous plains, which I really think
nature must have produced to *rest* herself, after the
strong excitement of composing the Caernarvonshire
hills.   But I cannot tell you how much I wanted to
express my feelings when at last that bold mountain
chain rose upon me, in all its grandeur, with the
crowning Snowdon (very superior, I assure you, in
'shape and feature,' to our friend Ben Lomond), main-
taining his 'pride of place' above the whole ridge.
And the Menai bridge, which I thought I should
scarcely have noticed in the presence of those glorious heights, really seems, from its magnificence, a
native feature of the scene, and nobly asserts the pre-
eminence of mind above all other things.   I could
scarcely have conceived such an union of strength
and grace; and its chain work is so airy in appearance, that to drive along it seems almost like passing
through the trellis of a bower; it is quite startling to
look down from any thing which appears so fragile, to
the immense depth below.

" Part of my journey lay along the sea-shore rather late at night, and I was surprised by quite a splendid vision of the northern lights, on the very spot where I had once, and once only, before seen them in early childhood. They shot up like slender pillars of white light, with a sort of arrowy motion, from a dark cloud above the sea; their colour varied in ascending, from that of silver to a faint orange, and then a very delicate green; and sometimes the motion was changed, and they chased each other along the edge of the cloud, with a dazzling brightness and rapidity. I was almost startled by seeing them *there* again; and after so long an interval of thoughts and years, it was like the effect produced by a sudden burst of familiar and yet long-forgotten music."

" I did not observe any object of interest on my voyage from Wales, excepting a new beacon at the extremity of the Liverpool Rock, and which I thought a good deal like the pictures of the Eddystone Lighthouse. There was something to me particularly stern and solemn in its appearance, as it rose darkly against a very wild sky, like a ' pillar of cloud,' with a capital of deep-coloured fire: but perhaps the gloom and stormy effect of the evening might have very much aided the impression left upon my fancy."

" Have you seen Rogers's *Italy*, with its exquisite embellishments? The whole book seems to me quite a triumph of art and taste. Some of Turner's Italian scenes, with their moonlit vestibules and pillared arcades, the shadows of which seem almost trembling

on the ground as you look at them, really might be fit
representations of Armida's enchanted gardens: and
there is one view of the Temples of Pæstum, standing
in their severe and lonely grandeur on the shore, and
lit up by a flash of lightning, which brought to my
mind those lines of Byron —

> ——'As I gazed, the place
> Became Religion, and the heart ran o'er
> With silent worship of the great of old.'

"I have not yet read Northcote's *Life of Titian*,
but I was much struck with a passage I lately saw
quoted from it, relating to that piercing, intellectual,
eagle-look, which I have so often remarked in Titian's
portraits. 'It is the intense personal character,'
Northcote says ' which gives the superiority to those
portraits over all others, and stamps them with a living and permanent interest. Whenever you turn to
look at them, they appear to be looking at you. There
seems to be some question pending between you, as if
an intimate friend or an inveterate foe were in the
room with you. They exert a kind of fascinating
power, and there is that exact resemblance to individual nature, which is always new and always interesting.' I suppose it was a feeling of this kind which
made Fuseli exclaim, on seeing Titian's picture of
Paul the Third with his two nephews, ' That is history !' "

"The account you sent me of the longevity of
artists (a privilege which I, at least, am far from envying them), seemed confirmed, or rather accounted for,
in some degree, by a paper I was reading on the same

20 *

day,—it is written, with great enthusiasm, on the
'Pleasures of Painting;' and the author (Hazlitt, I
believe), describes the studies of the artist as a kind
of sanctuary, a 'city of refuge' from worldly strife,
envy and littleness; and his communion with nature
as sufficient to fill the void, and satisfy all the cravings
of heart and soul. I wonder if this indeed can be.
I should like to go by night with a magician to the
Coliseum (as Benvenuto Cellini did), and call up the
spirits of those mighty Italian artists, and make them
all tell me whether they had been happy; but it
would not do to forget, as he also did—(have you ever
read those strange memoirs of his?)—the spell by
which the ghosts were laid, as the consequences were
extremely disagreeable."

———

" I was much interested a few days ago, in looking
over some beautiful engravings of antique English
portraits. I wonder whether you were ever impressed
by what struck me much during an examination of
them, the superior character of repose by which they
are distinguished from the portraits of the present
day. I found this, to a certain degree, the predominant trait in every one of them; not any thing like
nonchalance or apathy, but a certain high-minded
self-possession, something like what I think the ' Opium
Eater' calls the ' brooding of the majestic intellect
over all.' I scarcely ever see a trace of this quiet,
yet stately sweetness, in the expression of modern portraits; they all look so eager, so restless, so trying to
be *vieillé*. I wonder if this is owing to the feverish
excitement of the times in which we live, for I should

suppose that the world has never been in such a hurry during the whole course of its life before."

———

"Since I wrote last, I have been quite confined to the house; but before I caught my last very judicious cold, I went to see an exquisite piece of sculpture, which has been lately sent to this neighbourhood from Rome by Gibson, with whose name as an artist you are most likely familiar. It is a statue of Sappho, representing her at the moment she receives the tidings of Phaon's desertion. I think I prefer it to almost any thing I ever saw of Canova's, as it possesses all his delicacy and beauty of form, but is imbued with a far deeper sentiment. There is a sort of willowy drooping in the figure, which seems to express a weight of unutterable sadness, and one sinking arm holds the lyre so carelessly, that you almost fancy it will drop while you gaze. Altogether, it seems to speak piercingly and sorrowfully of the nothingness of Fame, at least to woman. There was a good collection of pictures in the same house, but they were almost unaccountably vulgarized in my sight by the presence of the lonely and graceful statue."

———

"I wish I could be with you to see Young's performance of Hamlet, of all Shakspeare's characters the one which interests me most; I suppose from the never-ending conjectures in which it involves one's mind. Did I ever mention to you Goethe's beautiful remark upon it? He says, that Hamlet's naturally gentle and tender spirit, overwhelmed with its mighty tasks and solemn responsibilities, is like a China vase, fit only for the reception of delicate flowers, but in which an oak tree has been planted; the roots of the strong tree expand, and the fair vase is shivered."

"I have lately met with an exquisite little book, a work upon the Classics, just published, by Henry Coleridge; it is written with all the fervour, and much of the rich imagination and flow of 'words that burn,' which characterise the writings of his celebrated relative."

"Some *Quarterly Reviews* have lately been sent to me, one of which contains an article on Byron, by which I have been deeply and sorrowfully impressed. His character, as there portrayed, reminded me of some of those old Eastern cities, where travellers constantly find a squalid mud hovel built against the ruins of a gorgeous temple; for alas! the best part of that fearfully mingled character is but ruin—the wreck of what might have been."

"I have been reading a great deal during all this gloomy winter, and have been charmed lately by an account of the life of my favourite musician Weber, in the *Foreign Quarterly Review*, with extracts from his letters. The flow of affectionate feeling in these —the love he everywhere manifests of excellence *for its own sake*—the earnestness and truth of heart revealed in all his actions—these things make up a character, like his own music, of perfect harmony. Is it not delightful, a foundation of gladness to our own hearts, when we are able to love what we admire? I shall play the waltz, and those beautiful airs from 'Der Freischütz,' with tenfold pleasure after reading the memoir."

"I hope you will be as much amused at the 'Analysis of a Lady's Tear,' which I inclose for your edification, as I have been. Only imagine the tear to have been one shed at parting, and then can you conceive any thing so unsentimental?"

The inclosure was the following extract, cut out of a newspaper:—"*Analysis of a Lady's Tear.*—This was really effected by the celebrated Smithson, one of the fellows of the Royal Society, whose loss the past week has had to deplore. Nothing, it seems, eluded the grasp of this enquiring man, who, not content with operating on the common objects which nature had placed before him, presumed to approach the shrine of beauty itself, wherewith to satisfy his curiosity. He had analysed more than a dew-drop—a lady's tear! He caught the pearly treasure as it fell from its source, and on submitting it to his tests, discovered that it contained two separate salts.'

"Since I last wrote to you, I have received a visit from a remarkable person, whose mind is full, even to overflowing, of intelligence and original thought. It is Dr. ——, the distinguished linguist, of whom I shall speak. I do not know when I have heard such a flow of varying conversation; it is like having a flood of mind poured out upon you, and that, too, evidently from the strong necessity of setting the current free, not from any design to shine or overpower.

I think I was most interested in his descriptions of
Spain, a country where he has lived much, and to
which he is strongly attached.   He spoke of the songs
which seem to fill the airs of the South, from the constant improvisation of the people at their work : he
described as a remarkable feature of the scenery, the
little rills and water-courses which were led through
the fields and gardens, and even over every low wall,
by the Moors of Andalusia, and which yet remain,
making the whole country vocal with pleasant sounds
of waters: he told me also several striking anecdotes
of a bandit chief in Murcia, a sort of Spanish Rob
Roy, who has carried on his predatory warfare there
for many years, and is so adored by the peasantry, for
whose sake he plunders the rich, that it is impossible
for the government ever to seize upon him.   Some
expressions of the old Biscayan (the Basque) language,
which he translated for me, I thought beautifully
poetical.   The sun is called, in that language, 'that
which pours the day ;' and the moon, 'the light of
the dead.'   Well, from Spain he travelled, or rather
shot off—like Robin Goodfellow, who could

> ——'put a girdle round about the earth
> In forty minutes,'—

away to Iceland, and told me of his having seen there
a MS. recording the visit of an Icelandic Prince to
the court of our old Saxon king, Athelstane.   Then
to Paris, Brussels, Warsaw, with a sort of 'open
sesame' for the panorama of each court and kingdom.

*   *   *   *   *

" A striking contrast to all this, was a visit I lately

paid to old Mr. Roscoe, who may be considered quite as the father of literature in this part of the world. He is a delightful old man, with a fine Roman style of head, which he had adorned with a green velvet cap to receive me in, because, as he playfully said, ' he knew I always admired him in it.'[1]   Altogether he put me rather in mind of one of Rembrandt's pictures; and, as he sat in his quiet study, surrounded by busts, and books, and flowers, and with a beautiful cast of Canova's Psyche in the back-ground, I thought that a painter, who wished to make old age look touching and venerable, could not have had a better subject."

The occasional society of Mr. Roscoe, in such bright intervals as were admitted by his failing health (which frequently obliged him to pass months in comparative seclusion, though it never impaired his mental energies and cheerful benevolence), was one of the greatest enjoyments of Mrs. Hemans's residence near Liverpool.   She never spoke of him but with affectionate deference, and had an honest pride in knowing that he appreciated her poetry, and took pleasure in having it read to him.   It was during the present winter and spring that she applied herself with some diligence to the study of music, under the instruction of Mr. J. Zeugheer Herrmann, who, as she wrote, " comes to me every week, and I should like him as a

---

[1] This is not the first instance of the attractions of a green velvet cap.   In one of Alexander Knox's letters, speaking of the picture for which he was then sitting, he says—" Sir Thomas Acland would have me in my invalid dress—my green velvet nightcap had taken hold of his heart."

master exceedingly, were it not that I am sure I give him the toothache whenever I play a wrong note, and a sympathising pang immediately shoots through my own compassionate heart."

About the same time, she began to be sensible of a newly-awakened power of inventing airs, adapted to the words of some of her own lyrics. The spontaneous flow of this stream of melody, was a source of great delight to her, though she found some difficulty in the mechanical part of noting down, or what she called "caging," her musical fancies. In this task she was most kindly aided by Mr. Lodge, the accomplished amateur already alluded to; and to whom she was indebted for the symphonies and accompaniments of two of her songs, "Go forth, for she is gone," and "By the mighty Minster's Bell," which were published by Lonsdale and Mills.[1]

The following note may be applicable to that numerous class of hieroglyphical writers, who would do well to adopt the ingenious device of a certain French nobleman of the *vieille cour :*—" Par respect, Monsieur" (he wrote, or rather scrawled, to a person of equal rank with himself), "je vous écris de ma propre main ; mais pour faciliter la lecture, je vous envoye une copie de ma lettre."—" I have the pleasure to inform you that you have attained a degree

---

[1] The copyright of four other songs, also composed by Mrs. Hemans, was purchased by the late Mr. Power, not long before his death ; but it is believed they have never been published. These were,—" The Wreck ;" " Thou'rt passing from the Lake's green side ;" (the Indian song from " Edith," in *Records of Woman*); " Death and the Warrior ;" and " Good Night."

of indistinctness positively sublime in the name of the day upon which you promise to visit me next. I was, as the Lady Cherubina says, in *The Heroine,* ' terribly ill off for mysteries,' before the arrival of your note; but this deficiency is now most happily supplied. Reasoning from analogy instead of wisdom, I should conclude it to be *Tuesday,* but then it has, if my senses fail me not, a dotted *i :* it seems to have rather too many letters for *Friday,* and into *Wednesday* it cannot be metamorphosed, even on the antiquarian system, that ' consonants are changeable at pleasure, and vowels go for nothing.' ' The force of nature can no further go ;' therefore I return the awful hieroglyphic for your inspection, and beg for some further light."

The next note refers to some of the works of an amiable young artist, whose distinguished talents excited in all who knew him a strong feeling of admiration, subdued into sorrowful interest by his early death.

" I return the very interesting collection of Mr. Austin's drawings, which I had great pleasure in looking over yesterday evening. I only regret that there were no names to them, as I am prevented from particularizing those which I most admired; but I recognised Tivoli, and was especially struck with one representing the interior of a church. There is also an exquisite little hermitage buried among trees, where I should like to pass at least a month after my late fatigues, and hear nothing but the sound of leaves and waters, and now and then some pleasant voice of a friend. I did not quite understand a message which

Henry brought me, about the dedication or advertisement to these drawings. I cannot help feeling interested in Mr. Austin, from all I have heard you say
of him; and if you think it would gratify him, I would
send you a few lines to be prefixed to this work, in
which I should try to express in poetry what I imagine
he wishes to convey—that the spirit of the artist was
wandering over the sunny fields of Italy, whilst he
himself was confined to the bed of sickness."

The " late fatigues" referred to in the above note,
were occasioned by all the harassing preparations for
removal, which were now assuming a " form and
pressure" absolutely overwhelming to one so little
used to worldly cares, and whose fitful strength was
so easily exhausted. Mrs. Hemans had continued
to be visited throughout the winter, by those distressing attacks of palpitation of the heart, which caused
her friends so much uneasiness, and were invariably
brought on by any unwonted excitement, or mental
agitation. " My chest is still strangely oppressed,"
she wrote in one of her letters, " and always makes
me think of Horatio's words:—

'I, in this harsh world, draw my breath with pain.' "

And the following, written at the point of departure, now seems fraught with a sad foreboding:—

" You will be surprised to hear, that notwithstanding my healthful looks, Dr. ——, who visited me after
you were gone, positively forbade the intended excursion to Ince, and gave me most serious admonitions
with regard to that complaint of the heart from which
I suffer. He says that nothing but great care and

perfect quiet will prevent its assuming a dangerous character; and I told him that he might as well prescribe for me the *powdered diamonds* which physicians of the olden time ordered for royal patients. I must own that this has somewhat deepened the melancholy impressions under which I am going to Ireland, for I cannot but feel assured that *he is right*."

On the subject of her new plans, she thus wrote to an attached friend in Scotland:—"One of my greatest inducements to take this step, is the constant want of protection and domestic support to which my situation exposes me, and my anxiety to have my brother's advice and guidance as to my boys, for whose future prospects in life I begin to feel painfully anxious. Ireland seems a troubled land to seek, just at present; but every place is troubled to a woman at once so conspicuous, so unprotected, and so little acquainted with the world as, from peculiar causes, I am. I shall not despair of seeing you again, as Scotland is just as attainable from Dublin as from Liverpool, and I have too many kind friends there, ever to forget the beautiful scenes in which I first knew them. Do not fancy that I was insensible to the external charms of Kinfauns, because the treasures of art *within* its walls were more attractive to me (who am passionately fond of such objects, and have had few opportunities of gratifying my taste for them) than the hills and woods *without*. You should recollect that I have been almost cradled amidst scenes of beauty, and almost all the forms and colours of nature are familiar to me, but it is not so with those of art."

Towards the latter end of April 1831, Mrs. Hemans

quitted England for the last time, and, after remaining
for a few weeks in Dublin, proceeded to visit her brother, then residing at the Hermitage, near Kilkenny.
" This," she wrote, " is a very pretty little spot, and I
should be really sorry that my brother is to leave it in
two or three months, were it not that the change will
be one of great advantage to himself, as he is appointed to a trust of high responsibility. I have a blue
mountain chain in sight of my window, and the voice
of the river comes in to me delightfully. My health
has been very unsettled, yet my friends are surprised
to see me *looking* so well. I think that, on the whole,
the soft climate agrees with me; my greatest foe is
' the over-beating of the heart.' My life in Dublin
was what might have been expected—one of constant
excitement, and more ' broken into fragments' than
ever. I very nearly gave up letter-writing in despair.
I must, however, gratefully acknowledge, that I met
there much true kindness. The state of the country
here, though Kilkenny is considered at present tranquil, is certainly, to say the least of it, very ominous.
We paid a visit yesterday evening at a clergyman's
house about five miles hence, and found a guard of
eight armed policemen stationed at the gate : the win-
dow-ledges were all provided with great stones for the
convenience of hurling down upon assailants; and the
master of the house had not, for a fortnight, taken a
walk without loaded pistols. You may imagine how
the boys, who are all here for the holidays, were
enchanted with this agreeable state of things; indeed,
I believe, they were not a little disappointed that we
reached home without having sustained an attack

from the Whitefeet. Do not, however, suppose that we are in the least danger, though there seems just ·possibility of danger enough all round us, to keep up a little pleasant excitement — (the tabooed word again !) There is this peculiarity in Irish disturbances, that those who are not obnoxious, from party or political motives, to the people, have really nothing to fear; and my brother is extremely popular. My sister-in-law and myself are often amused with the idea of what our English friends would think, did they know of our sitting, in this troubled land, with our doors and windows all open, till eleven o'clock at night."

The extracts which follow, are from letters written at the same place.

"I wish to give you an account of an interesting day I lately passed, before its images become faint in my recollection. We went to Woodstock, the place where the late Mrs. Tighe, whose poetry has always been very touching to my feelings, passed the latest years of her life, and near which she is buried. The scenery of the place is magnificent; of a style which, I think, I prefer to every other; wild, profound glens, rich with every hue and form of foliage, and a rapid river sweeping through them, now lost, and now lighting up the deep woods with sudden flashes of its waves. Altogether, it reminded me more of Hawthornden than anything I have seen since, though it wants the solemn rock pinnacles of that romantic place. I wish I could have been alone with Nature and my thoughts; but, to my surprise, I found myself the object of quite a *reception*. There was no help for it, though I never

21 *

felt so much as if I wanted a *large leaf* to wrap me
up and shelter me.   Still, one cannot but feel grateful
for kindness, and much was shown me.   I should have
told you that Woodstock is now the seat of Mr. and
Lady Louisa Tighe.   Amongst other persons of the
party was Mr. Henry Tighe, the widower of the
poetess.   He had just been exercising, I found, one
of his accomplishments in the translation into Latin
of a little poem of mine; and I am told that his ver-
sion is very elegant.   We went to the tomb, ' the
grave of a poetess,' where there is a monument by
Flaxman: it consists of a recumbent female figure,
with much of the repose, the mysterious sweetness of
happy death, which is to me so affecting in monu-
mental sculpture.   There is, however, a very small
Titania-looking sort of figure with wings, sitting at the
head of the sleeper, which I thought interfered with
the singleness of effect which the tomb would have
produced: unfortunately, too, the monument is carved
in very rough stone, which allows no delicacy of touch.
That place of rest made me very thoughtful; I could
not but reflect on the many changes which had
brought me to the spot I had commemorated three
years since, without the slightest idea of ever visiting
it; and, though surrounded by attention and the
appearance of interest, my heart was envying the
repose of her who slept there." [1]

---

[1] It is interesting to compare the ideal visit to "the grave of a
poetess," described in the little poem so named in the *Records
of Women*, with the real one commemorated in the lines " Written after visiting a tomb near Woodstock," which were published

" Mr. Tighe has just sent me his Latin translation of my lines, ' The Graves of a Household.' It seems very elegant, as far as I can venture to judge, but what strikes me most is the concluding thought, (so peculiarly belonging to Christianity), and the ancient language in which it is thus embodied : —

> ' Si nihil ulterius mundo, si sola voluptas
>   Esset terrenis — quid feret omnis Amor ?'

" I suppose the idea of an affection, powerful and spiritual enough to overcome the grave (of course the beauty of such an idea belongs not to me, but to the spirit of our faith), is not to be found in the loftiest strain of any classic writer."

Under the influence of similar feelings with those expressed in the last quotation, Mrs. Hemans thus alluded to her own lyric—" The Death Song of Alcestis," which was written at this time.

" It was with some difficulty that I refrained from making Alcestis express the hope of an immortal re-union : I know this would be out of character, and yet could scarcely imagine how love, so infinite in its

---

in the *National Lyrics.* The same train of feeling may be traced in both—the same " mournful iteration."

> " O love and song ! though of heaven your powers,
>   Dark is your fate in this world of ours."

But in each solemn picture, " the day-spring from on high" breaks through the " mists of earth ;" and " visions of brighter things" win us to heavenly contemplation.

The sonnet " On Records of immature Genius," (published in Mrs. Hemans's *Poetical Remains*), was written after reading some of the earlier poems of Mrs. Tighe, which had been lent to her in MS.

nature, could ever have existed without the hope
(even if undefined and unacknowledged) of a heavenly
country, an unchangeable resting-place.   This awoke
in me many other thoughts with regard to the state
of human affections, their hopes and their conflicts in
the days of ' the gay religions, full of pomp and gold,'
which, offering, as they did, so much of grace and
beauty to the imagination, yet held out so little comfort to the heart.   Then I thought how much these
affections owed to a deeper and more spiritual faith,
to the idea of a God who knows all our inward struggles, and pities our sufferings.   I think I shall weave
all these ideas into another little poem, which I will
call *Love in the Ancient World*." [1]

"I do not think I mentioned to you having seen
at Woodstock a large and beautifully painted copy of
Raphael's ' *Great Madonna*,' as it is called—the one
at Dresden.   I never was enabled to form so perfect
an idea of this noble work before.   The principal
figure certainly looks like the ' Queen of Heaven,' as
she stands serenely upon her footstool of clouds;' but
there is, I think, rather a want of human tenderness
in her calm eyes, and on her regal brow.   I visited
yesterday another lovely place, some miles from us—

[1] This design was afterwards partly, and *but* partly, fulfilled,
in the *Antique Greek Lament*, which was intended as one of a
series of poems, illustrating the insufficiency of aught but Christianity to heal and comfort the broken in heart; and its all-sus-
taining aid to those, " who, going through this vale of misery,
use it for a well," and apply to its living waters for " the strengthening and refreshing of their souls."

Kilfane; quite in a different style of beauty from Woodstock—soft, rich, and pastoral-looking. Such a tone of verdure, I think, I never beheld anywhere: It was quite an emerald darkness, a gorgeous gloom brooding over velvet turf, and deep silent streams, from such trees as I could fancy might have grown in Armida's enchanted wood. Some swans upon the dark waters made me think of that line of Spenser's, in which he speaks of the fair Una, as

' Making a sunshine in the shady place.'

The graceful play of water-birds is always particularly delightful to me ;—those bright creatures convey to my fancy a fuller impression of the joy of freedom than any others in nature—perhaps because they are lords of two elements."

"I heard a beautiful remark made by the Chief-Justice, when I met him at Kilfane. I think it was with regard to some of Canova's beautiful sculpture in the room, that he said—' Is not *perfection always affecting ?*' I thought he was quite right; for the highest degree of beauty in any art certainly always excites, if not tears, at least the inward feeling of tears." [1]

---

[1] " Is that strong passion for intellectual beauty a happy or a mournful gift, when so out of harmony with the rest of our earthly lot? Sometimes I think of it in sadness, but oftener it seems to me as a sort of rainbow, made up of light and tears, yet still the pledge of happiness to come." — From one of Mrs. Hemans's letters, written in 1829.

" I will now describe to you the scene I mentioned in my last letter, as having so much impressed me. It was a little green hill, rising darkly and abruptly against a very sunny background of sloping corn-fields and woods. It appeared smooth till near the summit, but was there crested — almost castellated indeed—by what I took for thickly-set, pointed rocks; but, on a nearer approach, discovered to be old tomb-stones, forming quite a little 'city of the silent.' I left our car to explore it, and discovered some ruins of a very affecting character: a small church laid open to the sky, forsaken and moss-grown; its font lying overturned on the green sod; some of the rude monuments themselves but ruins. One of these, which had fallen amongst thick heath and wild-flow-ers, was simply a wooden cross, with a female name, and the inscription —' May her soul rest in peace!' You will not wonder at the feeling which prompted me to stoop and raise it up again. My memory will often revert to that lonely spot, sacred to the hope of immortality, and touched by the deep quiet of the evening skies."

" Kilkenny is a singular-looking old place, full of ruins, or rather fragments of ruins, bits of old towers and abbey-windows; and its wild lazzaroni-looking population must, I should think, be tremendous when in a state of excitement. Many things in the condition of this country, even during its present temporary quiet, are very painful to English feeling. It is scarcely possible to conceive bitterness and hatred existing in the human heart, when one sees nature smiling so brightly and so peacefully all around; and yet those dark feelings *do* exist here to a degree which I could not have credited; and religious animosities are carried to a height which sometimes painfully reminds me of Moore's lines, where he speaks of the land in which

> ——'hearts fell off that ought to twine,
> And man profaned what God had given;
> Till some were heard to curse the shrine,
> Where others knelt to Heaven.'"

Early in the autumn of 1831, Mrs. Hemans took up her abode in Dublin, where she at first resided in Upper Pembroke Street. The two elder boys of those still with her, had been already placed at school, under the care of the Rev. Dr. Gwynne, of Castleknock; and her son Charles had the great privilege of having his education superintended by Mr. (now the Reverend) R. P. Graves, then a student at Trinity College, from whose valuable instruction he derived advantages far more permanent and important than any acquisitions of mere worldly learning. Mrs. Hemans entered very little into the general society of Dublin, but enjoyed, with a few real and attached friends, that kindly intercourse most congenial to her tastes and habits. Amongst these friends must be particularly mentioned the Graves family, their venerable relatives Dr. [1] and Mrs. Perceval, the household circle of

---

[1] The Sonnet "To an aged Friend," published in Mrs. Hemans's *Poetical Remains*, was addressed to Dr. Perceval. Its beginning,—

> "Not long thy voice amongst us may be heard,
> Servant of God! thy day is almost done,"—

Colonel D'Aquilar, and that of Professor, now Sir William Hamilton.

From an early period of intimacy she received the most friendly attentions from the Archbishop of Dublin, and Mrs. Whateley, whose subsequent kindness can never be forgotten; and she had great interest and pleasure in the acquaintance of Mr. Blanco White, who was at that time their inmate; his delightful conversational powers yet unimpaired by the infirm health which has now unfortunately withdrawn him from society. Few individuals, as she was herself always foremost to acknowledge, were ever blessed with more zealous and devoted friends than Mrs. Hemans; and if, in these slight memorials, little has been said of the constant solace and support she derived from the ministering affection of her brothers, it is because the gentle charities of domestic life are things too sacred to be held up to the public; and because all who personally knew her, knew from her continual and grateful allusions to it, that their kindness was "a fountain"—

> "Whose only business was to flow,
>   And flow it did; not taking heed
>   Of its own bounty, or her need;"

---

must be read with affecting interest by those who know that that voice is still heard, though feebly and failingly, — whilst the "Daughter of Music" has long been laid low. The sonnet 'To the Datura Arborea," in the same volume, was written after seeing a superb specimen of that striking plant, in Dr. Perceval's beautiful greenhouse at Annefield.

Dr. Perceval died 3d March, 1839, shortly after the above note was written.

Soon after her establishment in the Irish capital, Mrs. Hemans had an opportunity of hearing the wonderful performances of Paganini; and how completely she was wrought upon by the mighty master, will be seen by the following letters :—

" To begin with the appearance of the foreign wonder. It is very different from what the indiscriminating newspaper accounts would lead you to suppose : he is certainly singular-looking, pale, slight, and with long, neglected hair; but I saw nothing whatever of that *wild-fire*, that almost ferocious inspiration of mien. which has been ascribed to him. Indeed, I thought the expression of his countenance rather that of good-natured and mild *enjouement*, than of any thing else ; and his bearing altogether simple and natural. His first performance consisted of a *Tema* with variations, from the beautiful Preghiera in '*Mosé ;*' here I was rather disappointed, but merely because he did not play alone. I suppose the performance on the single string required the support of other instruments; but he occasionally drew from that string a tone of wailing, heart-piercing tenderness, almost too much to be sustained by any one whose soul can give the full response. It was not, however, till his second performance, on all the strings, that I could form a full idea of his varied magic. A very delicate accompaniment on the piano did not in the least interfere with the singleness of effect in this instance. The subject was the Venetian air ' Oh ! come to me when daylight sets.' How shall I give you an idea of all the versatility, the play of soul, embodied in the variations upon that simple air ? Imagine a passage of the most

VOL. I.——22

fairy-like delicacy, more aerial than you would suppose it possible for human touch to produce, suddenly
succeeded by an absolute *parody* of itself; the same
notes repeated with an expression of really comic
humour, which forced me to laugh, however reluctantly. It was as if an old man, the ' Ancient Mari-
ner' himself, were to sing an impassioned Italian air,
in a snoring voice, after Pasta. Well, after one of
these sudden travesties,[1] for I can call them nothing
else, the creature would look all around him, with an
air of the most delighted *bonhommie*, exactly like a
witty child, who has just accomplished a piece of suc-
cessful mischief. The *pizzicato* passages were also
wonderful; the indescribably rapid notes seemed flung
out in sparks of music, with a triumphant glee which
conveys the strongest impression I ever received, of
genius rejoicing over its own bright creations. But I
vainly wish that my words could impart to you a full
conception of this wizard-like music.

" There was nothing else of particular interest in
the evening's performance:—a good deal of silvery
warbling from Stockhausen; but I never find it leave
any more vivid remembrance on my mind than the
singing of birds. I am wrong, however; I must except
one thing, ' Napoleon's Midnight Review,' the music
of which, by Neukomm, I thought superb. The words
are translated from the German: they describe the
hollow sound of a drum at midnight, and the peal of
a ghostly trumpet, arousing the dead hosts of Napoleon
from their sleep under the northern snows, and along

---

[1] Wordsworth.

the Egyptian sands, and in the sunny fields of Italy.
Then another trumpet-blast, and the chief himself
arises, ' with his martial cloak around him,' to review
the whole army; and thus it concludes—

> " 'France!' 'tis their watchword; and again,
> The pass-word, 'St. Hélène!' "

The music, which is of a very wild, supernatural
character, a good deal in Weber's incantation style,
accords well with this grand idea: the single trumpet,
followed by a long, rolling, ominous sound from the
double drum, made me quite thrill with indefinable
feelings."

" I inclose you a programme of the concert at which
I again heard this triumphant music last night.　It is
impossible for me to describe how much of intense
feeling its full-swelling dreamy tones awoke within
me.　His second performance (the *Adagio a doppio
corde*) made me imagine that I was then first waken-
ing in what a German would call the ' music-land.'
Its predominant expression was that of overpowering,
passionate regret; such, at least, was the dying languor of the long *sostenuto* notes, that it seemed as if
the musician was himself about to let fall his instrument, and sink under the mastery of his own emotion.
It reminded me, by some secret and strange analogy,
of a statue I once described to you, representing Sappho about to drop her lyre, in utter desolation of heart.
This was immediately followed by the rapid, *flashing*
music—for the strings were as if they sent out lightning in their glee—of the most joyous *rondo* by Kreut-
zer you can imagine.　The last piece, the ' Dance of

the Witches,' is a complete exemplification of the grotesque in music. Some parts of it imitate the quavering, garrulous voices of very old women, half-complaining, and then would come a burst of wild, fantastic, half-fearful gladness. I think Burns's 'Tam O'Shanter' (not Mr. Thom's—by way of contrast to Sappho), something of a parallel in poetry to this strange production in music. I saw more of Paganini's countenance last night, and was still more pleased with it than before ; the original mould in which it has been cast, is of a decidedly fine and intellectual character, though the features are so worn by the wasting fire which appears his vital element."

———

"I did not hear Paganini again after the performance I described to you, but I have received a very eloquent description of a subsequent triumph of his genius. It was a *concerto*, of a dramatic character, and intended, as I was told, to embody the little tale of a wanderer sinking to sleep in a solitary place at midnight. He is supposed to be visited by a solemn and impressive vision, imaged in music of the most thrilling style. Then, after all his lonely fears and wild fantasies, the day-spring breaks upon him in a triumphant rondo, and all is joy and gladness."

" ———— related to me a most interesting conversation he had held with Paganini in a private circle. The latter was describing to him the sufferings (do you remember a line of Byron's,

'The starry Galileo, with his woes'")

by which he pays for his consummate excellence. He

scarcely knows what sleep is, and his nerves are wrought to such almost preternatural acuteness, that harsh, even common sounds, are often torture to him: he is sometimes unable to bear a whisper in his room. His passion for music he described as an all-absorbing, a consuming one: in fact, he looks as if no other life than that ethereal one of melody were circulating in his veins: but he added, with a glow of triumph kindling through deep sadness—'mais c'est un don du ciel.' I heard all this, which was no more than I had fully imagined, with a still deepening conviction, that it is the gifted, beyond all others—those whom the multitude believe to be rejoicing in their own fame, strong in their own resources—who have most need of true hearts to rest upon, and of hope in God to support them."

In the course of the same autumn, Mrs. Hemans made an excursion into the County of Wicklow, some records of which appear in the following extracts:

"I was very unwell for some days after my arrival here, as the mountains gave me such a stormy reception, that I reached this place with the dripping locks of a mermaid, and never was in a condition so utterly desolate. In the midst of my annoyances from the rain and storm, I was struck by one beautiful effect upon the hills; it was produced by a rainbow diving down into a gloomy mountain pass, which it seemed really to flood with its coloured glory. I could not help thinking that it was like our religion, piercing and carrying brightness into the depth of sorrow and of the tomb. All the rest of the scene around that one illumined spot, was wrapt in the most lowering

22 *

darkness. My impressions of the country here have not hitherto been very bright ones; but I will not yet judge of it :—the weather is most unfavourable, and I have not quite recovered the effect of my first day's adventures. The day before yesterday we visited the Vale of the Seven Churches and Lake Glendalough; the day was one of a kind which I like—soft, still, and grey,—such as makes the earth appear 'a pensive but a happy place.' I was a little disappointed in the scenery. I think it possesses much more for the imagination than the eye, though there are certainly some striking points of view; particularly that where 'a round tower of other days' rises amidst the remains of three churches, the principal one of which (considered, I find, as quite the Holy of Holies), is thickly surrounded with tombs. I was also much pleased with a little wild waterfall, quite buried among the trees. Its many cascades fell into pools of a dark green transparency, and in one of these I observed what seemed to me a remarkable effect. The body of water threw itself into its deep bed with scarcely any spray, and left an almost smooth and clear surface, through which, as if through ice, I saw its foamy clouds rising and working tumultuously from beneath. In following the course of this fall, down very slippery, mossy stones, I received from our guide (a female), the very flattering compliment of being 'the most *courageousest* and *lightest-footedest* lady' she had ever conducted there. We afterwards went upon the lake, the dark waters and treeless shores of which have something impressive in their stern desolation, though I do not think the rocks quite high enough for grandeur.

Several parties have been arranged for me to visit other celebrated scenes in the neighbourhood, but I do not think that St. Kevin, who, I suppose, presides over the weather here, seems more propitious to female intrusion than of old."

"It is time that I should tell you something of my adventures among these wild hills since I last wrote. I must own that the scenery still disappoints me, though I do not dare to make the confession openly. There certainly are scenes of beauty, lying deep, like veins of gold, in the heart of the country, but they must, like those veins, be sought through much that is dreary and desolate. I have been more struck with the Devil's Glen (I wish it had any other name), than all the other spots I have visited; it is certainly a noble ravine, a place where you might imagine the mountain Christians of old making their last stand, fighting the last battle of their faith—a deep glen of rocks, cleft all through by a sounding stream, of that clear brown 'cairn-gorm' colour, which I think Sir Walter somewhere describes as being among the characteristics of mountain waters.

"To-day has been one of most perfect loveliness. I enjoyed the change of the wild rough mountains for the softer wood landscapes, as we approached Powerscourt. I think I love wood scenery best of all others, for its kindly look of shelter."

"I returned to the country," wrote Mrs. Hemans, after this excursion, " rather wearied than refreshed, as I unfortunately found myself an object of much curiosity, and, in gratitude I ought to add, attention; still it fatigued my spirits, which were longing for full and quiet communion with nature. On my return to Dublin, I became a sufferer from the longest and severest attack of heart palpitation I have ever experienced; it was accompanied by almost daily fainting fits, and a languor quite indescribable. From this state I have again arisen, and that with an elasticity which has surprised myself."

A few weeks afterwards, she thus wrote of herself:—

"Your kind long letter found me quite alone: my brother had taken my elder boys to pass their holidays at Killaloe, and even little Charles was gone on a visit for a few days, which I could not be selfish enough to refuse him. But I can give you a better account of myself than has for a long time been in my power: my spirits and health are both greatly revived; and though I am yet unequal to any continuous exertion of mind, still I am not without hope, that if I go on improving, all my energies may be restored to me."

* * * * *

"You ask me what I have been reading lately: the access to new books here is not nearly as easy as in England, at least for me; and, in consequence, I have been much thrown back upon our old friends, especially the Germans—Goëthe, and Schiller, and Oehlenschlager more particularly—and I think I love them more and more for every perusal, so that I cannot regret the causes which have rendered my connexion with them more intimate than ever."

The improved health announced in the above letter, was, unfortunately, of very short continuance. In
another, written not long afterwards, she describes
herself as having just recovered from "a weary low
fever, from which I think I should scarcely have
revived, had not my spirits been calmer, and my mind
happier, than has for some years been the case.
During part of the time, when I could neither read
nor listen to reading, I lay very meekly upon the sofa,
reciting to myself almost all the poetry I have ever
read. I composed two or three melodies also, but
having no one here who can help me to catch the
fugitives, they have taken flight irrecoverably. I have
lately written what I consider one of my best pieces
—'A Poet's dying Hymn.' It appeared in the last
number of *Blackwood*."

—

It is impossible to read this affecting poem without
feeling how distinctly it breathes the inward echoes
of the soul to the frequent warnings of the Summoner;
those presentiments which must have long silently
possessed her, here for the first time finding utterance.
Still more strongly does it evidence that subdued and
serene frame of mind, into which her once vivacious
temperament and painfully vibrating sensibilities were
now so gently and happily subsiding. A delight in
sacred literature, and particularly in the writings of
some of our old divines, became from henceforward
her predominant taste ; and her earnest and diligent
study of the Scriptures was a well-spring of daily
increasing comfort. In these pursuits she derived
invaluable assistance and encouragement from the

friend already mentioned as so kindly directing the education of her son Charles. She now sought no longer to forget her trials—(" wild wish and longing vain !" as such attempts must ever have proved)—but rather to contemplate them through the only true and reconciling medium ; and that relief from sorrow and suffering for which she had once been apt to turn to the fictitious world of imagination, was now afforded her by calm and constant meditation on what can alone be called " *the things that are.*"

It was about this time that a circumstance occurred, by which Mrs. Hemans was greatly affected and impressed. A stranger one day called at her house, and begged earnestly to see her. She was then just recovering from one of her frequent illnesses, and was obliged to decline the visits of all but her immediate friends. The applicant was therefore told that she was unable to receive him; but he persisted in entreating for a few minutes' audience, with such urgent importunity, that at last the point was conceded. The moment he was admitted, the gentleman (for such his manner and appearance declared him to be), explained, in words and tones of the deepest feeling, that the object of his visit was to acknowledge a debt of obligation which he could not rest satisfied without avowing—that to her he owed, in the first instance, that faith and those hopes which were now more precious to him than life itself; for that it was by reading her poem of *The Sceptic* he had been first awakened from the miserable delusions of infidelity, and induced to " search the Scriptures." Having poured forth his thanks and benedictions in an uncontrollable gush of emotion, this strange, but interesting visitant took his departure, leaving her overwhelmed with a mingled sense of joyful gratitude and wondering humility.

The following letter was written during the awful visitation of cholera in Dublin, in the summer of 1832: —" I cannot describe to you the strange thrill that came over me, when, on accidentally going to the window yesterday, I saw one of the black covered litters, which convey the cholera patients to the hospital, passing by, followed by policemen with sabres in their hands. This last precaution is necessary to guard the litters from the infatuated populace, who imagine that the physicians are carrying on some nefarious work (*smothering* is, I believe, their favourite theory) within the vehicle. But the sight I have described to you was so like the actual presence of some dark power sweeping past, that I was for the moment, completely overcome;—and oh! the strange contrasts of life! there were May-dancers in the street scarcely a moment afterwards! Notwithstanding the sick sensation of which I have spoken, my spirits are perfectly composed, and I have not the least intention of taking flight, which many families are now doing. To me there is something extremely solemnizing, something which at once awes and calms the spirit, instead of agitating it, in the presence of this viewless danger, between which and ourselves, we cannot but feel that the only barrier is the mercy of God. I never felt so penetrated by the sense of an entire dependence upon Him; and though I adopt some necessary precautions on account of Charles, my mind is in a state of entire serenity."

The difficulty of keeping up any thing like regular correspondence, and the fear that her old friends might consequently think her negligent or ungrateful, would press upon her, at times, very painfully.

"You have judged me rightly and kindly," she wrote to one always considerate and indulgent. "I should have written to you before, but I have been in a state which made writing most painful, and *you* know too well how the calls for writing shower upon me—sometimes till my heart dies within me: and what I dread most are the reproaches of those who know not how the unsupported and lonely one is often borne down. The state of nervous suffering through which I have passed, is now again quietly subsiding. Yesterday I was able to go to church and receive the sacrament, and to-day, I am commencing an undertaking of which I think you will hear with pleasure —a volume of sacred poetry. My heart is much in it, and I hope to enshrine in its pages whatever I may have been endowed with of power and melody ; so that, should it be my last work, it may be a worthy close. I was grieved to hear that our dear, kind Nortons had been so severely tried ;[1] but they are still blessed in each other—and what earthly happiness can equal, what earthly sorrow counterbalance, that 'full bliss of hearts allied?' None—there is none. Do say how affectionately I think of them—how gratefully ;—but it is vain for me, situated as I am, to think of keeping up distant correspondences. My burthen is, in these things, 'greater than I can bear.'

---

[1] By the loss of children, and other dear relatives.

" I have removed here (36, Stephen's Green), much for the sake of having back rooms, as I suffered greatly from the street noises, where I lived before.'

———

" I have been in a state of great nervous suffering ever since I last wrote to you; it is as if I felt, and more particularly heard, every thing with *unsheathed* nerves.

" There is a line of Coleridge's—

'Oh! for a sleep, for *sleep itself* to rest in!'

I believe I shall require some such quintessence of repose to restore me. I have several literary plans for fulfilment as soon as my health allows. I enjoy much more leisure here than was the case in England, which is at least one great advantage.

" My state of health is such as to cause me frequently great distress and inconvenience. I do not mean so much from the actual *suffering* attendant upon it, as from its making the exertion of writing at times not merely irksome, but positively painful to me; this is, I believe, caused entirely by irregular action of the heart, which affects my head with oppressive fulness, and sudden flushing of the cheeks and temples. All my pursuits are thus constantly interfered with; but I do not wish this to convey to you the language of *complaint;* I am only anxious that it should give assurance of kind and grateful recollection; that it should convince you of my being unchanged in cordial interest, and silent only from causes beyond my power to overrule."

Vol. I.——23

" In my literary pursuits, I fear I shall be obliged to look out for a regular amanuensis. I sometimes retain a piece of poetry several weeks in my memory, from actual dread of writing it down.

" How sorry I was, not to see your friend Neukomm! We were playing at cross-purposes the whole time of his stay in Dublin ; but I *did* hear his organ-playing, and glorious it was — a mingling of many powers. I sent, too, for the volume you recommended to me — the *Saturday Evening* :—surely it is a noble work, so rich in the *thoughts that create thoughts*. I am so glad you liked my little summer-breathing song.[1] I

---

[1] " The Summer's Call." This faculty for realising images of the distant and the beautiful, amidst outward circumstances of apparently the most adverse influence, is thus gracefully illustrated by Washington Irving in the " Royal Poet" of his *Sketchbook:* — " Some minds corrode and grow inactive under the loss of personal liberty ; others grow morbid and irritable ; but it is the nature of the poet to become tender and imaginative in the loneliness of confinement. He banquets upon the honey of his own thoughts, and, like the captive bird, pours forth his soul in melody.

> ‘ Have you not seen the nightingale,
>   A pilgrim cooped into a cage,
> How doth she chant her wonted tale,
>   In that her lonely hermitage ?
> Even there her charming melody doth prove,
> That all her boughs are trees, her cage a grove ’ ”
> ROGER L'ESTRANGE.

Indeed, it is the divine attribute of the imagination, that it is irrepressible, unconfinable ; and that when the real world is shut out, it can create a world for itself, and with a necromantic power can conjure up glorious shapes and forms, and irradiate the gloom of the dungeon. Such was the world of pomp and pageant that lived round Tasso in his dismal cell at Ferrara, when he con-

assure you it quite consoled me for the want of natural objects of beauty around, to heap up their remembered images in one wild strain."

The mention of Neukomm's magnificent organ-playing brings to remembrance one great enjoyment of Mrs. Hemans's residence in Dublin — the exquisite " Music of St. Patrick's," of which she has recorded her impressions in the little poem so entitled. Its effect is, indeed, such as, once heard, can never be forgotten. If ever earthly music can be *satisfying*, it must surely be such as this, bringing home to our bosoms the solemn beauty of our own holy liturgy, with all its precious and endeared associations, in tones that make the heart swell with ecstasy, and the eyes overflow with unbidden tears. There was one anthem, frequently heard within those ancient walls, which Mrs. Hemans used to speak of with peculiar enthusiasm — that from the 3d Psalm — " Lord, how are they increased that trouble me !" The consummate skill exhibited in the adaptation of sound to sense in this noble composition, is, in truth, most admirable. The symphony to the 5th verse — " I laid me down and slept"—with its soft, dreamy vibrations, gentle as the hovering of an angel's wing — the utter *abandon*, the melting into slumber — implied by the half-whispered words, that come breathing as from a world of spirits, almost " steep the senses in forgetful-

---

ceived the splendid scenes of his *Jerusalem ;* and we may consider *The King's Quair,* composed by James of Scotland during his captivity at Windsor, as another of those beautiful breakings forth of the soul from the restraint and gloom of the prison-house."

ness;" when a sudden outbreak, as it were, of life
and light, bursts forth with the glad announcement,
" I awaked, for the Lord sustained me;" and then the
old sombre arches ring with an almost overpowering
peal of triumph, bearing to Heaven's gate the exulting chorus of the 6th and 8th verses.

The spring of 1833 brought somewhat of " healing
on its wings," to the gentle invalid, after all the distressing fluctuations of the winter. " I am sure," she
wrote, " you will have real pleasure in hearing that I
begin to feel something like symptoms of reviving
health; perseverance in the quiescent system, which
seems almost essential to my life, is producing, by slow
degrees, the desired effect. You must not think that
it is my own fault if this system is ever departed from.
I desire nothing but a still, calm, meditative life; but
this is exactly what my position, obliged as I am to
' breast a stormy world alone,' most precludes me
from. Hence, I truly believe, and from no original
disorder of constitution, arises all that I have to bear
of sickness and nervous agitation. Certainly, before
this last and severest attack, I had gone through
enough of annoyance, and even personal fatigue, to
try a far more robust frame. Imagine three removals,
and those *Irish* removals, for me, between October
and January. Each was unavoidable; but I am now,
I trust, settled with people of more civilized habits,
and think myself likely to remain here quietly.[1] How
difficult it is, amidst these weary, heart-wearing, narrow cares, to keep bright and pure the immortal spark

---

[1] This expectation was fully realized. The house to which
she had now removed (No. 20, Dawson Street,) was destined to
be her last earthly home.

within! Yet I strive above all things to be true in *this,* and turn with even deeper and more unswerving love to the holy 'Spirit-land,' and guard it, with more and more of watchful care, from the intrusion of all that is heartless and worldly."

There was, indeed, no fear that *she* would ever become "heartless or worldly." No part of her character was more remarkable than her placid indifference to those trifling annoyances, about which the unoccupied and the narrow-minded are for ever "disquieting themselves in vain." She would often quote the words of Madame l'Espinasse—"*Un grand chagrin tue tout le reste.*" "You know it is part of my philosophy," she once wrote, in allusion to some such every-day troubles, "not to let these kind of things prey upon my peace. Indeed, I believe, deep sorrows, such as have been my lot through life, have not only a tendency to elevate, but in some respects to calm the spirit; at least they so fill it, as to prevent the intrusion of little fretting cares. I have an ample share of these too, but they shall not fret me."

It is scarcely necessary to dwell more emphatically than has been already done, on another strong trait in her nature—her unfeigned dislike to every thing approaching invidious personality—to gossip, literary or otherwise, in any shape, however modified or disguised. Most warmly did she echo the sentiment of Mr. Wordsworth—

> "I am not one who much or oft delight
> To season my fireside with personal talk
> Of friends who live within an easy walk,
> Of neighbours, daily, weekly in my sight."

23 *

~ The following passage from Madame de Stael's *Allemagne* might, with perfect truth, have been applied to her, exemplifying, as it does, the natural kindliness (resulting from real superiority) which is, or ought to be, the unfailing attribute of genius, and which may perhaps be considered as a counter-balancing prerogative for that vain, quenchless yearning for sympathy which is but too often its penalty. " Il y a quelquefois de la méchanceté dans les gens d'esprit ; mais le génie est presque toujours plein de bonté. La méchanceté vient non pas de ce qu'on a trop d'esprit, mais de ce qu'on n'a pas assez. Si l'on pouvait parler des ides, on laisserait en paix les personnes ; si l'on se croyait assuré de l'emporter sur les autres par ses talens naturels, on ne chercherait pas à niveler le parterre sur lequel on veut dominer. Il y a des médiocrités d'âmes deguisées en esprit piquant et malicieux ; mais la vraie supériorité est rayonnante de bons sentimens comme de hautes pensées."

" Do not be surprised at these pencilled characters," wrote Mrs. Hemans to a friend, after a long silence. " I am obliged to write in a reclining posture, and can only accomplish it by these means, without much suffering. I pass a great deal of my time lying on the sofa, and composing my sacred pieces, in which I do hope you will recognise the growth of a more healthful and sustained power of mind, which I trust is springing up within me, even from the elements of deepest suffering. I fear it will be some time before I shall have completed a volume, as, notwithstanding all the retirement in which I live, I have, I think, more claims upon my time and thoughts than ever;

and, alas! fewer *helps,* to use the expressive American word."

In reference to a project for having one of her sons initiated into mercantile pursuits, she thus touchingly alludes to her own precarious state:—"I know not that I can make for him any better choice; and the many warnings which my health gives me, and the increasing reluctance of my spirit (which seems withdrawing itself more and more from earthly things as my health declines) to cope with worldly difficulties, make me very anxious to do what I can, ' whilst it is yet day.' " [1]

The following was addressed to a dear friend in Scotland:—"I could not but feel much affected by .your account of the visit to the tomb of your dear children. A peculiar feeling mingled, however, with my sympathy;—to me there seems something almost

---

[1] In alluding to the same subject some time afterwards, she thus expressed herself to a long-tried friend :—"You have heard, I conclude, that a path has been opened for Claude in America, for which land the poor fellow sailed last May. I the less regretted his destination thitherward, as his inclinations had always been pointed decidedly to that country. I dare say you remember his statistical tastes in early childhood; they continued, or indeed rather grew upon him, and rendered him far more fit for such a scene of action than any of his brothers." In the same letter she spoke with maternal pride and fondness of her son Willoughby (the "little George," of former days), then lately returned from the Military College at Sorèze, and engaged on the Ordnance Survey in the North of Ireland. "His superiors," she wrote, "make the best reports of him. He never loses an opportunity of writing me the most affectionate letters, and takes a delight in my poetry, which, I trust, may be attended with better and higher results than those of *mere* delight."

blessed, and holy, and tranquillizing, in our sorrow for
the dead—so heart-rending are at times the struggles
caused by our passionate affections for the living.
With those who are gone, ' the future cannot contra-
dict the past;' and, where no self-reproach is connected with the memory of former intercourse, the
thoughts arising from their graves must all tend to elevate our nature to the Father of Spirits.   Your description of your dear sister's life and death, was full
of beauty.   I remembered well the lovely picture I
had seen of her in Edinburgh; her mind must indeed
have resembled that sweet and radiant countenance.
Such a loss may well have left a void place in the
circle of which she was the central light.

" Alas, for our dear old friend, Sir Robert Liston!
and the lovely Milburn, with all its rich array of flowers!   I think I could scarcely bear to look on that
place again, where I have been so happy.

" I sincerely hope my kind friends the Alisons are
not to be visited by any more domestic trials.   What
a shock was the removal of that bright, affectionate
spirit, Dr. James Gregory!   Oh, what would this
world be, but for the reflected light from another!"

The autumn of this year (1833) witnessed a happy
meeting between Mrs. Hemans and her sister and brother-in-law, after a five years' separation.   The rav-
ages of sickness on her worn and faded form were
painfully apparent to those who had not seen her for
so long; yet her spirits rallied to all their wonted
cheerfulness, and the powers of her mind seemed more
vivid and vigorous than ever.   With all her own cordial kindliness, she busied herself in forming various

plans for the interest and amusement of her visiters;
and many happy hours of delightful converse and old
home communion were passed by her and her sister
in her two favourite resorts, the lawn of the once
stately mansion of the Duke of Leinster (now occupied by the Dublin Society), and the spacious gardens
of Stephen's Green, which, at certain times of the
day, are almost as retired as a private pleasure-ground.
There was something in the antique and foreign appearance of this fine old square, which made her prefer it to all the magnificence of modern architecture,
so conspicuous in other parts of Dublin ; and she would
describe, with much animation, the striking effect she
had often seen produced by the picturesque and quaint
outlines of its irregular buildings, thrown into dark
relief by the fiery back-ground of a sunset sky. She
spoke at this time, with steadfast earnestness of purpose, of the many projects with which her mind was
stored, referring to them all in the same spirit which
dictated, not long afterwards, what may be considered
as a lasting record of the intended dedication of her
powers, had it pleased God to allow of her continuance
in this imperfect state of being. " I have now," are
her memorable words, " passed through the feverish
and somewhat visionary state of mind, often connected
with the passionate study of art in early life: deep
affections and deep sorrows seem to have solemnized
my whole being, and I now feel as if bound to higher
and holier tasks, which, though I may occasionally lay
aside, I could not long wander from without some sense
of dereliction. I hope it is no self-delusion, but I cannot help sometimes feeling as if it were my true task

to enlarge the sphere of sacred poetry, and extend its influence. When you receive my volume of *Scenes and Hymns,* you will see what I mean by enlarging its sphere, though my plans are as yet imperfectly developed."

In another letter, alluding to the same series of poems, she continues thus:—" I regard it, however, as an undertaking to be carried on and thoroughly wrought out during several years; as the more I look for indications of the connexion between the human spirit and its eternal source, the more extensively I see those traces open before me, and the more indelibly they appear stamped upon our mysterious nature. I cannot but think that my mind has both expanded and strengthened during the contemplation of such things, and that it will thus by degrees arise to a higher and purer sphere of action than it has yet known. If any years of peace and affection be granted to my future life, I think I may prove that the discipline of storms has, at least, not been without a purifying and ennobling influence."

Early in the year 1834, the little volume of *Hymns for Childhood* (which, though written many years before, had never been published in England)[1] was brought out by Messrs. Curry of Dublin, who were also the publishers of the *National Lyrics,* which appeared in a collected form about the same time.

---

[1] They had been printed at Boston, New England, in 1827, at the recommendation; and under the kind auspices of Professor Norton, to whom they had been sent merely for the use of his own children.

Of the latter, Mrs. Hemans thus wrote to her friend Mrs. Lawrence, in the note which accompanied the volume : — " I think you will love my little book, though it contains but the broken music of a troubled heart—for all the hours it will recall to you beam fresh and bright as ever in my memory, though I have passed through but too many of sad and deep excitement, since that period."

And of what she called " the fairy volume of hymns," she wrote to the same friend :—" you will immediately see how unpretending a little book it is ; but it will give you pleasure to know that it has been received in the most gratifying manner, having seemed (as a playful child itself might have done) to win criticism into a benignant smile."

The long-contemplated collection of *Scenes and Hymns of Life* was published soon after the two little volumes above alluded to. In her original dedication of this work to Mr. Wordsworth, Mrs. Hemans had given free scope to the expression of her sentiments, not only of veneration for the poet, but of deep and grateful regard for the friend. From a fear, however, that delicacy on Mr. Wordsworth's part might prevent his wishing to receive in a public form, a testimonial of so much private feeling from a living individual, the intended letter was suppressed, and its substantial ideas conveyed in the brief inscription which was finally prefixed to the volume. It is now hoped that

---

[1] Some of the most interesting pieces in this volume are connected with associations of Wavertree Hall; particularly, " Books and Flowers," " The Haunted House," and " O'Connor's Child."

all such objections to its publication have vanished, and that the revered friend to whom it was addressed, will receive it as the heart-tribute of one to whom flattery was unknown—as consecrated by the solemn truth of a voice from the grave.

Intended Dedication of the " Scenes and Hymns of Life," to William Wordsworth, Esq.

" My dear Sir,

" I earnestly wish that the little volume here inscribed to you, in token of affectionate veneration, were pervaded by more numerous traces of those strengthening and elevating influences which breathe from all your poetry 'a power to virtue friendly.' I wish, too, that such a token could more adequately convey my deep sense, of gratitude for moral and intellectual benefit long derived from the study of that poetry—for the perpetual fountains of ' serious faith and inward glee' which I have never failed to discover amidst its pure and lofty regions—for the fresh green places of refuge which it has offered me in many an hour when

——'The fretful stir
Unprofitable, and the fever of the world
Have hung upon the beatings of my heart;'

and when I have found in your thoughts and images such relief as the vision of your ' Sylvan Wye,' may, at similar times, have afforded to yourself.

" May I be permitted, on the present occasion, to record my unfading recollections of enjoyment from your society—of delight in having heard from your own lips, and amidst your own lovely mountain-land, many of these compositions, the remembrance of which will ever spread over its hills and waters a softer colouring of spiritual beauty? Let me also express to you, as to a dear and most honoured friend, my fervent wishes for your long enjoyment of a widely-extended influence, which cannot but be blessed—of a domestic life, encircling you with yet nearer and deeper sources of happiness; and of those eternal hopes, on whose foundation you have built, as a Christian poet, the noble structure of your works.

"I rely upon your kindness, my dear Sir, for an indulgent reception of my offering, however lowly, since you will feel assured of the sincerity with which it is presented by

"Your ever grateful and affectionate

"FELICIA HEMANS."

The manner in which this work was received, was calculated to inspire its author with every feeling of emulation and encouragement. "I find in the *Athenæum* of last week," she wrote," "a brief, but very satisfactory notice of the *Scenes and Hymns*. The volume is recognised as my best work, and the course it opens out called 'a noble path.' My heart is growing faint—shall I have power given me to tread that way much further? I trust that God may make me at least submissive to his will, whatever that may be."

One of the many literary projects contemplated by Mrs. Hemans at this time, was a series of German studies, consisting of translations of scenes and passages from some of the most celebrated German authors, introduced and connected by illustrative remarks.

The only one of these papers which she ever completed, was that on Goethe's *Tasso*, published in the
New Monthly Magazine for January, 1834; a paper
which well deserves attention, as it embodies so much
of her individual feeling with respect to the high and
sacred mission of the Poet; as well as regarding that
mysterious analogy between the outer world of nature
and the inner world of the heart, which it was so
peculiarly the tendency of her writings to develope.
"Not alone," to quote her own words, "from the
things of the ' everlasting hills,' from the storms or the
silence of midnight skies, will he [the poet] seek the
grandeur and the beauty which have their central
residence in a far more majestic temple.   Mountains
and rivers, and mighty woods, the cathedrals of nature
—these will have their part in his pictures; but their
colouring and shadows will not be wholly the gift of
rising or departing suns, nor of the night with all her
stars; it will be a varying suffusion from the life
within, from the glowing clouds of thought and feeling,
which mantle with their changeful drapery all external creation.

> ——' We receive but what we give,
> And in *our* life alone does nature live.'

Let the poet bear into the recesses of woods and
shadowy hills a heart full-fraught with the sympathies
which will have been fostered by intercourse with his
kind, a memory covered with the secret inscriptions
which joy and sorrow fail not indelibly to write—then
will the voice of every stream respond to him in tones
of gladness or melancholy, accordant with those of his

own soul; and he himself, by the might of feelings
intensely human, may breathe the living spirit of the
,oracle into the resounding cavern or the whispering
oak.   We thus admit it essential to his high office,
that the chambers of imagery in the heart of the
poet must be filled with materials moulded from the
sorrows, the affections, the fiery trials, and immortal
longings of the human soul.   Where love, and faith,
and anguish, meet and contend — where the tones of
prayer are wrung from the suffering spirit — *there* lie
his veins of treasure ; there are the sweet waters
ready to flow from the stricken rock."

The news which arrived from India in the summer
of this year (1834), of the death of her friend Mrs.
Fletcher (the late Miss Jewsbury), affected Mrs. Hemans very deeply.   The early removal of this gifted
and high-minded woman was, indeed, an event to
excite the most sorrowful and startling reflections.
On the 1st of August, 1832, she was married, in a
little quiet church amongst the Welsh mountains,[1] to
the Rev. W. K. Fletcher, one of the chaplains to the
H. E. I. C.   Fourteen months afterwards, she was laid
in her last resting-place, at Poonah, in the "far East,"
having fallen a victim to cholera, whilst travelling
with her husband back to Bombay, from Sholapore,
their first station, which they had been obliged to quit,
in consequence of its extreme unhealthiness.   It is
affecting to retrace passages in her letters, fraught
with forebodings which are now invested with a sad

---

[1] At Penegoes, in Montgomeryshire, then the happy home of
Mrs. Hemans's sister.

solemnity—with " something of prophetic strain." **In**
the very first letter written after her marriage, describing the journey through a desolate tract of coun--
try between Aberystwyth and Rhaiadr, she thus
expressed herself: — " We travelled for seventeen
miles through the most solitary land I ever saw—high,
green, bare hills, inhabited only by sheep; no trees,
no houses, no human beings—it gave us on the land,
a feeling similar to being on the sea—and I believe
our hearts were mutually full of that strange, deep
sadness, that unutterable melancholy, which childish
minds would say was incompatible with happiness,
but which thinking natures know to be inseparable
from enjoyment. It is not the skeleton at the Egyptian feast, but the voice of the Macedonian herald,
bidding the conqueror remember his mortality."

In another letter, written shortly before her departure from England, she says, in alluding to her own
compositions,—" In the best of everything I have done,
you will find one leading idea—*Death:* all thoughts,
all images, all contrasts of thoughts and images, are
derived from living much in the valley of that shadow.

" My poetry, except some half-dozen pieces, may
be consigned to oblivion; but in all, you would find
the sober hue which, to my mind's eye, blends equally
with the golden glow of sunset, and the bright green
of spring, and is seen equally in the 'temple of delight,'
as in the tomb of decay and separation."

Still more striking are the words of one of the last
letters ever received from her, dated only six weeks
before the writer was called away; in which she
speaks of living in a land " where death is such a

swift and cunning hunter, that before you know you
are *ill*, you may be ready to become his prey—where
death, the grave, and forgetfulness, may be the work·
of two days!"

Mrs. Hemans's feelings on this occasion, will be best
shown by the following fragments :—

"I was indeed deeply and permanently affected by
the untimely fate of one so gifted, and so affectionately loving me, as our poor lost friend. It hung the
more solemnly upon my spirits, as the subject of death
and the mighty future had so many, many times been
that of our most confidential communion. How much
deeper power seemed to lie coiled up, as it were, in
the recesses of her mind, than was ever manifested to
the world in her writings! Strange and sad does it
seem that only the broken music of such a spirit
should have been given to the earth—the full and
finished harmony never drawn forth. Yet I would
rather a thousand times that she should have perished
thus, in the path of her chosen duties, than have seen
her become the merely brilliant creature of London
literary life, at once the queen and slave of some
heartless coterie, living upon those poor *succès de soci-
été*, which I think utterly ruinous to all that is lofty,
and holy, and delicate, in the nature of a highly
endowed woman. I put on mourning for her with a
deep feeling of sadness,—I never expected to meet her
again in this life, but there was a strong chain of interest between us, that spell of *mind on mind*, which,
once formed, can never be broken. I felt, too, that
my whole nature was understood and appreciated by
her, and this is a sort of happiness which I consider
24 *

the most rare in all earthly affection. Those who feel
and think deeply, whatever playfulness of manner
may brighten the surface of their character, are fully
unsealed to very few indeed."

" Will you tell Mr. Wordsworth this anecdote of
poor Mrs. Fletcher? I am sure it will interest him.
During the time that the famine in the Deccan was
raging, she heard that a poor Hindoo had been found
lying dead in one of the temples at the foot of an idol,
and with a female child, still living, in his arms. She
and her husband immediately repaired to the spot,
took the poor little orphan away with them, and conveyed it to their own home. She tended it assiduously,
and one of her last cares was to have it placed at a
female missionary school, to be brought up as a Christian."[1]

" I was not well when the news of our poor friend's
death arrived, and was much overcome by it; and
almost immediately afterwards, I was obliged to exert
myself in a way altogether at variance with my feelings. All these causes have thrown me back a good
deal; but I am now surmounting them, and was yesterday able to make one of a party in an excursion to
a little mountain *tarn*[2] about twelve miles from Dublin. The strangely deserted character of the country,
long before this object is reached—indeed, at only

---

[1] In *The Christian Keepsake* for 1838, there is an excellent
likeness of Mrs. Fletcher, with a slight but pleasing Memoir,
written with much feeling and appreciation.

[2] Lough Bray.

seven or eight miles' distance from the metropolis—is
quite astonishing to English eyes; a wide, mountain
tract of country, in many parts without a sign of
human life, or trace of culture or habitation as far as
the sight can reach—magnificent views bursting upon
you every now and then, but all deep solitude, and
the whole traversed by a noble road, a military work
I was told, the only object of which seemed to be a
large barrack in the heart of the hills, now untenanted,
but absolutely necessary for the safety of Dublin not
many years since. Then we reached a little lake,
lying clear, and still, and dark, but sparkling all over
to the sun, as with innumerable fire-flies; high green
hills sweeping down without shore or path, except on
one side, into its very bosom, and all around the same
deep silence. I was only sorry that one dwelling, and
that, of all things, a cottage *ornée*, stood on its bank;
for though it was like a scene of enchantment to enter
and look upon the lonely pool and solemn mountains,
through the coloured panes of a richly-carved and
oak-panelled apartment, still the charm of nature
was in some degree broken by the association of
wealth and refinement."

Mrs. Hemans had projected another visit to Westmoreland in the course of this summer, and a delightful plan had been formed of a meeting there with her
sister and brother-in-law, and of happy days to be
passed together amidst the lovely scenery of the Lakes.
But an attack of fever, by which she was visited in
the month of July, and which reduced her to an alarming state of languor and weakness, compelled her,
sadly and reluctantly, to relinquish all idea of carry-

ing this long-cherished scheme into execution. "I know you will regret my heavy disappointment," she wrote to one of her friends in Liverpool, "when I tell you that I have been obliged sorrowfully to give up the hope of visiting England at present. Whether from the great exertions I had made to clear away all my wearisome correspondence, and arrange my affairs, so as to give myself a month's holiday with a free conscience, or from the intense heat of the weather, which has long greatly oppressed me, I know not; but my fever, which had not been quite subdued, returned upon me the very day I last wrote to you, and in a very few hours rose to such a height, that my strength was completely prostrated. 'I am now pronounced, and indeed feel myself, quite unfit for the possible risk of the passage, and subsequent travelling by coach, and am going this very day, or rather in the cool of the evening, a few miles into the county of Wicklow, for immediate change of air. If my health improve in a day or two, I shall travel on very quietly to get more among the mountains, the fresh, wild, native air of which is to me always an *elixir vitæ ;* but I am going under much depression of feeling, both from my keen sense of disappointment, and because I hate wandering about by myself." [1]

This excursion, far from producing the good effects anticipated, led, on the contrary, to very disastrous ones; for, by a most unfortunate fatality, the little country inn to which Mrs. Hemans repaired for change of air, proved to be infected with scarlet fever, and

---

[1] Her son Charles was gone with a friend into Westmoreland.

this circumstance was concealed by the people of the house, till both herself and her maid had caught the contagion. She thus became again a prisoner from illness, under circumstances of far greater discomfort than before; and so entirely were her strength and spirits subdued by these repeated attacks, that she afterwards described herself as having passed hour after hour, in the beginning of her convalescence, sitting in the little garden of the inn, with her senses absorbed in the tremulous motions of a weeping willow, and tears rolling down her cheeks from absolute weakness and weariness. Like " Mariana in the moated grange,"

> " She said, 'I am aweary, aweary,
> I would that I were dead!' "[1]

As soon as her removal could be undertaken with safety, she returned to Dublin, and by degrees attained once more to a state of partial recovery. " My fever has left me," she wrote to her sister, " with a very great susceptibility to coughs, sore throats, and all that " grisly train," and this, I am afraid, is likely to continue my scourge for a long time. In order to surmount it, I am desired to pass as much time as possible in the open air, which I accordingly do, but with a great sense of languor clinging to me. I went for two or three days to the Archbishop's country-seat, just before Charles's return, and my spirits were cheered by the quiet and the intellectual society of the place. I am now, though often with a deep-sighing weariness (of which, I fear, your own anxieties must have given

---

[1] See the poem of *Mariana*, by Mr. Alfred Tennyson.

you experience also), gradually returning to my employments."—The same letter contained copies of her
two sonnets to Silvio Pellico, to which she thus alluded,
—" I wrote them only a few days ago (almost the first
awakening of my spirit, indeed, after a long silence
and darkness), upon reading that delightful book of
Pellico's,[1] which I borrowed in consequence of what
you had told me of it.   I know not when I have read
any thing which has so deeply impressed me : the gradual brightening of heart and soul into " the perfect
day" of Christian excellence through all those fiery
trials, presents, I think, one of the most touching, as
well as instructing pictures ever contemplated.   How
beautiful is the scene between him and Oroboni, in
which they mutually engage to shrink not from the
avowal of their faith, should they ever return into the
world !   But I could say so much on this subject, which
has quite taken hold of my thoughts, that it would
lead me to fill up my whole letter."
  In another letter she spoke further of this book, as
" a work with which I have been both impressed and
delighted, and one which I strongly recommend you
to procure.   It is the *Prigioni* of Silvio Pellico, a distinguished young Italian poet, who incurred the suspicions of the Austrian government, and was condemned
to the penalty of the *carcere duro* during ten years,
of which this most interesting work contains the narrative.   It is deeply affecting from the heart-springing
eloquence with which he details his varied sufferings.
What forms, however, the great charm of the work,

---

[1] *Le mie Prigioni.*

is the gradual and almost unconsciously-revealed exaltation of the sufferer's character, spiritualized, through suffering, into the purest Christian excellence. It is beautiful to see the lessons of trust in God and love to mankind, brought out more and more into shining light from the depth of the dungeon-gloom; and all this crowned at last by the release of the noble, all-forgiving captive, and his restoration to his aged father and mother, whose venerable faces seem perpetually to have haunted the solitude of his cell. The book is written in the most classic Italian, and will, I am sure, be one to afford you lasting delight."

The same letter, speaking of several books which she had read with strong and varied interest, proceeds thus:—" Amongst the chief of these has been the Correspondence of Bishop Jebb with Mr. Knox, which presents, I think, the most beautiful picture ever developed of a noble Christian friendship, brightening on and on through an uninterrupted period of thirty years. Knox's part of the correspondence is extremely rich in original thought and the highest views of enlightened Christian philosophy. There is much elegance, ' pure religion,' and refined intellectual taste, in the Bishop's letters also, but his mind is decidedly inferior both in fervour and power."

Another affecting allusion to Silvio Pellico's narrative occurs in a subsequent letter—" I have read it more than once, so powerful has been its effect upon my feelings. When the weary struggle with wrong and injustice leads to such results, I then feel that the *fearful mystery of life is solved for me.*"

" A friend kindly brought me yesterday the *Satur-day Magazine* containing Coleridge's letter to his godchild. It is, indeed, most beautiful, and, coming from that sovereign intellect, ought to be received as an invaluable record of faith and humility. It is scarcely possible to read it without tears."[1]

---

[1] As it seems impossible for such a composition to be read too often, the letter is subjoined, for the benefit of those who may not have the means of referring to it.

Coleridge's Letter to his godchild Adam Steinmetz Kinnaird, written only a few days before his death : —

" My dear Godchild,—I offer up the same fervent prayer for you now, as I did kneeling before the altar when you were baptised into Christ, and solemnly received as a living member of His spiritual body, the church. Years must pass before you will be able to read with an understanding heart what I now write. But I trust that the all-gracious God, the Father of our Lord Jesus Christ, the Father of Mercies, who, by his only-begotten Son (all mercies in one sovereign mercy!) has redeemed you from evil ground, and willed you to be born out of darkness, but into light; out of death, but into life ; out of sin, but into righteousness; even into ' the Lord, our righteousness,'—I trust that He will graciously hear the prayers of your dear parents, and be with you as the spirit of health and growth, in body and in mind. My dear godchild! you received from Christ's minister, at the baptismal font, as your Christian name, the name of a most dear friend of your father's, and who was to me even as a son—the late Adam Steinmetz, whose fervent aspirations, and paramount aim, even from early youth, were to be a Christian in thought, word, and deed—in will, mind, and affections I, too, your godfather, have known what the enjoyments of this life are, and what the more refined pleasures which learning and intellectual power can give; I now, on the eve of my departure, declare to you (and earnestly pray that you may hereafter live and act on the conviction), that health is a great blessing, competence

The following extract is from a letter of acknowledgment, on receiving a present of Retzsch's *Outlines* to Schiller's *Song of the Bell* :—" This last noble production of Retzsch's was quite new to me, and you may imagine with how many bright associations of friendship and poesy every leaf of it is teeming for me.   Again and again have I recurred to its beauty-embodied thoughts, and ever with the freshness of a new delight.   The volume, too, is so rich in materials for sweet and bitter fancies, that to an

---

obtained by honourable industry a great blessing, and a great blessing it is, to have kind, faithful, and loving friends and relatives; but that the greatest of all blessings, as it is the most ennobling of all privileges, is to be indeed a Christian.   But I have been, likewise, through a large portion of my later life, a sufferer, sorely affected with bodily pains, languor, and manifold infirmities; and for the last three or four years have, with few and brief intervals, been confined to a sick-room, and at this moment, in great weakness and heaviness, write from a sick-bed, hopeless of recovery, yet without prospect of a speedy removal. And I, thus on the brink of the grave, solemnly bear witness to you, that the Almighty Redeemer, most gracious in his promises to them that truly seek Him, is faithful to perform what He has promised; and has reserved, under all pains and infirmities, the peace that passeth all understanding, with the supporting assurances of a reconciled God, who will not withdraw His Spirit from the conflict, and in His own good time will deliver me from the evil one.   Oh! my dear godchild! eminently blessed are they who begin early to seek, fear, and love their God, trusting wholly in the righteousness and mediation of their Lord, Redeemer, Saviour, and everlasting High Priest, Jesus Christ. Oh! preserve this as a legacy and bequest from your unseen godfather and friend,

" S. T. Coleridge."

" *Grove, Highgate.*"

Vol. I. —— 25

imaginative nature it would be invaluable, were it for this alone. But how imbued it is throughout with grace—the delicate, spiritual grace breathed from the domestic affections, in the full play of their tenderness! I look upon it truly as a religious work; for it contains scarcely a design in which the eternal alliance between the human soul and its Creator is not shadowed forth by devotional expression. How admirably does this manifest itself in the group of the christening—the first scene of the betrothed lovers, with their uplifted eyes of speechless happiness—and, above all, in that exquisite group representing the father counting over his beloved heads, after the conflagration! I was much impressed, too, by that most poetic vision at the close, where the mighty bell, no more to proclaim the tidings of human weal or woe, is lying amidst ruins, and half mantled over by a veil of weeds and wild flowers. What a profusion of external beauty!—but, above all, what a deep 'inwardness of meaning' there is in all these speaking things!"

Very soon after the date of the above letter, that fatal cold was caught, which, following up, as it did, so many trying attacks, completed but too effectually the wreck of a prematurely shattered constitution. Having been recommended, as already mentioned, to be as much as possible in the open air, Mrs. Hemans passed a good deal of time in the Gardens of the Dublin Society, which have been before alluded to, as amongst her most favourite resorts. One day, having repaired there, as usual, with a book, she unfortunately became so absorbed in reading, as to forget how the hours were wearing away, till recalled to herself by the penetrating chill of an autumnal fog, which had suddenly closed around her. She hastened home; but not, alas! without having already imbibed the pestilential influence of the blighting atmosphere. A shuddering thrill pervaded her whole frame, and she felt, as she often afterwards declared, a presentiment that from that moment her hours were numbered. The same evening she was attacked by a fit of ague; and this insidious and harassing complaint continued its visitations for several weeks, reducing her poor wasted form to the most lamentable state of debility, and at length retiring only to make way for a train of symptoms still more fatal and distressing. Yet, while the work of decay was going on thus surely and progressively upon the earthly tabernacle, the bright flame within continued to burn with a pure and holy light, and, at times, even to flash forth with more than wonted brightness. The lyric of "Despondency and Aspiration," which may be considered as her noblest and highest effort, and in which, from a feeling that it might be her last work, she felt anxious to concentrate all her powers, was written during the few intervals accorded her from acute suffering or powerless languor. And in the same circumstances she wrote, or rather dictated, the series of sonnets called *Thoughts during Sickness*, which present so interesting a picture of the calm, submissive tone of her mind, whether engaged in tender remembrances of the past, or in solemn and reverential speculations on the future. The one entitled "Sickness like Night," discloses a view no less affecting than consolatory, of the sweet

and blessed peace which hovered round the couch
where

> "Mutely and helplessly she lay reposing."

> "Thou art like night, O sickness! deeply stilling
>   Within my heart the world's disturbing sound,
> And the dim quiet of my chamber filling
>   With low, sweet voices, by life's tumult drowned.
>
> Thou art like awful night! — thou gatherest round
>   The things that are unseen, though close they lie,
> And with a truth, clear, startling, and profound,
>   Giv'st their dread presence to our mortal eye.
>
> Thou art like starry, spiritual night!
>   High and immortal thoughts attend thy way,
> And revelations, which the common light
>   Brings not, though wakening with its rosy ray
> All outward life. Be welcome, then, thy rod,
> Before whose touch my soul unfolds itself to God."

The last sonnet of the series, entitled "Recovery,"
was written under temporary appearances of convalescence, which proved as fugitive as they were fal-
lacious.

Early in the month of December, Mrs. Hemans having been recommended to try change of air, and the
quiet of the country, her brother and sister-in-law,
who had come up from Kilkenny to see her, and have
a consultation of physicians, were about to remove
her into the County of Wicklow; when the thoughtful
kindness of the Archbishop and Mrs. Whateley placed
at her disposal their own country-seat of Redesdale,
a delightful retirement about seven miles from Dublin, where every comfort was provided for her that
the most delicate consideration could suggest, and

where, for a short season, she appeared to derive some slight benefit from the change. She occasionally exerted herself to write short letters in pencil, to allay the anxieties of her friends; from one of which affecting epistles the following passage is extracted:—

"Redesdale, Sunday Evening, Dec. 13, 1834.

"My fever, though still returning at its hours, is decidedly abated, with several of its most exhausting accompaniments; and those intense, throbbing headaches have left me, and allowed me gradually to resume the inestimable resource of reading, though frequent drowsiness obliges me to use this very moderately. But better far than these indications of recovery, is the sweet religious peace which I feel gradually overshadowing me with its dove-pinions, excluding all that would exclude thoughts of God. I would I could convey to you the deep feelings of repose and thankfulness with which I lay on Friday evening, gazing from my sofa upon a sunset sky of the richest suffusions—silvery green and amber kindling into the most glorious tints of the burning rose. I felt its holy beauty sinking through my inmost being, with an influence drawing me nearer and nearer to God. The stillness here is exquisite; broken only by the occasional notes of the robin, one of which faithful birds yesterday paid us a visit."

Her love of flowers not only continued undiminished, but seemed daily to strengthen into a deeper sentiment, realizing the feelings which had been already depicted in her poem, entitled "Flowers and Music in a room of Sickness."

25 *

——"God hath purified my spirit's eye,
And in the folds of this consummate rose
I read bright prophecies. I see not there,
Dimly and mournfully, the word *'farewell'*
On the rich petals traced: No—in soft veins
And characters of beauty, I can read—
'Look up, look heavenward!' "

"I really think that pure passion for flowers," she wrote, in one of her notes at this time to Mrs. Lawrence, "is the only one which long sickness leaves untouched with its chilling influence. Often during this weary illness of mine, have I looked upon new books with perfect apathy, when, if a friend has sent me a few flowers, my heart has 'leaped up' to their dreamy hues and odours, with a sudden sense of renovated childhood, which seems to me one of the mysteries of our being."

Her son Charles was the inseparable companion of these solemn, yet blessed hours; and he will ever look back with a thankful heart on the privilege granted to him of being thus constantly permitted to profit by her example, to soothe her loneliness by his pious devotion, to read to her, to write for her, to be in all things her gently ministering spirit. During the Christmas holidays, these grateful offices were affectionately shared by his brother Henry, then a schoolboy at Shrewsbury. How often must the earnest eyes of the languid sufferer have rested on these, her bright and blooming ones, with all a mother's tenderness and pride—how must her heart have overflowed with unutterable yearnings at the thoughts of leaving them! —how fervently must she have committed them in silent, inward supplication, to the love and care of their Heavenly Father!

It would be doing injustice to the memory of a humble, but not the less valuable friend, to omit mentioning the great comfort Mrs. Hemans derived from the indefatigable services of her faithful attendant, Anna Creer; a young person whose excellent principles, undeviating propriety, and real superiority of mind and manner, would have done honour to any station, while they made her a perfect treasure in the one of which she fulfilled the duties so admirably. She was born of respectable parents in the Isle of Man, and had been carefully educated in a manner befitting her line of life. Mrs. Hemans had taken great pains to improve her; and from the force of grateful attachment, and a certain inherent refinement which seemed a part of her nature, she almost insensibly acquired a sort of assimilation in her ideas and expressions to those of her kind mistress. The assiduity of her attendance, cheerful and unwearied by night and by day, cannot be remembered without thankful appreciation; and this is now blended with a touching interest, excited by many circumstances of·her subsequent illness and death.[1]

---

[1] Two years after the death of her mistress, she married a most respectable tradesman in Dublin, who had been long attached to her — the proprietor of the house in which Mrs. Hemans had latterly resided. In this house she herself died, in May, 1838 (having fallen into a decline, in consequence of a premature confinement), and was buried in the same vault which holds the remains of her dear mistress. The subjoined extract is given, as affording some idea of her warm heart and singularly

During her stay at Redesdale, Mrs. Hemans was
continually visited by the benevolent Mrs. Whateley,

---

delicate mind.   It is part of a letter written by her, a few months
after Mrs. Hemans's death ·—"It is a continual cause of thankfulness to me that I was so wonderfully supported, even to the
last sad hour;—sad it must ever be to me; it is a thing not to
wear off.   Oh no! with me it seems to deepen daily—remembrances grow dearer   My thought of her is like some hidden,
treasured thing, which no power could win from me.   I feel it
would be downright selfishness to wish her back· it may well be
said this was not her rest.   She ever seemed to me as a wanderer from her Heavenly Father's mansion, who knew too much of
that home to seek a resting-place here!   She often said to me,
'I feel like a tired child—wearied, and longing to mingle with
the pure in heart.'   At other times she would say,—'I feel as
if I were sitting with Mary at the feet of my Redeemer, hearing
the music of His voice, and learning of Him to be meek and
lowly.'   And then she would say, 'Oh, Anna, do not you love
your kind Saviour?   The plan of Redemption was indeed a
glorious one, humility was indeed the crowning work.   I am
like a quiet babe at His feet, and yet my spirit is full of His
strength.   When any body speaks of His love to me, I feel as
if they were too slow; my spirit can mount alone with Him into
those blissful realms, with far more rapidity.'

"My heart gets too full for utterance when I think of her
affectionate manner to me.   She often told me that she believed
I had been sent to her in answer to her earnest prayer, and said
that, whatever might be her fate, I might always feel that my
being with her had not been in vain.   These were her words;
and the Searcher of hearts only knows how thankful, yet hum-
bled, I feel for such an inestimable blessing.   It is one for which
I feel I shall have to render an account.   May it prove a blessed
one!   I wish I could tell you more of what 'she said, but my
language is so poor, so weak, that when I would try, it is as if I
were robbing her words of their brightness; but then I know
that none can speak as she did.   These are not words of course;
no, I can truly say my ties to earth are weakened, because she
is no longer here."

whose gentle sympathy was a balm to her heart. The true brotherly kindness of her excellent friend, Colonel D'Aquilar — his indefatigable and thoughtful attentions, prompted as well by his own generous regard as by the affectionate anxiety of his sister, Mrs. Lawrence, were a source of comfort, the consciousness of which must be its own reward, as words are inadequate to do justice to it. And the same must be said of the disinterested zeal and solicitude of Mrs. Hemans's medical friends, Dr. Graves and Dr. Croker.

Not long after her removal into the country, her sympathies were sorrowfully excited by an event which plunged into the deepest distress the family with which she was most intimate, and deprived herself, individually, of a valuable and paternal friend; — the death, after a very short illness, of the late J. C. Graves, Esq. Most touchingly did she lament her own inability to minister at such a moment to the griefs of those for whom she felt so sincerely. " Again and again have I thought of you," were the words of her letter on this occasion, to one of his afflicted daughters, " and wished that my health allowed me to be near you, that I might make some little efforts to comfort and sustain. Few can more deeply enter into all you have suffered than myself, in whose mind the death-bed scene of my beloved and excellent mother is still as mournfully distinct as the week when that bereavement occurred, which threw me to struggle upon a harsh and bitter world. But, dearest C., there comes a time when we feel that God has drawn us nearer to Himself by the chastening influence of

such trials, and when we thankfully acknowledge that
a higher state of spiritual purification — the great
object, I truly believe, of all our earthly discipline —
has been the blessed result of our calamities.   I am
sure that in your pure and pious mind this result will
ere long take place, and that a deep and reconciling
calm will follow the awakening sense of God's paren-
tal dealings with the spirit."

The following words are from a note dated January 27th :—"I cannot possibly describe to you the sub-
duing effect that long illness has produced upon my
mind.   I seem to have been passing ' through the valley of the shadow of death,' and all the vivid interests of life look dim and pale around me.   I am still
at the Archbishop's palace,[1] where I receive kindness
truly *heart-warm.*   Never could anything be more
cordial than the strong interest he and his amiable
wife have taken in my recovery.   My dear Henry
has enjoyed his holidays here greatly, as I should have
done too (he has been so mild and affectionate), but
for constant pain and sickness."

The future destination of this " dear Henry," now
of an age to enter upon the active duties of life, and
work out his own path to independence, had been for
some time a subject which pressed heavily upon the
mind of his anxious mother.   It may, therefore, well
be imagined with what unspeakable joy and gratitude

---

[1] Redesdale is not, properly speaking, the Archbishop's *palace,*
but his country-seat; but there were old and dear associations
attached to the former name, which made it very natural that
Mrs. Hemans should use it in connexion with "kindness *heart-
warm.*"

she hailed the arrival of a boon so utterly unexpected as a letter from Sir Robert Peel, (expressed in terms no less honourable to the writer, than gratifying to the receiver), appointing her son to a clerkship in the Admiralty, and accompanied by a most munificent donation, which, emanating from such a quarter, could create no feelings but those of heartfelt thankfulness, unmingled with any alloy of false delicacy or mistaken pride.

Mrs. Hemans was at first entirely at a loss to trace the channel through whose means this stream of bounty had found its way to her retirement; but it was with less of surprise than of grateful pleasure, that she at length discovered it to have been through the affectionate exertions of her friend Mrs. Lawrence, that an interest so powerful had been awakened in her favour. The joyful excitement of a happiness so unlooked for—the relief of having such a weight of anxiety thus lifted from her heart—roused her for a time from the almost lethargic languor into which her feeble frame was gradually sinking, and her energies broke forth once more, " as the tender grass springeth out of the earth by clear shining after rain." She exerted herself to write many letters to impart the glad tidings to her friends, speaking invariably of this noble act of kindness as having filled her mind with joy and thankfulness; as being " a sunshine without a cloud." Again must her own words be quoted from one of the last of her letters to Mrs. Lawrence :—

" Well, my dear friend, I hope my life, if it be spared, may now flow back into its native course of quiet thoughtfulness. You know in how rugged a channel

the poor little stream has been forced, and through
what rocks it has wrought its way; and it is now longing for repose in some still valley. It has ever been
one of my regrets that the constant necessity of pro-
viding sums of money to meet the exigencies of the
boys' education, has obliged me to waste my mind in
what I consider mere desultory effusions:

> ——— 'Pouring myself away,
> As a wild bird, amidst the foliage, turns
> That which within him thrills, and beats and burns,
> Into a fleeting lay.'

" My wish ever was to concentrate all my mental
energy in the production of some more noble and complete work; something of pure and holy excellence
(if there be not too much presumption in the thought),
which might permanently take its place as the work
of a British poetess. I have always, hitherto, written
as if in the breathing times of storms and billows.
Perhaps it may not even yet be too late to accomplish
what I wish, though I sometimes feel my health so
deeply prostated, that I cannot imagine how I am ever
to be raised up again. But a greater freedom from
those cares, of which I have been obliged to bear up
under the whole responsibility, may do much to restore
me; and though my spirits are greatly subdued by long
sickness, I feel the powers of my mind in full matu-
rity. . . . . The very idea of possessing such
friends as yourself and your dear, noble brother, is a
fountain of strength and hope. . . . . I am very,
very weary of writing so long; yet still feel as if I had
a thousand things to say to you.

" With regard to my health, I can only tell you that

what I now feel is a state of sinking languor, from which it seems impossible I should ever be raised. I am greatly exhausted with this long letter, so farewell."

A reaction of still more distressing debility, and an increase of other alarming symptoms, followed but too rapidly this temporary revival. "I cannot tell you how much I suffer," was the reluctant confession of a pencilled note to her sister, "nor what a state of utter childlike weakness my poor wasted limbs are reduced to. But my mind is, as I desired Charlie to tell you, in a state of the deepest resignation; to which is now added a warm thankfulness to God for this His latest mercy."

The increased danger of her situation making it advisable that she should return into Dawson Street to be nearer her physicians, she quitted Redesdale in the beginning of March, with a heart full of gratitude for the kindly shelter it had afforded her. She had now almost entirely lost the use of her limbs, and had to be lifted in and out of the carriage by her brother, who had come up from Kilkenny on purpose to superintend the arrangements for her removal, and who from this time to the hour of her death, never left her, but when summoned into the country by his official duties; whilst his affectionate wife, who arrived in Dublin the following week, continued unremitting in her devoted attendance to the last. The melancholy group was soon afterwards joined by her sister, who remained with her until called away by still more imperative claims; and for a few days by her son Willoughby, then employed (as has already been mentioned) upon the Ordnance Survey in the north of Ireland.

From this time, the daily declining invalid could only leave her bed to be laid upon a couch in the same room; and her sufferings, caused by the organic disease which had succeeded the ague, were occasionally most severe.   But all was borne uncomplainingly. Never was her mind overshadowed with gloom; never would she allow those around her to speak of her condition as one deserving commiseration.   The dark and silent chamber seemed illumined by light from above, and cheered with songs of angels; and she would say, that, in her intervals from pain, " no poetry could express, nor imagination conceive, the visions of blessedness that flitted across her fancy, and made her waking hours more delightful than those even that were given to temporary repose."   Her sleep was calm and happy; and none but pleasing dreams ever visited her couch.   This she acknowledged as a great and unexpected blessing; for, in all her former illnesses, she had been used to suffer either from painfully intense wakefulness, or disturbed and fitful slumbers, which exhausted, rather than refreshed, the worn and feverish frame.   Changeful as were the moods of her mind, they were invariably alike in this—that serenity and submission as to her own state, and the kindest consideration for others, shed their sweet influence over all.   At times, her spirit would appear to be already half-ethercalized; her mind would seem to be fraught with deep, and holy, and incommunicable thoughts, and she would entreat to be left perfectly alone, in stillness and darkness, " to commune with her

own heart," and reflect on the mercies of her.Saviour
She continually spoke of the unutterable comfort she
derived from dwelling on the contemplation of the
Atonement.   To one friend, for whom she dreaded
the influence of adverse opinions, she sent a solemn
exhortation, earnestly declaring that this alone was
her "rod and staff," when all earthly supports were
failing.   To another, she desired the assurance might
be given, that "the tenderness and affectionateness
of the Redeemer's character, which they had often
contemplated together, was now a source, not merely
of reliance, but of positive happiness to her—*the
sweetness of her couch*."   At less solemn moments she
would converse with much of her own kindly cheerfulness, sending affectionate messages to her various
friends, and recalling old remembrances with vivid
and endearing minuteness.   Her thoughts reverted
frequently to the days of childhood—to the old house
by the sea-shore—the mountain rambles—the haunts
and the books which had formed the delight of her
girlish years.   One evening, whilst her sister was sitting by her bed-side, a yellow gleam from the setting
sun, which streamed through the half-closed shutters,
produced a peculiar effect upon the wall, exactly similar to what used to be observed at sunset in their old
school-room at Gwrych.   They both remarked the
circumstance, and what a gush of recollections was
thus called forth!   The association was like that so
often produced by a peculiar scent, or a remembered
strain of music.[1]   Yet in all, save that streak of light,

---

[1] ————"It may be a sound —
A tone of music — summer's eve — or spring —

how different were the two scenes!—The one, a chamber of sickness in a busy city—its windows (for a backroom had been chosen, for the sake of quietness,) looking down into a dull court; the other, a cheerful apartment in an old country-house, every thing about it bespeaking the presence of happy childhood, and the wide, pleasant window opening out upon fresh green fields; beyond them the silver sea; and far in the west, the sun sinking behind the dark, bold promontory of the Orme's Head. And in the inmates of those two rooms, the contrast was no less striking. Of the two joyous children, one, " the favourite and the flower," now a worn and faded form, lay on her dying bed; the other, on the eve of partings worse than death, destined to feel the sad force of the affecting old epitaph:—

> " Why doe I live, in life a thralle,
>   Of joye and alle berefte?
> *Their* wings were growne, to heaven they're flowne—
>   'Cause I had none, I'm lefte."[1]

The powers of memory for which Mrs. Hemans had always been so remarkable, shone forth with increased brightness whilst her outward frame was so visibly decaying. She would lie for hours without speaking or moving, repeating to herself whole chapters of the Bible, and page after page of Milton and Wordsworth. The volume of *Yarrow Revisited*,

---

A flower — the wind — the ocean — which shall wound,
Striking the electric chain wherewith we are darkly bound."
                    Childe Harold, Canto iv. Stanza xxiii.

[1] In Crediton Church, near Exeter.

which was published at this time, and sent to her by
her revered friend, with an autograph inscription,
afforded her great delight.[1]   Amongst the many messages of cordial remembrance which she sent to her
personal friends, as well as to some of those with
whose minds alone she had held communion, was one
to Miss Mitford, desiring she might be told how often
some of her sweet woodland scenes rose up before
her, as in a camera obscura, filling the dark room
with pleasant rural sights; with the scent of the new-
mown hay or the fresh fern, and the soothing sound
of waters.   Her "Remembrances of Nature," described with so deep a feeling in one of her sonnets,
continued equally intense and affectionate to the last.
A passage from a work which had long been high in
her favour, was now brought home to her thoughts
with a truth equal to its eloquence.   "O unseen
Spirit of Creation! that watchest over all things—the
desert and the rock, no less than the fresh water,
bounding on like a hunter on his path, when his heart
is in his step—or the valley girded by the glad woods,
and living with the yellow corn—to me, thus sad and

---

[1] It would have been very dear to her, could she have foreseen the delicate and appropriate commemoration awarded to
her by Mr. Wordsworth, in the elegiac stanzas which record the
high names of some of his most distinguished contemporaries,
summoned, in quick succession, " to the land whence none return :"—

> "Mourn rather for that holy spirit,
>   Sweet as the spring, as ocean deep,
> For her, who, ere her summer faded,
>   Has sunk into a breathless sleep."
>   See WORDSWORTH'S *Poems* (*new edition*), *Vol. V.* p. 336.

26 *

baffled, thou hast ministered as to the happiest of thy
children !—thou hast whispered tidings of unutterable
comfort to a heart which the world sated while it de-
ceived. Thou gavest me a music, sweeter than that
of palaces, in the mountain wind — thou badest the
flowers and the common grass smile up to me as children to the face of their father." [1]

One of the few visiters admitted to her room, after
she became entirely confined to it, was that most
gifted and gracious child (for such he then was, both
in years and appearance), Giulio Regondi, in whose
wonderful musical genius she had previously taken
great delight, whilst his guileless and sensitive nature
inspired her with a warm feeling of interest. The
lines she had addressed to him in the preceding year,
flowed from that well-spring of maternal kindliness
which was ever gushing within her bosom, and which
made every child—still more every loving and motherless child—an object towards which her heart yearn-
ed with tender sympathy. The little fellow showed
the greatest anxiety during her illness, and was constant in his spontaneous enquiries. Sometimes he
would call to ask for her on his way to play at the
Castle concerts, or at some other evening party ; and
as he stood in the doorway, with his innocent face, his
delicate form, his long fair hair streaming down his
shoulders, and his whole air and bearing so different
from the everyday beings around him, one might
almost have taken him for a messenger from " the
better land."

---

[1] " The New Phædo," in *The Student*, Vol. II. p. 355.

It is impossible to describe the considerate and un
ceasing attentions which were continually bringing
assurance to the patient sufferer, not merely of the
watchful kindness of friends, but of the generous
interest of strangers.[1] All this she would acknowledge with the most grateful emotion, and even when
unable to partake of the luxuries which poured in so
lavishly from every imaginable quarter, they were
still welcomed and appreciated as tokens of thoughtful recollection. But " flowers, fresh flowers !"—these
were ever hailed as things of " deep meaning" and
happy omen ; and never was her couch unblessed by
their gentle presence. For this gratification she was
more than once indebted to the kindness of a fellow
sufferer, at that time under the care of her own
friendly physician, Dr. Croker; this was the Rev.
Hugh White (the author of *Meditations and Addresses on Prayer*, and of several other religious
works), who was then considered to be in a state
little less precarious than her own, though it pleased
God, after long chastening, to " heal his sickness,"
and enable him to resume the duties of a " good and

---

[1] This was particularly shown in the instance of one lady who
was most assiduous in her personal enquiries, and was continually bringing some new delicacy to tempt the capricious appetite
of the invalid. There was a sort of interesting mystery attached to these fairy favours, as it never could be discovered from
whom they proceeded. The lady used to alight from an elegant
equipage at the corner of the street, come up unattended to the
door, and ask to see Anna Creer, whose entreaties to be told her
name were proffered in vain, " *That*," she used to say, " was of
no consequence ; she only hoped that her attentions might be received as kindly as they were meant."

faithful servant." The impressions under which
these tokens were sent and received, as from one
dying Christian to another, invested them with a
peculiar interest. Mrs. Hemans had desired that a
copy of her sonnet to " Flowers in a Sick Room"
should be sent to Mr. White, and was sensibly touched by the note in which he wrote to thank her for it,
as " so sweetly expressing the pleasurable and pious
feelings their ' pure and lovely forms' are calculated
to awaken in the bosom of one who delights to be
reminded, by every object in creation, of that most
precious and consolatory truth, that ' God is love.' "
Another passage from the same note, was equally in
unison with her own feelings. " I have been sorry, in
one sense, to hear that you have latterly been so
great a sufferer, and I can indeed sympathize with
you in many of the trying feelings attendant on a
broken and declining state of health. But as I believe
I am writing to one who has tasted that the Lord is
gracious, and has been given to know something of
that love which passeth knowledge, I almost feel as if
it were wrong to say I am sorry, that a gracious, and
compassionate, and faithful Saviour is fulfilling to you
His own precious promise — ' As many as I love, I
rebuke and chasten.' "

The conviction of the inestimable value of such
discipline, was, indeed, ever present to her mind,
mingled with the deepest humility, the most entire
resignation — an equal readiness to live or die — a
saying with the whole heart — " Behold the hand
maid of the Lord — Be it unto me according to Thy
word."

"I feel," she would say, "as if hovering between heaven. and earth;" and she seemed, in truth, so raised towards the sky, that all worldly things were obscured and diminished to her view, whilst the ineffable glories of eternity dawned upon it more and more brightly. Even her affections, warm and eager, and sensitive as they had been, were subdued into the same holy calm; and meetings and partings, which in other days would have thrilled her with joy, or wrung her very heart with grief, were now sustained with the sweet, yet solemn composure, of one whose hopes have " surely there been fixed," where meetings are *for ever,* and partings unknown. Of all she had ever done in the exercise of the talents with which it had pleased God to intrust her, she spoke in the meekest and lowliest spirit; often declaring how much more ardently than ever, had life been prolonged, her powers would have been consecrated to His service: and if a gentle regret would sometimes intrude, as she thought of the many literary designs on which her mind and heart had latterly been bent, but which were now dissipated for ever, she would console herself with the line dictated by Milton under analogous circumstances—

"Those also serve who only stand and wait." [1]

There was at times an affecting inconsistency in the words she would let fall to those around her—sometimes as if anticipating a renewal of their earthly intercourse; at others, revealing, by some allusion or

---

[1] See Milton's Sonnet on his Blindness.

injunction fraught with farewell tenderness, how completely all idea of such a possibility had passed away
from her mind.   One day, when her sister was beside
her, she repeated, with calm emphasis, the old homely
verse—

> "Fear no more the heat o' the sun,
>   Nor the furious winter's rages,
> Thou thy worldly task hast done,
>   Home art gone and ta'en thy wages."

adding—" Those words may soon be said for me."
And the circumstance of her sinking to rest on the
Saturday night, brought them most touchingly back
to remembrance.

On Sunday evening, the 15th of March, it had been
arranged that she was to receive the sacrament from
the hands of the Rev. Dr. Dickinson (one of the Archbishop's chaplains), who was in the habit of visiting
and reading to her.   Shortly before the appointed
hour, she was seized with a paroxysm of coughing, so
violent and prolonged, that those who stood around
her bed, scarcely expected she could survive it; and
the exhaustion which followed was most alarming.
When a little revived, she desired that the sacred rite
might still be performed.   Sadly and solemnly did
those holiest words fall on the hearts of the little group
of mourners assembled in the quiet chamber—on one
young heart, more especially, that of the dear, innocent boy, admitted to his first communion beside his
mother's deathbed; while *she* alone was calm amongst
the trembling, placid amidst the weeping.[1]   A night

---

[1] "I came again: the place was bright
    ' With something of celestial light'—

of intense anxiety followed; yet not only did it pass without further alarm, but the morning brought revival, and even some symptoms of improvement, as though a sort of crisis had been gone through. Once more the idea of a hope—a chance—of recovery, gained unconscious admission in the minds of those who, a week before, would have thought the mere mention of such a possibility absolutely chimerical. The advance of spring appeared to give somewhat of a fresh impulse to her frame, as soft showers might, for a season, revive a drooping flower. The images of external nature haunted her, as by the working of a secret sympathy, more vividly than ever; and her "green books," as she would fancifully call them, were again laid on the little table beside her bed, which, with "the ruling passion, strong in death," she loved to see covered with volumes, one of which would

---

A simple altar by the bed,
For high communion meetly spread,
Chalice, and plate, and snowy vest —
We ate and drank: then calmly blest,
All mourners — one with dying breath,
We sate and talk'd of Jesus' death.

"Oh! soothe us, haunt us, night and day,
Ye gentle spirits far away,
With whom we shared the cup of grace,
Then parted; ye to Christ's embrace,
We to the lonesome world again,
Yet mindful of th' unearthly strain
Practised with you at Eden's door,
To be sung on, where angels soar
With blended voices evermore."

Visitation of the Sick, in Keeble's *Christian Year*.

always lie open. Amongst the works of this nature which she looked over or listened to with the greatest interest, were Gilpin's *Forest Scenery*, and Bucke's *Beauties, Harmonies, and Sublimities of Nature.* And the poetry of Bowles, one of her early favourites, whom for years she had scarcely read or thought of, was now recurred to with a sort of old home feeling, and affectionate recognition of its mild and soothing beauty. Another book must be mentioned as having been peculiarly pleasing to her at this time—the *Lives of Sacred Poets*, by R. A. Willmott, Esq. Her mind dwelt with much comfort and complacency on those records of the pure and good, whose pious thoughts and quaint expressions had latterly gained such a hold upon her heart. Many of the poetical extracts given in that volume are now tenderly associated with her remembrance, particularly those lines from Quarles's elegy on the death of Archbishop Usher:—

"Then weep no more; see how his peaceful breast
Rock'd by the hand of death, takes quiet rest.
Disturb him not! but let him sweetly take
A full repose; he hath been long awake."

And yet more intimately connected with the memory of these latter days, is the account of the death of Madame de Mornay, in the second volume of the *Lives of Eminent Christians;* which she entered into with the deepest interest, and earnestly recommended as a beautiful and consolatory picture, showing in bright, yet not exaggerated colours, " how a Christian can die."

Under the fond and fugitive delusions into which this unexpected turn in her malady had beguiled the anxious watchers round her, and occasionally, as it appeared, even the sufferer herself, her sister, recalled by yet stronger ties, bade her farewell, on the 1st of April. The same fluctuations of hope and fear continued to assert their alternate ascendency during the earlier part of that month; but it soon became but too evident that, though many of the most imminent and distressing symptoms had been subdued, they had only given place to a consuming hectic fever, which went on surely and insidiously wasting the last remnants of vitality; now lending to its victim an aspect of illusive energy, now sinking her into the deepest extreme of passive and helpless prostration.

After the exhausting vicissitudes of days when it seemed that the night of death was indeed at hand— of nights when it was thought that she could never see the light of morning; wonderful even to those who had witnessed, throughout her illness, the clearness and brightness of the never-dying principle, amidst the desolation and decay of its earthly companion, was the concentrated power and facility with which, on Sunday, the 26th of April, she dictated to her brother the "Sabbath Sonnet," the last strain of the "sweet singer," whose harp was henceforth to be hung upon the willows.

"How many blessed groups this hour are bending,
 Through England's primrose meadow-paths, their way
 Toward spire and tower, 'midst shadowy elms ascending,
 Whence the sweet chimes proclaim the hallow'd day!
 The halls, from old heroic ages grey,
 Pour their fair children forth; and hamlets low,
 With whose thick orchard blooms the soft winds play,

VOL. I.——27

Send out their inmates in a happy flow,
Like a freed vernal stream; *I* may not tread
With them those pathways—to the feverish bed
Of sickness bound; yet, O my God! I bless
Thy mercy, that with Sabbath peace hath fill'd
My chasten'd heart, and all its throbbings still'd
To one deep calm of lowliest thankfulness."[1]

Little now remains for the biographer, but—

"A soft, sad, miserere chant
For a soul about to go."

After this last effort, the shadows of death began
to close in apace. The wing, once so buoyant and
fearless, was now meekly folded, and the weary,
wounded bird longed only for rest. During the last
week of her life, she became subject to slight wanderings; but the images she dwelt upon were always
pleasing or beautiful. She still loved to be read to,
and seemed to feel a tranquillizing influence from the
sound of the words, even when incapable of attending

---

[1] Amongst the many tributes of interest and admiration elicited
by a poem, so remarkable to all readers—so precious to many
hearts—the following expressions, contained in a letter from the
late venerable Bishop of Salisbury to Mrs. Joanna Baillie (and
already published by the latter), are too pleasingly applicable not
to be inserted here. "There is something peculiarly touching in
the time, the subject, and the occasion of this death-bed sonnet,
and in the affecting contrast between the 'blessed groups' she
describes, and her own (humanly speaking) helpless state of sickness; and that again contrasted with the hopeful state of mind
with which the sonnet concludes, expressive both of the quiet
comforts of a Christian Sabbath, and the blessed fruits of profit-
able application. Her 'Sweet Chimes' on 'Sabbath Peace,'
appear to me very characteristic of the writer."

to their import. Four days before her death, she read to herself the Collect, Epistle, and Gospel for the preceding Sunday—the fourth Sunday after Easter. The gracious and "comfortable words" of that gospel, mingling the consolations of Divine compassion with the parting tenderness of human love, were, perhaps, the most appropriate on which her fading eyes could have rested; nor could she fail to apply to herself the coincidence of some of the expressions—" Now, I go my way to Him that sent me"—" I go to my Father, and ye see me no more"—and, " Because I have said these things unto you, sorrow hath filled your hearts." And, as her feeble hands still held the cherished book, how fervently must she have inwardly responded to the words of the dying George Herbert, when, being asked what prayers he would prefer, he replied — " O sir, the prayers of *my mother*, the Church of England—no other prayers are equal to them !"

In her kind friend Dr. Croker, she was wont to say that she had at once a physician and a pastor. He frequently read to her, and particularly out of a little book which she dearly loved, and which he had first made known to her—a selection from the works of Archbishop Leighton. The last time of her listening to it, she repeatedly exclaimed, "beautiful! beautiful!" and, with her eyes upraised, seemed occupied in communing with herself, and mentally praying. She was attended to the last with the most watchful affection by her brother and his wife, by her darling Charles, and her faithful Anna, to whom she said, when all was fast drawing to a close, that " she had been making her peace with God;—that she felt all at peace within her bosom."

On Saturday the 16th of May, she sank into a gentle slumber, which continued almost unbroken throughout the day; and at nine o'clock in the evening, her spirit passed away without pain or struggle, and, it is humbly hoped, was translated, through the mediation of her blessed Redeemer, to that rest which remaineth to the people of God.

And those who loved her best—in whose hearts her departure has left an aching void which they must bear with them to the grave—who feel that a light is taken from their path which nothing earthly can restore—can yet thankfully and submissively acknowledge that "it is well!"—can rejoice to think of her in safety and repose; and, with spirits chastened like her own, can bless their Heavenly Father, that now, "of his great mercy," after the toils and trials of her mortal career, "He giveth his beloved sleep."

Her remains were deposited in a vault beneath St. Anne's Church in Dublin, almost close to the house where she died. A small tablet has been placed above the spot where she is laid, inscribed with her name, her age, and the date of her death, and with the following lines from a dirge of her own :—

> "Calm on the bosom of thy God,
>   Fair Spirit! rest thee now!
> Ev'n while with us thy footsteps trode,
>   His seal was on thy brow.
> Dust to its narrow house beneath!
>   Soul to its place on high!
> They that have seen thy look in death,
>   No more may fear to die."

A similar memorial, bearing the following inscription, is erected in the Cathedral of St. Asaph, beneath one which is consecrated to the remembrance of her mother: —

THIS TABLET,

PLACED HERE BY HER BROTHERS,

IS

IN MEMORY OF

FELICIA HEMANS,

WHOSE CHARACTER IS BEST POURTRAYED

IN HER WRITINGS.

SHE DIED IN DUBLIN, MAY 16th, 1835.

AGED 41

END OF MEMOIR.

MRS. HEMANS.

LEA & BLANCHARD,

PHILADELPHIA,

WILL SHORTLY PUBLISH

A COMPLETE AND UNIFORM EDITION

OF

MRS. HEMANS'S WORKS;

TO WHICH IS PREFIXED

A MEMOIR BY HER SISTER,

MRS. HUGHES.

In Six Volumes, Royal Duodecimo.

PROSPECTUS.

FROM the high reputation which the writings of MRS. HEMANS have attained, and from the influence which they seem destined to exercise over the public mind, alike by their loftiness of sentiment, by their purity of moral and religious feeling, and by their beauty of language, there can be no doubt that their Author has taken a permanent place amongst the Classics of Great Britain. Hitherto her compositions have only appeared in compact volumes, while others have never been presented in an acknowledged form. The Publishers have, therefore, resolved upon making a complete and uniform edition of the whole, in a style similar to their recent issue of the Poetical Works of SCOTT, and his Life, by Lockhart.

·In accomplishing this object more satisfactorily, they have deemed it of importance to adhere, in some measure, to the chronological order in which the various writings of Mrs. Hemans appeared—that the developement of her mind may be thus more distinctly shown; and, as intellectual efforts formed its epochs, each volume will open with one or other of her more elaborate productions. It is also here proper to mention, that such of her MS. relics, as her literary executors think fit will be now for the first time submitted to the public eye.

GENERAL CONTENTS.

Volume I., consists of a memoir of Mrs. Hemans, from the pen of her sister, containing authentic records of her life, together with such a selection from her correspondence and unpublished writings, as most accurately convey her habits of thought, her opinions of men and books, and her own literary plans and occupations—Wallace and Bruce. It also comprehends a variety of extracts from her juvenile poetry.

Volume II.—Tales and historic scenes.—The restoration of the works of art to Italy.—Modern Greece, &c., &c.

Volume III.—The Siege of Valencia.—The Last Constantine—The Sceptic.—Greek Songs.—Welsh Melodies, &c., &c.

Volume IV.—The Vespers of Palermo.—De Chatillon, a tragedy (hitherto unpublished).—The Forest Sanctuary.—Lays of Many Lands, &c., &c.

Volume V.—Records of Woman.—Sebastian of Portugal.—Songs of the Affections, and Miscellaneous Poems.

Volume VI.—Scenes and Hymns of Life,—Lyrics and Songs for music.—Despondency and aspiration, &c.

₊ *A specimen of the type and size of page is here presented.*

Then crowded round its free and simple race,
Amazement pictured wild on ev'ry face;
Who deem'd that beings of celestial birth,
Sprung from the sun, descended to the earth—
Then first another world, another sky,
Beheld Iberia's banner blaze on high!

Still prouder glories beam on history's page,
Imperial CHARLES! to mark thy prosperous age:
Those golden days of arts and fancy bright,
When Science pour'd her mild, refulgent light;
When Painting bade the glowing canvas breathe,
Creative Sculpture claim'd the living wreath;
When roved the Muses in Ausonian bowers,
Weaving immortal crowns of fairest flowers
When angel-truth dispersed, with beam divine,
The clouds that veil'd religion's hallow'd shrine;
Those golden days beheld Iberia tower
High on the pyramid of fame and power;
Vain all the efforts of her numerous foes,
Her might, superior still, triumphant rose.
Thus, on proud Lebanon's exalted brow,
The cedar, frowning o'er the plains below
Though storms assail, its regal pomp to rend,
Majestic, still aspires, disdaining e'er to bend!

When Gallia pour'd, to Pavia's trophied plain,
Her youthful knights, a bold, impetuous train;
When, after many a toil and danger past,
The fatal morn of conflict rose at last;
That morning saw her glittering host combine,
And form in close array the threat'ning line;

Fire in each eye, and force in ev'ry arm,
With hope exulting, and with ardour warm;
Saw to the gale their streaming ensigns play,
Their armour flashing to the beam of day;
Their gen'rous chargers panting, spurn the ground,
Roused by the trumpet's animating sound;
And heard in air their warlike music float,
The martial pipe, the drum's inspiring note!

   Pale set the sun—the shades of evening fell,
The mournful night-wind rung their funeral knell;
And the same day beheld their warriors dead,
Their sovereign captive, and their glories fled!
Fled, like the lightning's evanescent fire,
Bright, blazing, dreadful—only to expire!
Then, then, while prostrate Gaul confess'd her might
Iberia's planet shed meridian light!
Nor less, on famed St. Quintin's deathful day,
Castilian spirit bore the prize away;
Laurels that still their verdure shall retain,
And trophies beaming high in glory's fane!
And lo! her heroes, warm with kindred flame,
Still proudly emulate their fathers' fame;
Still with the soul of patriot-valour glow,
Still rush impetuous to repel the foe;
Wave the bright faulchion, lift the beamy spear,
And bid oppressive Gallia learn to fear!
Be theirs, be theirs, unfading honour's crown,
The living amaranths of bright renown!
Be theirs th' inspiring tribute of applause,
Due to the champions of their country's cause!
Be theirs the purest bliss that virtue loves,
The joy when conscience whispers and approves!

A fine edition in Six Volumes, Royal 12mo., printed on beautiful paper, and handsomely bound in embossed cloth, or in full-coloured calf, of

THE
POETICAL WORKS OF SIR WALTER SCOTT,
COMPLETE.

Also, to match the above, in Seven Royal 12mo. Volumes,
MEMOIRS OF THE LIFE OF
SIR WALTER SCOTT.
BY J. G. LOCKHART, Esq.

A cheaper edition of the last work may also be had in two volumes octavo, done up in embossed cloth.

THE NOVELS OF JANE AUSTEN.
CONTAINING
PRIDE AND PREJUDICE, SENSE AND SENSIBILITY,
MANSFIELD PARK, EMMA, AND
PERSUASION, NORTHANGER ABBEY.

Complete in One Large Volume.

Bound in embossed cloth, or neatly half bound with calf backs and corners.

THE LANGUAGE OF FLOWERS.
With Illustrative Poetry.
To which is now first added,
THE CALENDAR OF FLOWERS.
Revised by the Editor of " FORGET ME NOT."
A New Edition, with New Plates.
Handsomely done up in embossed leather, with gilt edges.

A New and Handsome Edition of
Picciola, the Prisoner of Fenestrella;
OR, CAPTIVITY CAPTIVE.
BY M. D. SANTAINE.
In One neat Royal 18mo. Volume.

THE

BRIDGEWATER TREATISES.

Complete in Seven Octavo Volumes.

CONTAINING

PROUT, CHALMERS, KIDD, BELL, WHEWELL,
ROGET, KIRBY, AND BUCKLAND.

Handsomely bound in half-coloured calf, or embossed cloth.

———

Illustrated editions of the following works by (BOZ) Charles Dickens, Esq., printed on fine paper, and handsomely bound in embossed cloth, to match.

𝕿𝖍𝖊 𝕻𝖔𝖘𝖙𝖍𝖚𝖒𝖔𝖚𝖘 𝕻𝖆𝖕𝖊𝖗𝖘 𝖔𝖋

THE PICKWICK CLUB,

WITH NUMEROUS DESIGNS,

ILLUSTRATED BY

SAM WELLER, JR., AND ALFRED CROWQUILL, ESQ

—

OLIVER TWIST;

OR, THE PARISH BOY'S PROGRESS.

WITH TWENTY-FOUR ILLUSTRATIONS.

DESIGNED BY CRUIKSHANK.

—

SKETCHES BY "BOZ,"

Illustrative of Every-Day Life, and Every-Day People.

A NEW EDITION.

COMPRISING BOTH THE SERIES,

𝕬𝖓𝖉 𝕰𝖒𝖇𝖊𝖑𝖑𝖎𝖘𝖍𝖊𝖉 𝖜𝖎𝖙𝖍 𝕹𝖚𝖒𝖊𝖗𝖔𝖚𝖘 𝕴𝖑𝖑𝖚𝖘𝖙𝖗𝖆𝖙𝖎𝖔𝖓𝖘

BY GEORGE CRUIKSHANK.

4

THE POCKET LACON,

Comprising nearly One Thousand Extracts from the best Authors, selected by John Taylor.

A work, that, dip where the reader may, he will find a fund of knowledge: and which he may continue to peruse, lay down, and take up at pleasure, without breaking the thread, or interrupting the chain of reasoning.

In two handsome pocket volumes, bound in embossed cloth.

ROB OF THE BOWL.

A LEGEND OF ST. INIGOES.

By the Author of " Horseshoe Robinson," &c.

Two Volumes, 12mo.

THE ADVENTURES OF ROBIN DAY.

By the Author of " Calavar," " Nick of the Woods," &c.

In Two Volumes, 12mo.

By the same Author.

PETER PILGRIM;

OR, A RAMBLER'S RECOLLECTIONS.

In Two Volumes, 12mo.

STANLEY;

OR, RECOLLECTIONS OF A MAN OF THE WORLD.

By an Anonymous Writer.

In Two Vols. 12mo.

Advice to a Young Gentleman,

UPON ENTERING SOCIETY.

By the Author of the " Laws of Etiquette."

A small volume, in embossed cloth.

PRECAUTION.

A NOVEL.

By the Author of " The Spy," " The Pioneers," &c.

"Be wise to-day; 'tis madness to defer—
To-morrow's caution may arrive too late."

A new edition, revised by the Author.—In Two Volumes, 12mo.

HOMEWARD BOUND;

OR, THE CHASE.

A STORY OF THE SEA.

BY J. FENIMORE COOPER, Esq.
Author of " The Pilot," " The Red Rover," &c.

A new edition, in 2 vols. 12mo.

HOME AS FOUND;

BEING A SEQUEL TO "HOMEWARD BOUND."

BY MR. COOPER.

In Two Volumes, 12mo.

THE AMERICAN LOUNGER; or, Tales, Sketches and Legends. By the author of " Lafitte," " Captain Kyd," &c. One volume, 12mo.

THE LITTLE FRENCHMAN AND HIS WATER LOTS, and other Hits at the Times. By George P. Morris, Esq., of New York. With illustrations by Johnson. One vol. 12mo.

A CONTINUATION OF THE DIARY ILLUSTRATIVE OF THE TIMES OF GEORGE IV., interspersed with Original Letters from Queen Caroline, the Princess Charlotte, and other distinguished persons. Edited by John Galt, Esq. In 2 vols. 12mo.

BROUGHAM'S HISTORICAL SKETCHES OF STATES-MEN WHO FLOURISHED IN THE TIMES OF GEORGE III. First and second series. In 4 vols. 12mo.

BIRTHS, DEATHS AND MARRIAGES. By Theodore Hook. In 2 vols. 12mo.

BUBBLES IN CANADA. By Sam Slick. In 1 vol. 12mo.

SOLOMON SEESAW. A Novel. In 2 vols. 12mo.

ELVIRA; or, the Nabob's Wife. In 2 vols. 12mo.

CONCEALMENT. A Novel. In 2 vols. 12mo.

ADAM BUFF. By Douglass Jerrold. In 2 vols. 12mo.

ISABEL, OR SICILY. A Pilgrimage. By Henry T. Tucker-man. In 1 vol. 12mo.

NICHOLAS NICKLEBY. By Boz. Nos. 1 to 17. To be completed in 20 numbers.

JACK SHEPPARD. A Romance. By the author of "Rook-wood," "Crichton," &c.

HORACE VERNON; or, Fashionable Life. In 2 vols. 12mo.

PASCAL BRUNO. A Sicilian Story. Edited by Theodore Hook. 1 vol. 12mo.

LIFE OF MATHEWS, THE COMEDIAN. By his Wife. In 2 vols. 12mo.

ELLIOTT'S TRAVELS IN AUSTRIA, RUSSIA AND TURKEY. In 2 vols. 12mo.

GURNEY MARRIED. By Theodore Hook. In 2 vols. 12mo.

MARY RAYMOND, and Other Tales. By Mrs. Gore. In 2 vols. 12mo.

A cheap Edition of OLIVER TWIST. By Boz. With two plates. In one volume.

A cheap edition of SKETCHES BY BOZ. With two plates. In one volume.

ALTHEA VERNON. By Miss Leslie. In 1 vol. 12mo.

LORD BROUGHAM'S OPINIONS on Politics, Theology, Law, &c. In 2 vols. 12mo.

THE NAVAL FOUNDLING. By "The Old Sailor." In 3 vols. 12mo.

WERT

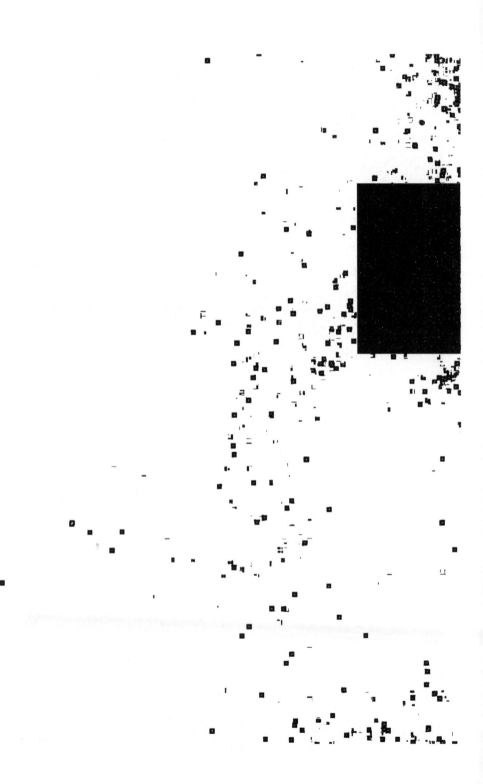

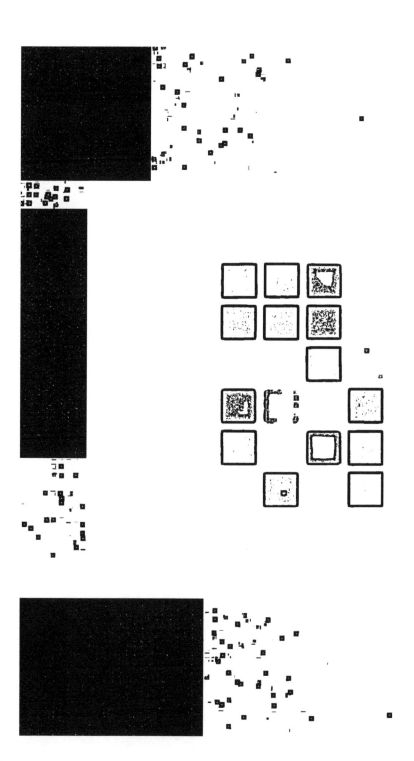